THE GOOD YEARS

THE
GOOD YEARS
YOUR LIFE IN THE TWENTY-FIRST CENTURY

Caroline Bird

E. P. Dutton, Inc.   New York

Published in the United States by E. P. Dutton, Inc.,
2 Park Avenue, New York, N.Y. 10016

Library of Congress Cataloging in Publication Data

Bird, Caroline.
  The good years, your life in the 21st century.

  1. Social indicators—United States. 2. Quality of life—United States. 3. Social prediction. I. Title.
HN60.B57   1983   303.4'973   82-25121

ISBN: 0-525-93284-4

Designed by Earl Tidwell

Published simultaneously in Canada by
Clarke, Irwin & Company Limited, Toronto and Vancouver

10 9 8 7 6 5 4 3 2 1

First Edition

To the years that
Marge, Libby, Karen,
and my daughter Carol
will spend in the twenty-first century

Contents

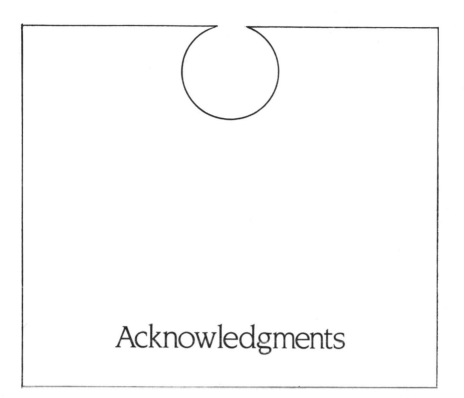

Acknowledgments

I am indebted, first of all, to the scores of older people who shared with me the uses they were making of their later years, particularly those who for various reasons are not identified by name. My visits with them, and the book that resulted, would not have been possible if the Ford Foundation had not staked me to the out-of-pocket expenses of visiting people who disproved the stereotypes of age at a time when I was not able to interest a publisher in what sounded like a downbeat subject.

Karen Braziller, my editor at Dutton, contributed to the thesis of the book by asking creative questions that forced me to articulate the bases for my optimism about the future. Another important influence was the patient ear of my friend Marjorie Godfrey, who gently pointed out how some of my wilder flights of fancy would sound to the general reader. I am indebted to Elizabeth Manion not only for double-checking the sources of the facts but for moral and logistical support when I was trying to work on the book through my husband's last illness and death.

The contribution of the many specialists on aging who helped me are recognized in the chapter notes, but help above and beyond normal scholarly duty came from Dr. Paul T. Costa, Jr., of the Gerontology Research Center of the National Institute on Aging; Marjorie Fiske, a sociologist specializing in life-stage research at the University of California, San Francisco; Christine Fry, an anthropologist specializing in gerontology at Loyola University in Chicago; Morris Ordover, Director of the External Affairs Staff of the Social Security Administration; as well as from the staffs of the National Center for Health Statistics, the Bureau of the Census, and the Bureau of Labor Statistics. Virginia Mekos, a sociologist specializing in labor issues, and John Applegath, author of *Working Free*, took time out from busy schedules to read the first draft of the manuscript and make helpful suggestions.

THE GOOD YEARS

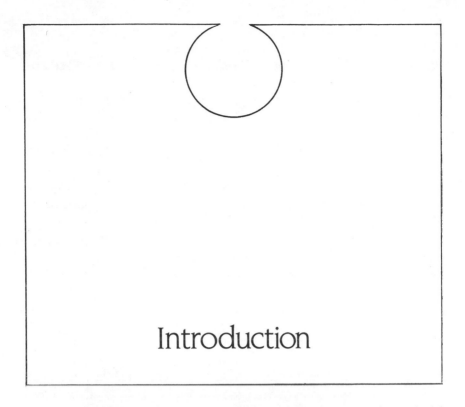

Introduction

In the 1980s I have begun to feel like a ridiculous gray-haired old woman trying to sell hope to college students who think the future is going to be terrible.

I would have given my eyeteeth to go to law school, but when my granddaughter went, she found it grim. According to her, the talk in 1982 was mostly about money: how to finance the tuition, how to make the most money after getting out. In addition to money, women law students talked about the Baby Problem: whether to have one before or after taking the bar, how to manage without falling behind.

Would that I had had such problems at twenty-five! I must have made the mistake of smiling.

"I can see that you don't take the Baby Problem seriously," she huffed.

"Oh, but I do, I do," I protested. "I was thinking of how much better your world is going to be than the one I've managed to survive. More schooling, less poverty, better housing, less dull and dangerous work, more options for women, longer life expectancies..."

But she shook her head and gave up trying to explain.

For two hundred years Americans have looked forward to the future. In the 1980s we are afraid of it. Angus Campbell and his team of psychologists found that young people polled in 1978 were less happy and less hopeful about the future than their counterparts asked similar questions in 1957. Workers were less satisfied with their jobs, and the decline was sharpest for those with a college degree.

The pessimism deepened. As early as 1977, nearly 60 percent of the readers of *Better Homes and Gardens* thought that there would be a major depression, a term associated with the prolonged hard times of the 1930s. In 1981 the percentage of Americans who expected to be better off in the next five years was lower than that of counterparts queried by Gallup in 1974 and 1964. By 1983, thousands were hoarding foodstuffs and buying gold against a collapse of the currency.

The interesting thing about these feelings is that they respond to the future rather than to the present. People may say that things in general are worse, but in 1982 very few of the individuals with whom I talked could identify exactly how their daily lives were worse than those of counterparts five or ten years earlier.

This was true to an astonishing degree even for the rising ranks of the unemployed. As late as the spring of 1982, unemployed auto workers were still drawing union benefits. Unemployment was rising, but unemployment benefits were only beginning to run out. Social workers in contact with the welfare population were afraid of what projected budget cuts would do to the poor in the future. They were outraged. Welfare checks had failed to keep up with rising prices, but the poor with whom they were in personal contact seemed to be scrounging what they needed, much as they had always done. Poor people freezing to death because of budget cuts were about as representative of the condition of the poor as welfare queens riding around in Cadillacs.

What we lost was hope of material advancement. It has been a grievous loss, and for young people a cruel betrayal. We told them that with a little bit of luck and a lot of hard work they could expect to enjoy more money and status than their parents or their peers. We led them to expect that people with talent could always make a place to express it. We told them that there was always room at the top.

This was the American Dream. It was a valid promise during the centuries it took to exploit a continent of untapped resources, but it could not last forever. There is room for all talents only when an economy is growing, and no economy, not even ours, can go on growing forever. We have had reprieves—usually by wars—but now that war is unthinkable the slowdown is upon us.

In the 1980s we are passing through the uncomfortable moment when the car comes to a stop in the garage after a long fast drive in the night and the children waken and fret. The awkward moment of stepping off the escalator. Beginning with 1981, there was little gain in productivity and no gain in real national income, our measure of all payments made to individuals, corrected for inflation. In 1983 the pileup of budget deficits showed how violently the unexpected slowdown had thrown the economy to the ground.

Everyone wanted to go back to the days of pleasant forward motion, but opinion differed only on how far back it would be nice to go. Democrats wanted to go back to the Great Society of the 1960s, but without the military buildup that seemed to be paying for it. Republicans with big-company jobs wanted to go back to the suburban, child-oriented, booming military-industrial complex of the 1950s, when a rising GNP seemed to be making jobs for the poor so that their narrow slices of the pie were more nourishing. The Republican whom right wing nostalgia elected in 1980 wanted to go even further back, to the western frontier, where every man made his own living and there wasn't any government at all.

But we can't go back, and in our bones we know it. We are going to have to learn to live in a slower-growing economy, and in some ways this is going to be a relief.

A steady-state economy does not encourage postponing satisfactions available today in favor of bigger ones promised in the future. It does not reward pushers, shovers, or driven workaholics. People can afford to be cheerful and friendly while they wait in line for a job or a bus.

When you aren't looking ahead to promotion, you choose the

job that you like to do today, rather than the one that leads to opportunities for the future. You stay with one task long enough to develop real competence. You can afford to take pride in what you have accomplished at the end of each day's work, instead of valuing it in terms of where it will lead you tomorrow.

Working conditions become more important. When employers cannot use the carrot of promotion to exact sixty-hour weeks from ambitious young lawyers and editors, they are going to have to make the tasks themselves interesting enough to engage the talent required to do them.

Fair shares for all is more important when the size of the total pie isn't growing: it's harder to ignore the people getting along on tiny slivers of it, and more obvious that there will always be some who, through no fault of their own, will be left without any share at all. And there's a deeper sense of community, because people have more time to pay attention to their neighbors as unique individuals instead of as ''contacts.''

The most enjoyable benefit of the steady-state economy will be the opportunity for leisure. The single biggest complaint of people on the fast upward track is that they don't have time to enjoy life now, because anything that is merely pleasure may at any moment have to be relegated to the future. When the pace is slower there will be time to find out what happened to the postman's little boy, to marvel at the tree uprooted in the storm, to make mincemeat from scratch, to watch a sunset out to its end. Time for family, friends, the nuances of relations between men and women, the daily pleasures that cannot be saved or banked.

Interest in these alternatives to the American Dream is growing. People are beginning to get the message that satisfaction can no longer be located in the future, as it was for our immigrants. Some of them are turning down the high-powered job, fleeing the high-powered city, and moving toward the pleasures that don't pay off in status. There is a deep weariness with the rat race, and only the most ambitious dismiss the disaffection as sour grapes.

In the 1980s some Americans are already living by the values that make sense in a slower-growing economy. They are the people past middle age who are going back to goals and activities that they had to defer when they were building their careers and rearing their families.

These quiet few are finding work and relationships that are ends instead of means, and lifestyles that are satisfying rather than symbols of success. They are going back to the identity-finding that they laid aside after college, and even to love affairs that might have been impractical in the heat of mid-life.

They are our older people, and we need to know much more about them. I first became interested in what happens to people in their later years because I suspected that the elderly are kept down by the same disingenuous myths that keep blacks and women out of the mainstream. In 1968, what was most hotly attacked in *Born Female*, my book about the status of women, was the parallel I drew between blacks and women. In discussing it I occasionally wondered whether similar stereotypes applied to old people.

During the 1970s, when the birthrate continued to drop, I found myself daydreaming about a world full of adults no longer preoccupied with bringing up children. Demographers didn't waste much time on the implications of the aging of the population, because they thought the decline in the birthrate was temporary. Or so they hoped. At that time, a world full of old people impressed everyone as dull and dreary.

But why? We classify people by race, sex, and age, and sometimes we classify them unfairly. And when you think about it, the stereotypes are strikingly similar.

Blacks, women, and the old are praised when they are like whites, males, or the young. Tiny little modifiers slip into statements about people who transcend the limitations of their race, sex, or age. A woman stockbroker who "thinks like a man" can be said to be "attractive for her age" and earn a salary that is "good for a black."

All three groups have at times conceded their inferiority by emulating their opposites. Before the triumph of the Afro haircut, blacks used to straighten their hair. Girls used to climb trees to prove that they could do anything that boys did. The consciousness of the old has yet to be raised, so many of them continue to lie about their age, dye their hair, lift their faces, and find ways to demonstrate that they are just as good as they ever were.

All three adapt by living down to their reputations. Blacks, women, and seniors have a handy excuse for taking it easy on the job, and they protect it by enforcing the stereotypes on each other. Blacks badmouth "brothers" who pass into so-called white jobs, women clerical workers resent women bosses, and the old are the first to criticize contemporaries who don't "act their age." In 1979 politicians suspected that elderly voters might think Ronald Reagan too old to run.

The analogy goes further. Blacks and females have been valued in the past for the contributions they can make to whites or to males. Blacks were supposed to be good at waiting on white people, women at the detail work men were too busy to do. We now suspect this praise, but we continue to patronize old people by suggesting that they have special talents for the baby-sitting and unpaid community chores that women used to do when we didn't need them in offices.

Of course there are differences. Women aren't segregated: as a bitter wit put it, they are the only minority who get to live with the master race. In the same vein it can be said that the old are the only minority that all but the unluckiest of us will one day join. But one of the unexplored differences is that chronological age isn't as inescapable a marker as race or sex.

If you look around at the people you know who are over sixty, you see that they are divided into two nations: the old, who are in need of welfare services, and people who aren't called old because they are doing all right.

The difference between these two nations isn't based on birthdays. "Ugly, decrepit, stupid, forgetful, toothless, sexless, and ready to fall on the conveyor belt of life after sixty-five" is the way Lydia Bragger summarized the media depiction of the old for the 1981 White House Conference on Aging. But when I have had occasion to mention that I was born in 1915, people feel obliged to say, "Oh, but I don't think of you as old!" Actually, of course, each of Bragger's adjectives applies to some young people, too.

So we have these two nations: the old and the ageless.

What makes the difference? We need to know, not only because the number of people over sixty-five is expected to double by

2030, and because you and I are going to live longer than we think, but because the ageless of today are exemplars for everyone destined to live in the steady-state economy of the future.

In 1980, thanks to a Ford Foundation travel and study grant, I was able to talk with scores of the ageless. I asked them about their health, their habits, their work, their families, their money, the use they were making of the uncommitted years of later life. They talked about their past mistakes and their hopes for the future. I had fun. The ageless are among the most interesting people around, but they had little to say that was helpful to the old.

The trouble was that they were too lucky to be good role models. It's all very well to be George Burns or Margaret Mead or William S. Paley. It's very nice to be able to turn handsprings at ninety. But most of us aren't rich, famous, smart, learned, energetic, or vibrantly healthy, and we are frankly sick and tired of hearing about people who are. Like the successful career women I interviewed in 1966, these older men and women kept telling me that their experience wouldn't help me, because they were exceptions.

But there is something to learn from exceptions. What precisely is it about money and privilege and power that makes it so much easier for a person to be ageless? Take education. How does a college education ward off old age? It did not seem to me to be the schooling itself, but something in the makeup of the ageless that attracted them to schooling in the first place. Even those who had not been to college were usually articulate, interested in ideas, well informed, and as curious about the world around them as children.

And then it dawned on me. When the ageless were young, you had to be privileged to go to college, to read books and talk ideas, to escape the environment that dulls curiosity—school chairs bolted to the floor, repetitive machine-tending that bolted the worker to the machine. But no more. In the 1980s many more adults have easy access not only to higher education but to the sea of information and stimulation that pours into every home. If words and ideas prolong active life, then many more of today's young adults will be ageless.

And the same thing was true of other characteristics of the ageless. Opportunities for sociability, enjoyable work, good health habits, companionable family relationships were once limited to the privileged. But now they are available to more of us—and this trend is continuing.

If this is so, then the ageless are lucky, not so much in enjoying privileges intrinsically limited to a few, but in enjoying them a generation early. They are important because they are bellwethers, living now the way more people of every age are going to live more of their lives in the future: without children, in small or special-purpose quarters, committed to a higher quality of intimate relationships and nonmaterial satisfactions in their work, cultivating habits that make them feel good.

My granddaughter isn't as optimistic as I am. She sees that she is living in a time of troubles, when the conventional wisdom fails and no one seems to know what to do. I tell her that a different world is going to emerge, a world she is going to like better. Our complaints are the arrows that point us in the direction we want to go, and our anger is the engine that is moving us there.

For this is not the first time of troubles. The last one was the Great Depression of the thirties. If we look at others we have survived we can see first of all that we always cope with them by trying to bring back the conditions for which the failed conventional wisdom was designed. In the 1930s, for instance, some people suggested going back to subsistence farming or opening new frontiers in Alaska. But you can't turn back the clock. In the 1980s the first lesson is that no President or policy can bring back the freakish spurt of growth following World War II.

The second lesson is that instead of changing the situation, we end up by changing the conventional wisdom. Our religion of growth was a logical response to an expanding economy, but we are already replacing it with values appropriate to a steady state.

Finally, the new insights created by times of trouble move us in new directions that make life better in unanticipated ways. For instance, in the Great Depression of the thirties we accepted the alien but fruitful notion that the government is responsible for the economy and has to put a safety net under the unfortunate, doctrines that were the cornerstones of our postwar prosperity.

Where will this present time of troubles lead? In the 1980s our slowdown looks like a passage to a present-oriented, adult society, richer, more various, and more humane than the society based on the ethic of success it seems destined to replace. More and more of us believe that work should bring pleasure to the worker, that money is only one of the measures of value, and that the end result of love need not be a child. In spite of discouraging headlines, most of us can expect to spend our later years in a world in which the ageless will outnumber the old.

This is the argument of this book. Part I establishes the long historical perspective that is moving us toward an adult society. Part II introduces us to the ageless individuals who are trying out the lifestyles we can all expect to live in the twenty-first century. Part III visualizes some of the good and bad things that could happen in the future.

My case for optimism is basically naïve. I think we have the wit and the urge to live. After we dropped the atom bomb, a great many people thought our days were numbered. I remember how shocked I was when Margaret Mead casually admitted that she gave the human race a fifty-fifty chance to survive for the next twenty years.

We were sitting in her Greenwich Village backyard in the 1950s, talking about the future and the work she was doing for the National Aeronautics and Space Administration. She hoped that space would buy us time by shifting the arena to peaceful competition, but she took it for granted that sooner or later we were bound to pull the fatal trigger. It was like guns. If you had them, eventually you would use them.

I told her no. I didn't believe it, but I couldn't come up with a coherent reason. We had managed to squeak by since we dropped the first bomb, and every year we succeeded in resisting the urge, the chance of resisting another year ought to get better.

Since then, we have resisted for almost forty years. Humans are wily survivors. If this is blind faith, then maybe it is the kind of turning toward life that has seen us through all those changes of environment since the primeval beginnings.

The case for optimism is even simpler. It is the only case worth considering.

I

Potentials

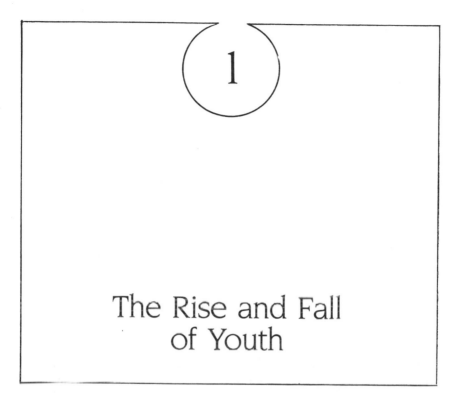

The Rise and Fall
of Youth

We are beginning to fall out of love with youth. In the long historical perspective, this may be the most important thing that is happening in the 1980s.

Young people are fewer and less evident. They haven't been marching or shouting. And instead of inflicting their favorite sound on strangers, they absent themselves from the scene by plugging themselves into earphones that keep their music a secret for them alone.

This is something new in America. It used to be children first, and women for the sake of children, ever since we declared our independence from the parent land. Many American families began with an immigrant who rebelled against a particularly oppressive parent. In my family, it was my mother's father, Ole Brattrud.

Around 1850, this fourteen-year-old Norwegian boy quarreled with his stepfather. As the older man turned away, the boy threw an awl after him that stuck in his buttock. Terrified, young Ole ran out of the house and went to sea. His ship was wrecked off Canada, but Ole saved himself and a baby girl by clinging to a mast. From

Canada he worked his way inland to Wisconsin and saved up enough money to buy 120 acres, a quarter section of dollar-an-acre wilderness land. At sixteen, an age at which his great-grandson had not qualified for the driver's license needed to leave our carbound home on his own, Ole had founded not only a farm but a family. He and another boy his age cleared enough ground to put in a crop of wheat and build, with the logs, two cabins close enough so that their brides could attend each other in childbirth. When the Civil War broke out a few years later, Ole managed to get a load of wheat to Madison and sell it for a hundred dollars, enough to pay for a replacement in the Union Army.

Back on the farm, the women had babies almost every year. The isolation got to the other bride. "I'm going to go to town and buy some new clothes," she raved to my grandmother, "and I don't care who pays for them." It is still our family saying for a situation that is truly desperate.

Grandmother Kari, for whom I am named, was of sterner stuff. When Ole died, of a stomachache allegedly caused by the kick of a horse (no one knows, because there was no doctor, but my mother thinks it was really a ruptured appendix), she rented the farm and took her eight children to Madison. There they grew up, a series of steps, each younger one better provided for than the one just ahead. The oldest (and brightest) never got more than three years of country school, but in town she worked as a dressmaker to send the two youngest through the University of Wisconsin. The next to the youngest was my mother.

This reversed the traditional hierarchy of age. In Europe the old were always preferred to their juniors. They held the land and passed it to the oldest child first. It paid to look older than you were. Wigs were powdered. In the eighteenth century tailors narrowed and rounded the shoulders of coats and broadened the hips and waists to make the wearer look bent by the weight of years, a fashion that flattered Benjamin Franklin in his later years. Analyses of colonial censuses have convinced historians that men lied about their ages to make themselves out to be older rather than younger. In the New World rebellious sons need not have waited around for their fathers to die, but it didn't occur to them to venture into the scary woods to found farms of their own until revolution, both the French and the American, gave them permission.

The revolutions liberated the young to pursue their own goals. They taught that the young were better than the old and morally charged with surpassing them. Revolt became a duty. Old was out. Young was in. Revolutionary fashions helped old men look younger. Toupees for the bald replaced the powdered wigs colonial young men had affected. Tailors slenderized waists. Our philosopher Ralph Waldo Emerson insisted that people could "grow younger in spirit," as if that were a compliment. Henry David Thoreau, our sage of Walden Pond, publicly doubted that the young had anything at all to learn from the old.

The most lasting impact of the youth revolution was demographic. The sons turned their backs on the coast, on Europe, and plunged into the woods, where nobody owned the land. The highest rate of natural increase recorded for any population of the world may have been scored during the opening decades of the nineteenth century, when most of the land east of the Mississippi was settled. It was the original Third World, teeming with babies, but on the American frontier there was food, so instead of dying like flies, almost all of the babies lived. (Of the nine children my grandmother bore, only the child born during that first hard winter died before adulthood.) And all of them were needed. We needed muscle. We imported slaves. We lured immigrants. But most of our labor supply we grew ourselves, and it didn't stay put. Young men went west, often at tender ages.

Our West was a teenage ghetto—lawless, reckless, brash, idealistic, as impractical as the brawling knights of the clamorous fourteenth century, or the students who made the Revolution of 1978 in Iran. These three societies have one thing in common: a median age under twenty.

Europeans were appalled at the impertinence of our children and the meekness of parents in putting up with them. Foreign visitors quoted by Richard Rapson in *The Cult of Youth in Middle-Class America* found American youngsters precocious. One described children often "calling for liquor at the bar"; another labeled them "cigar-smoking cherubs." A visitor of 1900 reported that the old were "shouldered unmercifully out of existence," so that in America there were no old people at all. Europeans thought that Americans never really grew up but continued to act like children all of their lives.

Observers marveled at the freedom enjoyed by our women and children and admired their mutual respect and affection. De Tocqueville, the French aristocrat, noted with approval that inheritances were divided among brothers and sisters instead of being saved for the eldest alone. American parents expected their children to surpass them, and gave them the benefit of the doubt in a disagreement.

My father's career is a good example. He didn't join his father's law firm, although his father begged him to, according to family legend, with tears in his eyes. Yet for a good ten years, he could count on money from home for projects that bewildered his father and sometimes embarrassed his father's political friends. But, loyal to my grandfather and tolerant of his spirited son, Wisconsin senators in Washington regularly got President Theodore Roosevelt to spring my father from jail, where he frequently landed, when as a newspaper publisher he defended the constitutional rights of Puerto Ricans against the military government that ruled the island after we seized it.

Back in New York, my father saw firsthand the reversal of the father-son relationship in the immigrant families he often defended against immigration authorities. From my childhood I remember a real estate closing common enough in the 1920s. The purchaser, a crinkle-faced Neapolitan, uncomfortable in his one Sunday suit, had brought his English-speaking teenage son to translate the papers being handed around. The boy's face reddened in shame as his father opened a suitcase and began to count out loudly, in Italian, fifty thousand dollars for the purchase, all in cash, and much of it in dollar bills earned one by one over years of washing windows. The louder and more suspicious-sounding the father's questions, the lower the boy's voice as he explained to the illiterate old man who had to sign with a cross for his mark.

These Americanized children generally despaired of their Old World parents, and so did the social reformers of the early twentieth century. Like my father, the Progressives believed that children could and should do better than their parents, either morally or materially, whichever happened to attract them at the moment, and ideally, of course, both ways. By a tacit triage, early social workers channeled their efforts to the young. The foreign-born immigrants were quick to get the unintentionally cruel message: the American Dream was not for them; they could live it only through their children.

And how were these children to surpass their own parents? By education, of course. John Dewey, the Progressive, gave the world fair warning: "Education is the fundamental method of social prog-ress and reform." And since children were held to be basically curious, they would have to learn by following their impulses. It sounded good, but during the 1920s the details were not yet in place.

I was one of the guinea pigs. At Lincoln School of Teachers College, followers of Dewey tried to find out how far a selected group of children could educate themselves through their own curiosity. To the relief of our parents, we managed to get into college and even do well, although we were a handpicked bunch who would probably have done just as well with no schooling at all.

One thing we did learn was how much fun it could be to make adults nervous. At one sixth-grade birthday party, for instance, we fingerpainted a mural in ice cream on the damasked dining room walls of our hostess. What I remember most vividly is my mother's attempt to conceal her shock. Parents had been conditioned not to interfere with our self-expression.

America was the first country where parents lived for their children, followed their children, feared their children, and worried about whether the best they could do was good enough for them. The Soviets and the Zionists in Israel pinned their hopes on their children too, but they—and the children—had the advantage of a detailed vision of the perfect society they were expected to create. Our burden was ambiguous: to be better than our parents each in his or her own, unspecified way. And like the biblical curse, this burden was descended even unto the third and fourth generations.

Children were never more glorified than in the Spock-run suburbs that sprang up all over the United States after World War II. At the peak of the baby boom we produced 4.3 million babies in a single year, more than in any year of our history before, and very probably more than we will ever produce in a single year again. We are invited to feel sorry for these children because they have had to compete all their lives for everything from cribs in the maternity ward and the attention of their parents to places in schools, colleges, and the job market.

But their very numbers were an advantage. There were so many of them that they were able to set the style for everyone older. When this generation came to puberty, they brought sex out into the open. They overturned the parietal rules of colleges, and demanded a say in running them. They succeeded in lowering the legal drinking and voting ages, and won not only an end to the draft but an end to the Vietnam War their elders had expected them to fight.

In the 1960s teenagers developed a generational solidarity. They developed a slang of their own, at least in part for the pleasure of baffling their elders, which only whetted the appetite of admiring adults to find out what youth was really doing. Marketers employed teenage spies to inform on the fashions, the music, and the language that was really ''in.'' In hopes of pleasing or keeping up with the young, graying professors wore Nehru jackets, beads, bushy beards, jeans, and even taught classes in railroad overalls while they seemed to be in vogue. (By then, of course, young people had already abandoned them and moved on to something else.)

The Turnaround

But even in the 1950s, adults began to revolt, particularly the mothers, who had borne the brunt of the youth boom. Covertly at first, and sometimes with shame, they wrote passionate letters to women's magazines complaining of the self-sacrifice expected of mothers. They didn't exactly say that they didn't want all those children, but that's what they probably meant, and my own obstetrician confirmed this.

''You really *want* this baby,'' he explained when I asked why the young suburban wives in his waiting room were so much sicker and sadder than I, a pregnant forty-five-year-old woman with a demanding job. "Most of those women out there are having third or fourth babies to impress the neighbors."

Disenchantment with large families was one of the reasons it was possible to legalize abortion in the 1960s. The movement to control population exploded on Earth Day 1970, when young people gathered to save the planet from pollution. Some of them boasted to each other about their vasectomies and wore buttons that said "Stop at Two" and, since you couldn't really be against children, "Have One, Adopt One."

The campaign caught fire because it provided a noble reason for doing what young people wanted to do anyway. It was well funded and it captivated the media. At some moments the whole campaign looked like a plot hatched by the Club of Rome, that vaguely sinister long-range-planning organization of European aristocrats and superrich American conservatives—all of whom, come to think of it, had an interest in protecting the status quo from the pressure of rising populations, and the connections for media attention. By 1980 the antinatalists were cooperating with the fundamentalists who opposed technological progress, the conservationists, the consumer movement, the antinuclear movement, advocates of safety in the workplace, and the women's movement, to name a few causes with a stake in fewer people.

Almost every interest seemed to be served by a smaller population. Business leaders had always welcomed a rising population of future consumers, but now they were not so sure. In 1972 the distinguished economists of the Commission on Population Growth and the American Future concluded that slower population growth would improve the quality of life in America and ensure our continued prosperity.

The energy crisis and inflation persuaded many couples that there was no point in trying to live for your children. It wasn't that you didn't love them, merely that there was nothing you could do to improve their lot in the future, so the best thing to do was to live it up now. In 1977 Yankelovich, Skelly & White, the opinion research firm, discovered a "new breed" of prosperous, college-educated parents who don't feel that they have to sacrifice in order to give the best to their children. (By what may be merely coincidence,

Yankelovich turns out to be a card-carrying member of the Club of Rome elite.)

But there was no denying the trend. In 1980, the humorist Russell Baker delineated the shift in a column:

> OLD You want your children to have a better life than you had.
>
> AGING FAST You want your child to have it just as good as you had it, except for the really heavy drugs.
>
> YOUNG You wouldn't mind having children if you could afford a house to put them in and if the Government rewrote the law to make children a profitable tax shelter.

As it became clearer, during the 1970s, that children could no longer be expected to surpass their parents, they began to lose the benefit of the doubt that had made them a privileged class. Landlords were emboldened to reject them. In 1980 nearly 29 percent of landlords in predominantly white neighborhoods (but only 18 percent in black ones) refused to rent to families with children under eighteen, and nearly half of all families with children reported trouble in finding a place to live.

Most violent crimes are committed by young people. Students of law enforcement were not surprised to find that the crime rate rose with the tide of teenagers, but ordinary citizens began to revise their faith in the natural goodness of the child. Some people faulted the juvenile courts set up by the Progressive movement at the turn of the century for being soft on the young, others for denying child criminals the constitutional rights available in the regular courts. Newspapers responded to the cooler view of childhood by reporting brutal crimes by children, formerly suppressed as distasteful, and urging that parents be held responsible for damage caused by unsupervised or incorrigible children.

Doubts about the value of children undermined commitment to public education. School bond issues began to fail. No longer the hope of an undefined future, children were once again expected to measure up to the standards of their parents. The mood was "out with the frills" that fostered aspiration, and "back to the basics" required to maintain the established order. Meanwhile, a slower job market for college graduates discouraged the less bookish high school graduates' interest in college, and parents supplied less and less of the money for those who went. Alvin Eurich, president of the Academy for Educational Development, Inc., warned that we might be creating the first generation in history to average fewer years of education than their parents.

Fewer Babies

In the early 1960s the birthrate began to slide. We didn't notice it much at first. Demographers had warned of a population explosion when the tidal wave of babies born after World War II began to have babies of their own, but it didn't come off. In the 1970s we had more women of childbearing age than ever before, but they actually produced fewer babies than in the 1950s. With a "sigh of relief" the *New York Times* reported that the much-feared "Mother Bomb" looked like a dud. In 1957 the number of babies born per thousand women fifteen to forty-four was at its postwar high. By 1976 it had fallen to an all-time low.

In the 1980 Virginia Slims poll, four out of five women didn't think children were essential to a happy marriage. Organizations like the National Alliance for Optional Parenthood urged young couples to weigh the pros and cons of parenthood as coolly as they calculated the purchase of a house. "Some people may get a special joy from holding, caring for a new baby, or from breastfeeding," an Alliance workbook advised. "Other people find child care boring and lonely, keeping them from adult companionship, and some men prefer their partners to have a job rather than be homemakers." By 1980 newlyweds no longer expected to have a baby right away, as a matter of course.

Nor could it be argued that the Mother Bomb would come later. By 1980 more women were waiting until they were over thirty to have their first babies, it's true, but in spite of the attention attracted by celebrated career women, women who wait that long are too few to have much impact on the birthrate. In the early 1980s only 7 percent of first mothers were over thirty. Meanwhile, a growing proportion of women were closing off their options for future births in their thirties. According to surveys of family growth made under the auspices of the National Center for Health Statistics, the proportion of white married women between thirty-five and forty-four who reported that either they or their husbands had been sterilized rose to 48 percent in the 1970s. Women were waiting longer to start their families and stopping sooner, a trend as portentous for change as the decline in the birthrate itself.

The fertility collapse of the 1970s surprised demographers as much as the baby boom twenty years earlier. At first they ignored it. The rates spewed out of the computers were "too low" and would "have to go up," although they couldn't say why. The pill and the legalization of abortion accounted for some of the drop, but a United Nations analysis attributed only half of the decline in developed nations to the avoidance of unwanted babies. The other half was because women wanted fewer children.

Why did they choose to have fewer? Some analysts blamed the drop on affluence. Traditionally the birthrate goes up in good times and down in bad—but the correlation reverses for wives who are working. According to a Rand Corporation study, the birthrate rose in the recession years 1970 and 1974. A wife who isn't getting ahead on the job may decide that the time has come to drop out and have a baby.

Economists suggested that children had become a burden rather than an asset to their parents. Children were a good investment in my grandfather's day. He needed eight children to run the farm, and there was plenty of room and food to support them. Now one of his great-granddaughters and her husband run it without any extra help, and the expense of rearing a child is formidable. According to the U.S. Department of Agriculture, the out-of-pocket cost of rearing a child born in 1979 will be $134,414 by the time he or she is seventeen, and at the rate that college tuitions have been rising, college could mean an outlay of $50,000 more. This estimate does not include the much bigger cost of the care required to replace a parent who works outside the home, or the loss of the income the care-giving parent would otherwise earn.

A child is the most expensive luxury a couple can undertake if the mother forgoes dollar earning to care for the child herself. The higher her pay, the more the child costs. For a couple living on two professional salaries, a child costs more than a second home or a trip around the world or a modest yacht, and unlike material possessions, it cannot be sold or cut out of the family budget if lifestyle priorities change.

Moralists tended to ignore the economic explanations for the dwindling birthrate. Some of them maintained that pessimism about the future could explain it. Why bring children into a world doomed to war, destruction, and the slow erosion of our standard of living? Prospective parents may talk this way, but very few people actually make personal decisions on the basis of general abstractions.

One of the most imaginative contemporary theories holds that the number of persons in an age group determines not only their birthrate but the birthrate that can be expected of their children. Economist Richard A. Easterlin of the University of Pennsylvania argues that the few children born during the Depression of the 1930s were so badly "needed" by the expanding postwar economy that they married early and had big families. Now that these big families are grown and having trouble finding jobs, they are postponing getting married and having children of their own. According to the Easterlin theory, we are condemned to ride a roller coaster: small cohorts are happy and successful, so they marry early and produce big cohorts, who have so much trouble getting jobs that they produce a small cohort to begin the cycle all over again.

The theory is pat but implausible. It stands the usual direction of cause and effect on its head: instead of the economy determining the size of families, the size of families determines the economy. The theory assumes that the aspirations of women never change, so that they always choose to have babies if they can afford them; that the market for labor never changes, so employment and wages are always determined by the number of people in the generation. In real life, of course, nothing ever holds steady.

Few demographers buy the Easterlin theory. The Mother Bomb had failed to explode by 1983, and there did not seem to be any mystical life force that would keep us having enough babies to reproduce ourselves. Brides of 1967 expected to have three or more children, but their counterparts in 1977 expected to stop at two. Two, not three, was the goal of the average bride of 1980, but if these young women undershoot their goal, as those ahead of them did, the typical young family of the year 2000 could be a father, a mother, and a single child.

The one-child family is now the norm in Germany. Germans have never made up the deficit of births following World War II. In the 1980s deaths outnumber births, so that there are fewer native-born Germans every year. Our baby boom will keep our population from dropping for many years, but sometime in the twenty-first century the number of native-born Americans could begin to shrink too.

Adults First

Whatever the reasons, adults are accepting responsibility for fulfilling themselves in their own lifetimes instead of investing in a future only their children can enjoy. Cultural history may have something to do with it. Adults of the 1980s were born into center stage, and as they move through their lives they are carrying the spotlight with them. Children were favored when they were children, and adults are favored now that they are adults.

An adult society could be either good or bad. We could become a stable, law-abiding, civil, but slightly stodgy society, like Britain or Sweden. We could preserve ourselves in amber, like Ireland, where the population has been kept down to a level that can be supported on the farms by delaying marriage and exporting the surplus children the farms can't employ. Or we could fall into the kind of guerrilla sniping between the young and the old that is well developed around the retirement communities of Florida.

Numbers aren't the whole story, but the changing ratio of young to old will upset relationships we now take for granted. If you stack people by age, in the past they always formed a pyramid, bottom-heavy with children, thinning with deaths at each higher age to the point at the top that represents the oldest person alive. The numbers of people by age have formed a pyramid ever since the pharaohs of Egypt built the first one. In Third World countries, including the frontier in America, the pyramid is broadly based. When the birth and death rates are low, the pyramid is steeper.

Now something new is happening. Fewer births at the bottom are making the pyramid into a barrel. We are going to have almost as many fifty-year-olds as forty-year-olds, thirty-year-olds, and twenty-year-olds, and none of them weighed down by big families of little children.

In 1980 little more than 25 percent of the population was under eighteen, and only 21 percent were over fifty-five. But the proportion can change. If we continue to have fewer children than we need to reproduce ourselves, there could be as many people over fifty-five as under eighteen. Then in the twenty-first century, when the postwar babies begin to reach fifty-five, more than 33 percent of our population will be over fifty-five and less than 20 percent under eighteen.

That prospect raises questions.

What would happen if we had twice as many older people collecting Social Security as we have now, and only a few more people of working age to support them?

Will more older people make us a different kind of country? Older adults differ from their juniors in ways that could make for a much stabler society. They are more apt to vote and to pay attention to politics. They commit fewer crimes of violence. Older adults who continue to earn save more of their money: they already have a house and a car, and they aren't as tempted by the things that can be charged to a credit card. They are more contented with their jobs, less likely to quit one for another, and less likely to be fired in a layoff. It's the young who swell the ranks of the unemployed.

Women live and remain active longer than men, and their advantage is rising, yet they continue to marry men older than themselves. What can we expect from this rising tide of healthy (and lusty) old widows?

What's going to happen to the army, the schools, and the colleges when there aren't enough young people to keep them going?

Are small families good or bad for the children themselves? We know that children who grow up alone or with only one brother or sister are more independent, more verbal, more ambitious, better students, higher achievers, more self-sufficient, and, according to a study made by Toni Falbo, a psychologist at the University of Texas at Austin, less selfish than children growing up in large families.

Blacks have a higher birthrate than whites, but Hispanics, many of them here illegally, may have the highest birthrate of all, and a higher death rate, too. In fact, a white is three times as likely to reach sixty-five as a Hispanic. It is conceivable that all the population increase after 1990 will be foreign-born immigrants. Will elderly white property owners tax themselves to support schools for poor black and Hispanic children?

What kind of lives are the childless going to live? We know some things about adults who avoid or postpone having children. The childless spend less of their lives in marriage. A very high proportion of marriages would not occur if the bride were not pregnant, and the fewer the children, the easier it is for a couple to decide to divorce.

Then, childless women are more apt to earn money. The fewer children a woman has, the more likely she is to earn money, and the more money she makes, the less likely she is to have children. It's the chicken and the egg.

Finally, the childless have money to spend on themselves, and they spend it in ways that aren't as predictable as the spending of families meeting the needs of children.

All these things are true for now, but they are not inevitable. We are all so used to life in the pyramid of ages that it is hard to imagine what the world will be like when a preponderance of children no longer determines what adults must do. Perhaps the simplest difference is that adults will have more freedom. They will no longer expect to go through a series of crises and stages at predictable ages.

Flexible Life Stages

We think of our lives as a journey with a rigid timetable. The most poetic model is the one proposed by Erik Erikson, the psychoanalyst, who attaches a crisis to each of his eight life stages. His four adult stages begin with adolescence, which confronts the teenager with the choice between "identity and role diffusion." Next comes young adulthood, when he (and, but less clearly, she) must chose between "intimacy and isolation." After that comes adulthood, where the choice is between "generativity and stagnation." Finally comes maturity, where the choice is between "ego integrity" on the one hand and "disgust and despair" on the other.

Life schedules proposed by behavioral scientists purport to be norms established by the impersonal testing of people of various ages. The most popular is the timetable of problems author Gail Sheehy distilled from several life-cycle researchers for her book *Passages: Predictable Crises of Adult Life*. It is:

18–20 Pulling Up Roots: Getting away from parent
The Trying 20s Preparing for a life work, shaping a dream
Catch-30: Dissatisfaction with marriage, career, family
Early 30s Rooting and Extending: Children, houses, careers
35–45 Deadline Decade: Last chance for babies or success
Mid-40s: Renewal or resignation

Now the interesting thing about all the maps on which Sheehy drew is that none of them goes very far beyond middle age. When they do, they fill out the remaining years with leisure, retrospection, and preparation for death. Anthropologist Christine Fry finds that older people tend to see more divisions in adulthood than younger people see. Children, for instance, see only two stages—children and adults.

But from antiquity to Sheehy, life-stage maps have one thing in common: all of them are based on the reproductive cycle. Whatever the stages are called, they prepare for bearing and rearing children and then getting out of the way or otherwise serving these children when they have children of their own. They may not all be as explicit as the charming nineteenth-century cartoon that put the Bride at the pinnacle of the Seven Ages of Women, with Baby, Girl, and Daughter before, and Mother, Grandmother, and Widow descending on the other side, but they all define the stages of life by the same family measure. Women become adult when they are ready to bear children, men when they are able to support a family.

Even the sophisticated contemporary social scientists imply that stages of adult life are biologically inevitable. This seemed self-evident when normal, healthy adults expected children as a matter of course. The parents of the postwar baby boom called birth control "family planning." They used it to get big families of children over with early, as if children were an inevitable burden, like taxes. They did not question the sequence of school, marriage, career, children, and the new addition to the American Dream, if your company had it—the reward of paid leisure at the end of the line. A hit tune of the 1950s asserted that love and marriage went together like a horse and carriage, and a houseful of children was part of the deal.

These children were born in the postwar baby boom, and when they grew up they were no longer willing to follow the conventional program. They asserted their right to premarital sex, not on the sly in the back seats of cars, but openly, in the homes of their parents. They declared themselves sexually active, autonomous adults before they had committed themselves to children or careers. Instead of planning their lives around children and hoping to "get it over with" by thirty, they scheduled a child or two around the other things they wanted to do with their lives.

Meanwhile, their parents had come to the end of the programmed idyll. Disenchanted with their jobs, envious of the sexual freedom of their sons, fathers looked for new personal intimacy and found it, as often as not, with another partner. Disenchanted with child rearing and bed making, envious of the aspirations of their daughters, mothers dreamed of the careers they had given up to marry. Many parents separated. A new stage emerged: mid-life crisis.

Mid-life crisis looked inevitable in the 1970s, because everyone in mid-life seemed to be going through it. One of the reasons was that the entire generation of people who were in their forties in the 1970s had married and had children and bought houses on the same timetable during the conformist 1950s. In earlier periods of history the life stages of individuals of similar age had not coincided so neatly, nor had these stages followed each other as inevitably as the steps of different colors on the dust cover of *Passages*. These younger rebels weren't marching along together at all.

Bernice Neugarten, University of Chicago pioneer in life-stage studies, finds that lives are becoming more various and fluid. She has reminded us that we are becoming accustomed to "the 28-year-old mayor, the 30-year-old college president, the 35-year-old grandmother, the 50-year-old retiree, the 65-year-old father of a pre-schooler, the 70-year-old student, and even the 85-year-old mother caring for a 65-year-old son."

Willard Wirtz, former Secretary of Labor and chairman of the National Manpower Institute, made fun of the whole idea of life stages. It would, he liked to say, make more sense in reverse, so that you would come in, if you will, at age eighty, spend fifteen years of total meaninglessness, to which the old are now consigned, go on to the satisfactions of thirty-five to forty years of working, advance from there to the pleasure of education, and then enjoy six years of lack of responsibility attended by tender loving care until the doctor patted you good-bye instead of hello.

The truth is that situations themselves make the difference we have lazily attributed to the age at which the situations are supposed to occur. I had been keeping house for twenty-five years when my son was born, but I tried new recipes, bought new furniture, and resolved to reform myself as enthusiastically as younger mothers. Friends said that having a baby had made me young, but a woman becomes interested in improving the home environment when she's about to bring a newcomer into it, at any age.

Old people lose interest in work not because they can no longer do it but because their work has been taken away from them. Executives retired against their will can grow fat and flabby at sixty-six, but Ronald Reagan was trim and alert at sixty-nine because he was running for President.

Athletes in their thirties whose careers are drawing to a close can actually behave like senile old men. According to sportswriter Roger Kahn, Muhammad Ali "spoke in the crabbed tones of age" about defending his heavyweight title at thirty-six. Kahn reports the desperate attempt of a big-league pitcher "without many games left in his arm" to attract the attention of a particular tennis star for whom he lusted. "He was 39. He was well-conditioned and black-haired and every movement he made suggested physical strength," Kahn wrote. "He had won premature fame at 22 and now he was paying with a kind of senility at 39. Already his manner with attractive women had regressed."

The Myths

The stereotypes of age are myths. They serve a variety of special interests, some more commendable than others. Managers of business enterprises like to employ "young blood" because it is cheaper as well as more docile. Advocates for the elderly unwittingly reinforce the stereotype of rigidity in later years by their attempts to sell programs for helping them. Marie Blank of the National Institute of Mental Health warned her fellow social workers that the image they were creating could hurt the very people they were trying to help:

"One would quickly come to the conclusion that at least half of the population over the age of 65 is in a long-term care facility, that at least 85 percent of aged persons in the community were mentally and physically frail, rather than the reverse, and that at least 75 percent of aged persons were either below the poverty level or close to it, though just the opposite is true."

More than 90 percent of people over sixty-five are living with family, friends, or on their own. Less than 5 percent are in institutional care, and many of those are there only because they don't want to live alone and have outlived anyone they would like to live with, or because the outpatient treatment they need is not reimbursed by Medicare.

Most people over sixty-five can work. When they do, according to a report by the Work in America Institute, a research organization, they are more reliable workers than their juniors, with fewer absences and fewer accidents. They like their work better and do it with less stress.

Most old people are active. The National Health Survey finds that ill health does not keep people over sixty-five from normal activities. Chronic diseases are more frequent in later life, but they can be treated or prevented. None of them is inevitable, according to Alex Comfort, the gerontologist best known for his book *The Joy of Sex*, and Robert N. Butler, the psychiatrist who was the first director of the National Institute on Aging.

Most old people are mentally competent: 90 percent of those

over sixty-five show no decline in any mental power, including memory. Among the men followed over the years at the Baltimore laboratory of the National Institute on Aging, those who had spent their lives solving problems improved their scores on tests of problem solving as they grew older. If you're smart when you are young, you will be smart when you are old.

Old people are happy. A Louis Harris study of 1974 found that they don't feel as lonely, neglected, rejected, bored, poor, or fearful of death as young people think they are. Gail Sheehy found that the older respondents to her magazine questionnaire on well-being were more apt to say they were happy than the young ones. Happiness rose with age straight into the seventies. The self-ratings of happiness she used were cross-checked with reports of boredom, recollections of failures, enjoyment of work, and psychosomatic symptoms such as headache and fatigue.

Sex doesn't stop, but it does taper off. A Duke University study that has followed 268 people over sixty for several decades found that the frequency of sexual intercourse declines over the decades. Alex Comfort points out that the erections of older men don't rise as fast or as far, and they need longer rests in between, but the response itself depends more on physical and mental health than it does on age. A television personality says that she gave up sex at seventy-eight because she didn't want strange men to see her sunken armpits, but she may be unusually vain. Widespread acceptance of nudity and aging bodies was one of the surprises of the *Starr-Weiner Report* of 1981 on sex and sexuality after sixty.

Most people over sixty-five aren't desperately poor. In 1981, 15 percent of Americans over sixty-five were below the Census poverty level, only 1 percent more than for the rest of the population, and although the percentage in poverty rose after 1979, the gap between young and old had actually narrowed a bit.

The old aren't powerless. On the contrary, those who wield real power are very apt to be over sixty-five. Most of them are high officials who cannot be removed by politicians, like Supreme Court Justices and members of the Federal Reserve Board, public figures whose power grows with their years in the spotlight, and stockholders looking after their interests on the self-perpetuating boards of major corporations.

When Henry Luce founded *Time* magazine, he thought of it as a young man's enterprise. In order to keep it that way, he set up one of the country's first mandatory retirement plans, but like other founders, he influenced policy (and sometimes unpredictably) at an age when no one else in the corporation would have been allowed to continue working.

The rule of the old is even more dramatic abroad. In 1980 candidate Reagan pointed out that the other heads of state he would have to deal with as President were his age—all but Margaret Thatcher of Britain, whom he gallantly named as an exception because she was only fifty-five.

These are the myths of age. The old people who bear them out are victims not of their age but of their particular experience. The myths won't apply to the later years of people born after World War II, because these younger people will have lived through a different period of history.

Mid-life adults of the 1980s were not crippled by the Great Depression of the 1930s. They were not immigrants who sacrificed themselves to give the American Dream to their children, but the children who were supposed to be realizing it. They are having fewer children and investing fewer years of their lives in the arduous task of rearing them. Many have liberated themselves from the arbitrary constraints of the family life cycle.

Some observers fear this freedom. They don't see how society can hold together unless most people travel together along a generally accepted path. The New Breed who invest in themselves instead of their children are faulted for the sin of Narcissus, the mythological youth who fell in love with his reflection in the water.

Erik Erikson reports that young women patients on the contraceptive pill are suffering from a new kind of neurosis: repression of their parental rather than their sexual urges. He does not describe these urges or explain how their repression damages the individuals concerned. Glen Elder, a life-stage historian at Cornell, worries that an age-irrelevant society would be "rudderless." According to him, people need age norms to anchor and structure their lives.

None of the worriers has any very explicit suggestions for the score or more of active years newly available to most Americans after middle age. Based on the past, these later stages are usually filled with negatives: retirement, disengagement, retrospection. But the postwar babies have improved the options of every age they have passed through so far, and there is every reason to believe that their later years will be no exception. Their lives to date have been like the lives of people who become ageless along the way instead of old, and the long historical trend will make this easier to achieve in the twenty-first century.

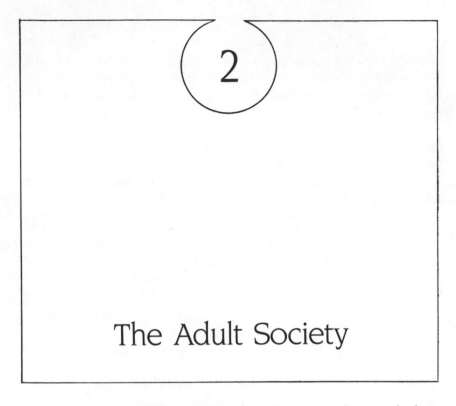

The Adult Society

Twenty-first-century America is going to be a nicer place in which to live for everyone, but especially for the adults of the 1980s who will be spending their later years in it.

It doesn't look that way now. Theodore White, the veteran analyst of presidential elections, believes that Americans are held together only by "an idea of opportunity and equality—as it were, a culture of hope," and that the conservatives won the election of 1980 because this consensus is unraveling. White was so shaken that he decided never to report another election.

We are losing our bearings, but that is exactly what we have to lose if they are leading us in the wrong direction. The suspicion that this may be true is one of life's most unnerving experiences. As Major Barbara was told in Shaw's play of that name, "When you learn something, it feels at first as if you have lost something."

What we have lost is a vista of endless growth that will bail us out of all of our social problems. We have begun to doubt that there will ever be enough jobs to go around, that able people will always be able to market their talents, that we can count on a rising tide to float all boats.

By 1982 even President Reagan had been forced to concede that his program of cutting government spending and taxes had not resulted in the surge of investment, employment, and profits he had promised. Tight control of the money supply had slowed inflation, but this control had kept interest rates so high that housing, automobiles, steel, and other basic industries had been paralyzed, major enterprises were close to bankruptcy, and projected federal deficits had risen so fast that the Administration had reluctantly supported an increase in taxes to contain them.

We are beginning to recognize that no President or government program can put us, as the saying goes, "back" on the track of the kind of economic growth for which so many of our cherished beliefs were crafted. We are even beginning to suspect that those cherished premises are exactly what makes the problems of the 1980s insoluble.

People will endure a great deal of pain in the defense of a premise, but in the long historical perspective, they eventually abandon theories they can't make work. After a century of religious warfare, Europeans of the seventeenth century gave up the idea of killing each other over theology, and adopted, if only in exhaustion, the practical notion that each individual had a right to worship God in his or her own way.

The Great Depression of the thirties moved theory even faster. After waiting a few years for free enterprise to repair the damage it had done in the 1929 crash, we adopted the heretical notion that the federal government has to take some responsibility for the economy. In the 1980s only a tiny minority of nostalgic Libertarians still hold to the premises that made Herbert Hoover helpless.

In the 1980s we are going through a similar crisis. This time, circumstances are forcing us to doubt a number of basic principles: that economic growth can continue indefinitely; that it solved our most pressing problems in the past; that the market will create enough jobs to go around and allocate income fairly; that we would be better off with less government; that you earn your money by your efforts alone and have a right to spend it any way you please;

that your money income is a rough but generally reliable measure of the quality of your life and your value to the community; that the Gross National Product is a measure of the well-being of the nation.

We had not recognized the extent to which we were all borrowing from tomorrow. Plans based on rapid growth can come to grief if the rate of growth so much as falters, and that is what is happening in the 1980s, to governments and business enterprises as well as to families. Social Security is a particularly good example. Like deficits projected for the national budget, the projected health of the Social Security system depends on what various government agencies think will happen to the economy. The forecasts of the Congressional Budget Office seldom agree with the optimistic prophecies of the President, and neither has a very good track record.

Social Security

Social Security is not a reserve, like a bank account, but a claim on current paychecks. Since pensioners are paid out of money currently taken in, the funds available for the old and disabled go up and down with the size of the nation's payrolls.

After his 1982 State of the Union address, President Reagan quipped that the law requiring the report made him into a liar because nobody could tell what the economy was going to do in the year ahead. The law is less kind to the three cabinet members and the presidentially appointed commissioner of Social Security who are its trustees. They are required to estimate taxes and benefits for seventy-five years in the future, when the fund will be paying old people who haven't yet been born.

It is a formidable task. In their 1981 report the trustees said that the future health of the fund would depend on "fertility, mortality, net immigration, marriage, divorce, labor force participation, unemployment, productivity, inflation, retirement patterns, and disability incidence and duration." All of these have to be estimated for every year ahead, and since precise forecasting of any or all is impossible, the trustees presented four projections and a "worst case" scenario of disaster. By the end of 1981 unemployment was worse than the worst case projected.

Social Security is a big chunk of money, and when the economy is rising it is an irresistible fiscal bonanza. During the prosperous 1950s and 1960s, the money kept pouring in. The trustees are supposed to begin the year with 9 percent of the year's obligations in the till, but they started some years with almost twice as much. Legally, the money was a trust outside the federal budget, but the billions piling up were a standing temptation to politicians.

The only thing they could legally do with the billions was to pay them out in benefits. In 1956 they added disability insurance; in 1965 Medicare. Each was set up as a separate fund with its own legal claim on a fixed percentage of the money collected, based on its own actuarial assumptions.

Then, in the late 1960s, when the Vietnam War ran the federal budget into the red, Lyndon Johnson found a way to use the Social Security funds to make the deficit look smaller. He incorporated the trust funds into a unified budget and provided that a surplus in any of the funds could be applied to the federal deficit in calculating the overall balance. The money was still in trust. It couldn't be used to buy a bomber. But it was supposed to make everyone feel better, especially fiscal conservatives who made the money markets on which the Treasury depended to finance the national debt.

Other goodies were added as the billions continued to grow. In 1965, benefits were provided beyond the cutoff age of eighteen for dependent children trying to get through college. In 1972 inflation was a cloud on the horizon the size of a man's hand, but the elderly were on fixed incomes, and Congress decided to protect them against it. Every year after 1974, benefits reflected rises in the Consumer Price Index and the benefits of older workers were calculated on the wages they would have received if they were earning them at current pay levels.

Then, with inflation, came a time of troubles. Shrinking payrolls mean that the funds produce little more than they have to pay out, and sometimes less. Unexpectedly high unemployment could put the funds in the red. A real depression could threaten the system as it is presently funded, so it needs reform to provide against this contingency. But the money collected from payroll taxes is still in trust for beneficiaries and can't be used to retire the federal debt or buy a bomber. Cutting benefits would make the federal deficit look smaller because the funds are counted in the federal budget.

The funds available for pensioners at any future date are going to depend on the taxes collected from future payrolls. The relative numbers of young and old are not the most important factor in the forecast, and they are not a problem in the foreseeable future. The big generation of babies born in the 1950s are working now and swelling the income of the funds, and they will continue paying these taxes until they begin to retire in 2010. According to the Report of the Technical Committee on Retirement Income prepared for the 1981 White House Conference, the aging of the population won't be a strain on the funds for another half century.

So many factors go into the equation that there is no reason to assume that fewer young adults won't be able to support a growing retired population. This ability depends, among other things, on how many of them work, how much they earn, and how productive they are. On the other side of the equation, we know how many old people there are likely to be, but we don't know how long they will live, how many will continue to earn, how many dependents (including former spouses) will have to be cared for, and how their benefits will be adjusted to reflect the changing purchasing power of the dollar.

So many trends can go so many ways that you can get whatever future you please by letting the right ones run for another thirty or forty years. If you are pessimistic, you can project disaster by assuming that productivity will level off, that people will insist on retiring earlier and earlier, that women will give up their jobs and go back to the home, that unemployment will rise, or that the GNP will continue to slide for a dozen years.

On the other hand, the strain of the aging population could be wiped out if better health reduced the proportion of workers disabled, if productivity improved, or if young immigrants increased taxable payrolls by swarming into the country to take the unpleasant jobs that now go begging because native-born Americans don't want to do them. Social Security actuaries have even figured in this possibility. In 1981 they estimated that the small deficit they were projecting on the basis of the aging of the population over the next seventy-five years could be cut by more than half if 1.2 million immigrants came into the country to work every year instead of the 400,000 officials think are coming in now.

The estimates don't attempt to deal with the most important changes ahead. It is, for instance, highly unlikely that jobs of the 2040s, or even the 2010s, will be anything like the jobs of the 1980s. There might be no solvency problem at all if work was organized so that old and young would want to spend more time in taxable employment.

Social Security can't go broke unless we have an atomic war or a revolution. If, as it now appears, our payrolls are going to grow more slowly than we figured they would, benefits are not apt to be increased, as they were during the 1960s. Future beneficiaries cannot expect the fivefold return of their contributions that pensioners of the 1980s enjoy. But neither President Reagan nor anyone else is suggesting that old people will ever get less than the share of the GNP to which the present level of benefits now entitles them.

The plight of Social Security is a good example of what has been happening to the country in general. As a nation, we are used to growing pains. Shrinking pains are a new experience, but as we entered the 1980s it was possible to see the ways in which a permanently sluggish economy was beginning to change how we spend our money, what we want from our jobs, and what we expect from the government.

Spending Values

When it doesn't look as if you are going to get a raise this year after all, what do you do?

You don't buy the new things you had been planning to get, but as long as you have as much to spend as the year before, instead of the more you expected, you find it surprisingly easy to substitute satisfactions that don't cost money.

For starters, you don't slosh through the mud in your party shoes, as a friend of mine did several years ago, explaining that "they are worn at the heel and it's just as easy to buy a new pair as it is to make two trips to have them repaired." Throwing half-used things away makes sense when you expect to be able to afford better things next year, but in the 1980s most of us are thinking of ways to conserve.

The pain is surprisingly small. The United States of America is still the world's most productive economy, and it's not declining. If it is growing a little more slowly than in the past, it is stabilizing at a very high level. In the 1980s we are able to satisfy a wide variety of material needs even though a quarter of our factories are down and more than 11 million of our workers are jobless. Wallace Peterson, an economist at the University of Nebraska, figures that in 1981 private industry produced enough to supply every man, woman, and child with consumer goods and services worth $7,500 a year.

A standard of living as high as ours is easy to defend because it gives us so many options. When we can't afford to buy a new car, we don't go carless, we find a way to keep the old one running. When we can't afford to have the house professionally cleaned, the family pitches in to do the work, and the house may even be better kept and cleaner. When food prices go up, we discover it's fun to keep a kitchen garden. We have the time to do more things around the house because we are making a short visit to friends instead of vacationing at a costly resort this summer. There's so much waste in the GNP that cutting the money we pass around may not always cut our standard of living.

Consider how noiselessly we adjusted to the gas shortage, once the gas lines and the pump prices alerted us to the problem! Some people warned that Americans would rather die than give up their cars—if need be, in a war—to keep the gasoline flowing.

But what happened? There were not as many car pools as there might have been, because Americans like to stay in control of their wheels. But people invented ways to make out. The woman who cleans my house stacked me back to back with a neighboring customer. The lady who sews added mileage charges to her bills, and was happy to visit me because it financed a trip to town on which she could do her other errands. Living rooms got chillier when husbands set the thermostat down, and wives took to knitting sweaters.

Piddling stuff, but it added up. By 1982, to the surprise (and perhaps dismay) of the oil industry, we were getting along on 2 to 3 million barrels of oil a day less than we had used in the late 1970s, and according to the American Petroleum Institute, only one-quarter of the savings was due to the recession.

Many of the adjustments we have been making are so painless that we hardly think of them as economies. Jogging instead of joining a health club. Visiting friends instead of going to Europe. Recording a song from a friend's tape instead of buying it from the store. Unfortunately for sales and profits, it is easy to dispense with some of the innovations on which American industry relies to keep the GNP rising.

My family and I tried all sorts of things in the microwave oven the first few weeks we had it, but for most things it wasn't better than the regular oven. When it was stolen, I figured I'd had my fun with it, so I spent the insurance money equipping my home computer to connect with other computers and data available by telephone. My behavior was a perfect example of the fickleness of new consumption patterns that worries marketers.

Doing without is often a reminder of the nonmaterial pleasure that made us want to make the expenditure in the first place. People who bought microwave ovens thought they were buying freedom and leisure, benefits that, at the very least, are quite separable from the product. When the price of an edible restaurant meal deterred women office workers from meeting each other for lunch, they discovered that eating their brown-bag lunches together was often just as satisfying as trying to talk through the noise of a bustling restaurant.

Work Values

A slower-growing economy changes patterns of work as well as patterns of spending. How do you feel about your job when you discover that you aren't going to get a raise and there's no point in quitting because you know that you can't do better anywhere else?

At first you are angry or depressed, but eventually you relax and say to yourself, well, it's a job. And instead of thinking about how to get promoted out of it, you look for ways to be more comfortable doing it and to pay more attention to the life you lead outside of working hours.

People whose opportunities are blocked expend their energy on friends, family, hobbies, weekends, vacations, and volunteer work. In her study of the motivations of men and women in a major corporation, Rosabeth Kanter found that workers who had little opportunity to advance tended to "talk more often and more openly about life outside." One man she studied used his office to do work for outside involvements and was described as always on his way to a meeting.

But the most important difference was that those who had given up hope for promotion found their satisfactions in their relationships with the people they met through their work rather than in the work itself. Instead of competing with their co-workers, they enjoyed being one of them. Kanter's study documented the suspicion that women, like blacks, appear to be less ambitious because they are restricted to dead-end jobs.

Young adults starting careers in the 1980s are making some of these adjustments at the very outset. They look lazy or spoiled to older colleagues because while they worry about future income, they don't seem willing to work very hard to get ahead. It's not the moral fiber of workers that has declined, but the payoff for career dedication.

Declining payoff reduces the commitment of all but the most energetic. The ambitious who continue to compete for the top are already beginning to feel like a suspect minority. They conceal or apologize for their dedication and worry more about the satisfactions they are missing than their opposite numbers did twenty years ago, when ambition was highly regarded. Some of them respond to the crowded ladder by inventing new ladders of their own: one young lawyer plans to pull away from the crowd by creating a specialty in aviation law.

These are the exceptions. We now have doctors, lawyers, college professors, and editors who are less dedicated than professional workers used to be when chances for advancement were high because demand for their services was growing. In the 1980s even professionals become like the low-opportunity employees of the corporation that Kanter studied. When advancement is slow, employers will have to motivate workers by making the work more interesting and the workplace a more pleasant place to spend time.

Political Values

Slower growth threatens the values of business-oriented free enterprise, as well as the party in power that espouses them.

Conservatives talk as if they fear a rising up of the poor against the rich. Will the unemployed protest in the streets? Will they march on Washington demanding handouts?

The answer is no. There was little public commotion when one out of four was unemployed during the Great Depression of the thirties—nothing as big as the Civil War draft riots in New York, or the race riots following World War II in Detroit or Watts. What really happened was a return of the sense of community we had mislaid in the scramble to get rich quick during the country's dramatic expansion.

The same sense of community is beginning to return in the 1980s. We can no longer rely on growth to take care of those who have never been able to make it. We see too many people left out through no fault of their own. We are social animals, and when we see people left out we feel as if we have to do something about it.

Luckily, there is no such thing as a purely economic man or woman. In his famous essay "The Tragedy of the Commons," the environmentalist Garrett Hardin suggests putting a contraceptive in the water supply in order to save the planet from overpopulation. He argues that people cannot be expected to forgo having children for the common good. Common pastures will always be overgrazed, he points out, because each shepherd has more interest in grazing his own sheep on them than in doing his part to save them for everyone.

It is a plausible theory, especially in America, where farmers exploited their land and then abandoned it to move west. But the sense of community is older and deeper than the American experience, and easier to invoke than Hardin imagined.

In 1981, when New York City's reservoirs were running low,

authorities beamed appeals to save water over radio and television. Water wasn't metered in New York, and although all would suffer if the reservoirs fell below the danger point, it was perfectly obvious that no individual could be better off in such a disaster because he had put a brick in the toilet tank, refrained from flushing "for everything," or soaped up before turning on the shower. How many people would shiver in four inches of water instead of luxuriating in a full tub, where no one could see them?

According to Garrett Hardin, individuals would be much too smart to do anything of the kind. But they weren't. New Yorkers just didn't feel comfortable preferring their comfort to the general good when it was pointed out to them. A few months after the first appeals, the consumption of water had fallen to below the level the campaign to conserve had set as a target.

Boom times suppress the sense of community, but when no one is getting very rich it is easier to feel that we are all in the same boat. Business analysts are a bit too smart by far when they say that the spontaneous cooperation of Japanese workers won't work in the United States because of our individualistic culture. Let them speak for themselves, not for American workers. In spring 1982, thirteen workers for the Department of Public Works in Plymouth, Michigan, gave up a week's pay to save the job of a junior truck driver.

We cannot shake the feeling that each of us owes something to the general pot and each of us has an overriding claim to a share of that pot regardless of input, merit, or legalities. Financially sophisticated young workers complain that Social Security won't be as good a deal for them as it has been for beneficiaries now drawing their pensions. Given the right circumstances, they might even do better if they could invest the taxes they have to pay in private insurance.

But this is theory. Even the young who expect to be shafted aren't sure that they want the Social Security system to be run like a private insurance business, which pays each insured a benefit based on his or her individual contribution. Most people feel that benefits should be based at least in part on need. In a Harris poll of 1981 a majority said that they were willing to pay heavier taxes to maintain Social Security benefits, and even more favored paying them, if necessary, out of general revenues, much of which comes from unearned income.

When it comes to the crunch, it is not the strength of the old-age lobby that politicians fear, but a pervasive feeling that annuitants ought to share in whatever the economy is producing. There is a very strong feeling that retired workers deserve a fair share of what younger workers are producing, regardless of what they produced or paid in during the years when they were earning.

None of us would now be willing to go back to the boxlike little house, the half day's work on Saturday, and the clothes that had to be washed by hand that the wages of annuitants provided them in the 1950s, so we don't expect them to live that way in the 1980s. In 1972 we retroactively raised the wages on which benefits were figured to bring the standard of living of our parents up to our own. Would we have given them more to maintain their former standard if, instead of rising, the standards of active workers were actually shrinking? Of course we wouldn't.

It's easy to dish out bigger helpings when the pie is growing. People are not so apt to question their share when there's more to divide. But they look very carefully at who gets what and why when the pie to be divvied up is shrinking or even when it is growing more slowly than expected. When unemployment is chronic, we can no longer rely on the market to do this job fairly.

Before the Great Depression of the 1930s a great many people believed that the progressive income tax was "immoral" because it took from the rich to give to the poor, and some of President Reagan's conservative associates believe this still. But as a practical matter, every civilized nation of the world was forced into making the rich help the poor before that depression was over. The only reason that conservatives can revive the notion of an absolute right to property now is that, after World War II, the free market seemed for a time to be doing a reasonably equitable job of distributing income. Property rights will be once again suspect if the disparity between rich and poor is widened by a new depression.

In the 1980s it is easier to see that our free market has never been able to provide enough jobs to go around in peacetime. In January 1982, when unemployment rose to almost 9 percent, President Reagan said he had counted twenty-four pages of help-wanted ads in Washington newspapers. If the unemployed couldn't type or program computers, well, then they should learn these skills. And if jobs were scarce in Michigan, maybe they ought to go to Texas, where business was booming.

The remark boomeranged. The unemployed complained that very few of those jobs were for baby-sitters or clerks or any of the other jobs the umemployed could do. Reporters dug into the story. Michiganders were coming back from Texas to report that there were no jobs there, either. And programs of job training at federal expense had been cut from the budget, on the ground that not enough of those trained were able to get private-sector jobs to warrant the cost of training them.

In the roaring 1950s technological unemployment could be declared a fallacy. Business leaders promised that workers displaced by machines would find jobs in new industries that the machines would make possible. Computers were heralded as the creators of a whole new profession of specialists skilled in programming, using, and repairing them. But it wasn't that simple.

SHARP RISE IN COMPUTER JOBS IS FORECAST FOR NEXT 8 YEARS a headline of 1982 promised. But how many? The story went on to say that most of the new jobs would be for "computer service technicians, where the 83,000 positions in 1980 are expected to increase by 93 percent to 112 percent in this decade." A gain, over the decade, of 100,000, while many more that number of existing jobs are eliminated.

We have a labor force increasingly split between a few well-paid, high-skilled technical specialists and a growing army of unskilled workers who are unemployed because they are being replaced by machines, or because the work that they do has been moved to Hong Kong or Taiwan, or because it isn't worth the minimum wage to the people who might employ them here.

This ominous split in the labor force is growing. The steady rise in peacetime unemployment since World War II has been ignored because the principal victims have been teenagers, blacks, and women newly attracted into the labor force. It has been easy to tell them that they can get jobs if they train for the skills in demand and make themselves personally more employable.

But sometimes the view from below is clearer. Black teenagers know that there aren't enough jobs to go around, because they are the ones who lose out in the game of musical chairs. A third are unemployed. In 1979 no less an authority than the Nobel Prize–winning economist Wassily Leontief warned that there will be so few jobs in the future that we will have to learn to share them.

The sense of community is old and deep, and it reasserts itself when technological advances increase the quantity of things individuals want to consume without creating, in the process, enough jobs to allow everyone to claim them. The sense of community is older and deeper in humankind than is our parochial American dream of taking care of yourself without any help from anybody else.

None of us made ourselves. We do not earn our paychecks by our unaided individual efforts. They are merely pieces of the common pie that are allocated to us on a more or less arbitrary basis. When promotions are few we ponder the basis on which they are handed out. We would like to feel that people are actually earning their incomes.

Unfortunately, there will never be any way of knowing whether they do. Most people provide services whose value is measured only in terms of the pay that has to be justified. Some teachers are better than others, but their salaries are set by negotiations with school boards that consider merit, if at all, on a highly subjective basis.

Organizations go to great lengths to justify salary differentials. They conduct salary reviews in which worker and boss check boxes labeled "leadership ability," "team player," "initiative." They may quantify progress toward predetermined goals. But everybody knows it's a game.

Market forces look as if they play a bigger part in the compensation of business owners and fee-paid professionals, but this possibility recedes the closer you look at it. Lawyers are sometimes paid out of the verdicts they collect, but most business, managerial, and professional workers are paid on the basis of custom. For instance, Park Avenue doctors say they have to charge more not because they are better but because their rent is higher than that of doctors rendering the identical service in Poughkeepsie.

Book authors paid royalties are among the few whose incomes are determined in a really competitive market. This may be the reason that authors are much less likely to believe in the benevolent workings of Adam Smith's Invisible Hand than are bank presidents and telephone company executives, whose income is sheltered from it. The most interesting case, of course, is that of farmers who are paid not for what they grow but for what they refrain from growing.

Slower economic growth challenges not only the legitimacy of the free market but its ability to provide the goods and services people most desperately want. Reagan was elected in 1980 on a promise to cut government spending so that taxpayers could spend more of "their own money" in the private sector, and most of them welcomed the rhetoric. But whenever Americans are asked what would improve the quality of their lives, they generally give priority to peace, health, safety, and other goods available only from the public sector. If forced to choose, the vote might be surprisingly high for giving up microwave ovens for safer streets or even the satisfaction of living in a just society.

People complain obsessively about crime, violence, dirt, fraud, pollution, and the waste of collective resources ranging from our remaining unspoiled wilderness to our scientific and artistic talent. We make heavier demands on the common good when we can no longer expect a dramatic rise in our private consumption. The unmet needs of the 1980s are not in the private sector but in the government services people really want, and that is where the new jobs are going to have to be created. Programs shelved by the Reagan Administration will be rediscovered and voted in as if they were brand-new initiatives.

A Different Future

The fallout of slower growth is heading us toward a future different from the one adults born after World War II have been led to expect, but one that many of them are going to like better—more communal, more equal, less competitive—a world of people less willing to sacrifice the pleasures of the here and now for material rewards in the future. Come to think of it, these were the values they espoused in opposition to those of their parents when they were rebelling in the 1960s.

They are quieter now, but they have not lost their concern for minorities and the environment or their intolerance of violence, meaningless consumption, and what they still call greed. Their careers are less likely to tempt them into the tunnel vision of material advance they decried in their parents, and many of them have delayed careers and families to develop alternative interests.

Those who have been so inclined have had the time as well as the education to pursue activities formerly available only to the privileged few. Never before has so large a minority of Americans pursued the arts, the crafts, science, nature, politics, cooking, hobbies, and the wilder shores of recreational sex, to name a few of the embellishments of life that don't depend on age or stage in the family cycle.

There's no reason to expect that a future increase in the proportion of old people will make the whole country more conservative. People do not become more rigid and prejudiced, or less likely to read a newspaper, join a club, try a new product, or make new friends, as the years go by; nor are they converted to believing in a domestic role for women and a literal interpretation of the Bible. These attitudes have nothing to do with age or arteries. They are simply the characteristics of people with less than a high school education that show up on opinion surveys. We think of them as "old" because most of them ended their education in grade school.

In the year 2000 half the people over sixty-five will be high school graduates. They will have lived more widely and deeply than their parents. In 1980 they are only halfway through their lives, but they have already done more, seen more, learned more, and earned more. They are even more likely to know how to swim, play tennis, and dance, to name a few of the skills that last a lifetime.

Up to now, the babies of the postwar boom have changed the conventions of every age they have been through. They have loosened the grip of every institution they have encountered. Schools, colleges, military service, marriage, and jobs are permanently less constricting than they were before the boom babies hit them. They are not likely to fade away into the background when they turn sixty-five, as the retired have been expected to do. Liberated from the myths of age, they will do many things that the youth-oriented elders of 1980 have been programmed not to attempt. Most likely, they will once again be lifestyle leaders, the bearers of the values that will be adopted by the whole society.

We do not know for sure what new ground they will break in the twenty-first century, but there is one clue. A sense of the human community as a whole, concern for individuals overlooked, the pleasures of leisure and the task itself—these are the steady-state values on the rise, but they are also the values that characterize the ageless individuals who never seem old.

The old who make an agenda out of these values are exceptional now, but they are exceptions to the history that has kept their agemates down. A lucky minority of people now over sixty-five have had the good fortune to enjoy the education, comforts, choices, and encouraging environment that were a birthright for almost everybody born after World War II.

We may be able to find out what later years will be like for the average elder of the twenty-first century by looking at what this lucky minority is doing now.

II

Pioneers

3

The Human Years

The ageless are people who seem to have succeeded in outwitting Mother Nature. One of them was Margaret Mead. The last time I saw her she was seventy-six. Clinging to the rostrum at the National Women's Conference at Houston, she begged an audience of thousands to stop clapping. "I am only allowed ten minutes to speak," she scolded, "so let's not waste any of it in demonstrations."

The word *demonstrations* set the huge, tense audience rustling. The feminist majority was expecting a camera-catching walkout of the conservative minority who had come to defend a traditional family role for women, and Mead's sharp eyes had been following the movement of the whips on the floor who could set it off.

"Demonstrations about *me*, I mean. . ." she added. Both camps laughed, and then listened. "It has been women's task throughout history to go on believing in life, when there was almost no hope," she told them. "If we will act unitedly, forget every other consideration, as we do when our children are at stake, we may be able to

53

produce a world in which our children and other people's children will be safe."

Feminists had expected Mead to champion women's rights, but the appeal for women to work for peace established a common ground on which every woman in the room could agree. Television newsmen were cheated of a walkout scene they could have played for laughs that would have discredited the purposes of the conference.

She certainly did not look like a woman suffering from pancreatic cancer that would end her life in a matter of months. When cancer was diagnosed, she simply denied it. As she grew weaker, she drew more heavily on people who helped her to get from one appointment to another. But she maintained her influence in public affairs by refusing to admit that she was sick up to the last few weeks of her life.

The Ageless and the Old

The ageless are not slow, timid, or disengaged from society. Their lives are not "characterized by a reduction in physical activities and social interaction," as one textbook of psychology describes them. Nor do they suffer from a "reduction of energy" that makes them "willing accomplices in the process of separation from active society."

Consider Armand Hammer, chairman of Occidental Petroleum. During a few months of his eighty-second year he bid on Leonardo da Vinci's notebooks at a London auction, swung by the Kremlin to discuss the Afghan uprising with his old friend Leonid Brezhnev, clarified the conversation with reporters, and suggested an oil deal with Mexico via an op-ed article in the *New York Times*.

The ageless don't waste time. Hoyt Catlin, founder of Fertl Cubes, Inc., a small seed-starting business in Norwalk, Connecticut, celebrated his eighty-ninth birthday by driving four hundred miles to visit relatives on Cape Cod. Between the drive and the party they gave for him after he arrived, he stayed up twenty hours.

And they don't let anything stop them. When Eleanor Roosevelt was seventy-six, a car backed into her on Eighth Street, the bustling main thoroughfare of Greenwich Village in New York, and knocked her down.

"I was up at once & no crowd gathered, & I walked away but I found my right foot functioned less & less well," she wrote her daughter. "I opened the cancer benefit I was going to. I greeted and fed a group of some 24 kids 8–10 with their chaperones . . . & then I called David [her physician] because I had to speak at a Cloak & Suit Industry dinner for Brandeis."

The doctor found torn ligaments and ordered her into the hospital, but she simply transferred her schedule there. "Yesterday at least 40 reform N.Y. City candidates were photographed here with Sen. Lehman & me," she wrote her daughter. "I've done 3 recordings, tons of mail each day & seen all the people who intended to see me."

Instead of disengaging, the ageless are almost foolishly sociable. As they outlive their friends they work at attracting new ones. Some, like CBS chairman William S. Paley, have money and clout on their side. In his eightieth year he worked in his office every day and went out on the town with a pretty young woman on his arm every night. And what can we make of the hundred-and-five-year-old black woman who managed to have a cheery word every day with every patient on her ward when she was in the hospital getting her pacemaker replaced?

We expect the old to mumble or fail to finish their sentences, but words are a way of reaching out to other people, and the ageless take pains to write and speak distinctly. Even when they look physically fragile, their speech remains dry, sharp, and as clear as rarefied mountain air. Millicent Fenwick, former U.S. Senator from New Jersey, is a good example. Her seemingly effortless flow of perfect speech was a formidable political asset. Although she lost in the general election of 1982, she simply outtalked the young man half her age who challenged her in the Republican primary. Her charm, to which he attributed his defeat, was primarily a gift for calling a spade a spade and for finishing her sentences.

We expect the old to mull over the past, but the ageless look to the future, however long or short they can expect it to be. A ninety-four-year-old retired businessman and his wife are crossing orchids that can't be expected to bloom for at least five years. Francetta

Barberis, the former head of Webster College, thinks of her life as "a novel that keeps you turning the pages." At her seventy-fifth birthday party, she told her friends she looked forward to the thrill of her voluntary retirement from the Job Corps. And the next page? "The thrill of seeing heaven." V. S. Pritchett, the British man of letters, tells about an eighty-four-year-old friend who was so depressed that he wanted to die at once—but not, he said, until he had found out what was going to happen in Poland, and after that, in Iran. If that's his plan, then it seems unlikely that the world will ever calm down long enough to let him die.

The ageless exceptions to the stereotypes surprise us most by their curiosity. Instead of aches and pains, they are full of what they just saw in China. They are as eager as children to try new things. If they are authors, they are learning to write with a computer. If they are swimmers, they are altering the crawl that has served them for half a century to take advantage of the new, more efficient S stroke. Mary Calderone, the sex educator, spent her seventy-eighth birthday learning how to program a computer. According to her friend Richard Rodgers, the composer, Eleanor Roosevelt learned to dive in her later years because her grandchildren made fun of the awkward way she slid into the swimming pool at her cottage in Hyde Park.

Life-Stage Anomalies

Disengagement doesn't describe the later years of the ageless, but neither do any of the other life-stage theories. The study by Daniel Levinson of Yale reported in *The Seasons of a Man's Life*, the ongoing study of a Harvard class by George Valliant, the *Transformations* reported by California psychiatrist Roger Gould, and Gail Sheehy's *Passages* have very little to say about the stages they label "old age," "late adulthood," "the thoughtful sixties," or the large territory Gould sweepingly describes as "after 50."

European-bred thinkers have been a little more imaginative. Danish-born Erik Erikson promises "generativity," or concern for future generations. Carl Jung, the Swiss psychoanalyst, promises deeper understanding of the meaning of life. But until recently the youth-oriented behavioral scientists of America described what happens after middle age in terms of decrements.

Bernice Neugarten, now at Northwestern University, was the first sociologist to notice that we are becoming an age-irrelevant nation, but in 1965 she was classifying the old on the basis of their response to waning capacity. Even at that time she found that the largest group of people over sixty-five had "integrated" personalities, among whom some were "reorganizers" who had adjusted to their new situation.

The ageless I talked with didn't see themselves in terms of decline. When I asked them what had changed in their lives after middle age, they did not regret that their children were grown and gone, nor did they look back wistfully at the years they spent building careers. When asked to describe the course of their lives, they responded with metaphors of continued growth. An educator thought of the course of his life as "a snowball, gathering size and strength." Jacqueline Wexler, the former president of Hunter College, described it as a "spiral that brings you back to the same problems, but you resolve them each time on a higher plane."

Many thought of their lives as a journey rather than an arrival, but all of the modes of travel suggested were self-directed and self-propelled: nobody felt like a ship being passively tugged through the predictable locks of the Panama Canal. Margaret Hickey, the veteran editor of the *Ladies' Home Journal*, thinks of her life as "a voyage of discovery through stormy seas." For Pauli Murray, the civil rights activist who was the first Negro, male or female, to earn a doctorate from the Yale Law School, it's a "pilgrimage": in her seventies, she has just embarked on a new career as an Episcopal priest. Henry Chauncey, the first president of Educational Testing Service, thinks of his life as "an obstacle race." I think of mine as a climb up a mountain that rewards each step with a longer view.

Looking back on their lives, none could identify the classic stages of any of the life-cycle programs I described to them. They thought of the course of their lives as a series of lucky accidents. "I seem to have been at the right place at the right time" is the comment Alvin Eurich added to his *Who's Who* listing.

Eurich started out to be a teacher of psychology at Stanford University and the University of Minnesota, because he liked teaching, but in World War II the Bureau of Naval Personnel drafted him to organize military training on college campuses. This war service gave him firsthand knowledge of the country's colleges, and when the war ended he was called back to Stanford as vice-president and later acting president to help reorganize the university and set up the Stanford Research Institute. This experience, in turn, made him a natural choice to be the first chancellor of the State University of New York, where he put together a consortium of state colleges and universities, now the biggest postsecondary organization in the world. After getting SUNY established in three years, he became the first director of the Ford Foundation's Fund for the Advancement of Education.

Giving away all this money proved a frustrating experience. Academics didn't know how to make a ten-year budget. All they knew how to do was to keep their institutions going by the stopgap measures devised to cope with the Depression of the thirties. Eurich's wartime experience had forced him to apply the rudiments of budgeting to colleges, so once again he had unique experience in a skill that was badly needed, and as the date for mandatory retirement from the Ford Foundation approached he set up an organization of his own to put that special knowledge to work.

At eighty Eurich is busier—and making more money—than ever before in his life. When I saw him in the Rockefeller Center offices of his Academy for Educational Development, he had just returned from a worldwide trip, including Sri Lanka, where he had arranged for several American colleges to sponsor an agricultural development program. As head of his own Academy for Educational Development, he was exempt from all retirement laws and policies.

The right place at the right time. The way he puts it, luck was with him all along the way. But a surprising number of the ageless credit bad luck, instead.

A cousin of mine ascribes the health and affluence she enjoys in her seventies to the bankruptcy of her husband. She was a fashion model before she retired to become a picture-perfect wife and mother during the family-oriented 1950s. When she was fifty-eight her husband, an inventor, went broke, and she ran up a twelve-thousand-dollar hospital bill in a vain attempt to cure an ailing back that confined her to bed.

What to do? She knew that she could never pay the staggering bill out of earnings at a regular job, even if she could get one at her age. The only hope she could see was to start a business, but she couldn't think of one for which she was fitted. She insists that desperation forced her to invent one. Thinking back to her brief experience as an office worker, she recalled how indignant she used to feel at the insensitive way personnel interviewers had treated her when she was applying for a job. She used to complain that they did not even try to find out what special talents any of the applicants had to offer.

Friends who worked for major corporations assured her not only that interview techniques had not improved but that personnel departments were unable to locate candidates for the growing number of jobs that required an unusual combination of skills (for instance, a chemist fluent in French). Personnel officers admitted they simply didn't have time or money to fill these unusual requests, and agreed to pay her a fee for every successful search. Eventually she built a business that supported her family comfortably, and seemed, in addition, to cure her back.

My cousin isn't unusual. By a kind of semantic shortcut, people often ascribe their success to the obstacle that challenged them instead of the way they responded to it. Rosser Reeves, the advertising man, thinks he decided early in life to make money because his family was poor. René Dubos, the microbiologist and historian of science, told me he turned to books because rheumatic fever left him too fragile to play games with other boys or to become a butcher like his father. Irregular schooling abroad was mentioned by two distinguished women: Margaret Hickey, the *Ladies' Home Journal* editor, in Switzerland while her parents were posted to a foreign-service assignment in the Middle East, and Mary Calderone, in France, where her father, the famous photographer Edward Steichen, was beginning his career in art.

Off-Track Potentials

It may be easier to keep on breaking new ground if something happened early on to keep you from doing what the people around you were doing. Mary Calderone, the sex educator, is a good example. In her late seventies, she is an erect, slight, fast-moving woman with straightforward china-blue eyes that look straight at you. Perfectly groomed, she claims she buys her clothes by mail order to save time. Unfailingly articulate, she speaks in seemingly effortless torrents of well-shaped paragraphs.

Like her public service achievements, Mary Calderone's late-life vigor stems from her steadily increasing skill in seeing her way around conventional obstacles. It began as a necessity for survival. All her early life she had reason to consider herself an outsider. Born in 1904, she remembers herself as the ugly duckling of the family, a lanky child with stringy brown hair, who seemed to herself painfully less attractive than her round, cuddly, curly-haired younger sister.

Alienation was greater as she grew older. She was a stranger in her own country when the Steichens fled to America after the outbreak of World War I. A fiercely independent eleven-year-old with a French accent, she didn't fit into grade school in Sharon, Connecticut, where the Steichens lived as refugees in the summer house of a rich American family. At the fashionable Brearley School for Girls in New York and at Vassar College, she felt like a poor relative in hand-me-down clothes, admired for her brains and talent, but not particularly liked by her well-to-do classmates.

It was even worse after college. For a time she drifted. She married and divorced. She studied for the stage, but knew she would never be as good as Katharine Cornell and gave it up after three years. She tried to support herself and her two children as a clerk in a department store, but couldn't learn to write sales checks. She was psychoanalyzed. When she sought vocational advice from Johnson O'Connor, the pioneer aptitude tester, he classified her as a "too many aptituded woman," doomed to wander restlessly until she found an occupation that could use her diversity of talents. He suggested that a woman with interests as broad as hers should consider medicine.

It sounded impossible. She was thirty years old and responsible for an eight-year-old daughter. Her college grades weren't good, and she had dropped chemistry after completing the requirements for medical school because she found it boring. In 1934 only the most brilliant, dedicated women could hope to get into medical school, but in her innocence she simply informed the startled Dean of the University of Rochester Medical School that she was going to be a doctor, and an hour and a half later he agreed to let her try. Four years later she graduated. Her biggest complaint against medical school was that it deprived her of a social life. She was ten years older than the other students and never met a man who interested her.

After acquiring a degree in public health, she married Dr. Frank Calderone, and spent the next four years having four pregnancies and two more children. To keep her tie to medicine, she took a part-time job as a physician in the local school system. Instead of treating it as a dead-end job made to order for a doctor with family responsibilities, she undertook to redefine it in larger terms. She was supposed to confine herself to looking down the throats of the pupils for signs of contagious diseases, but she instantly saw the golden chance to give the children general information that they could take home to their parents. The school board gave her a raise and told her to stick to inspecting throats. Instead of shutting up, as they expected her to do, she quit, not only because she thought she was being overpaid to look down throats but also to jolt the school board into broadening the job to include community health education.

Her next redefinition was more successful. When her youngest child was seven, she accepted the then minor job of medical director of the Planned Parenthood Federation of America. Characteristically, she did not realize at first that she got the job because no male physician would take it. Birth control was an embarrassing subject, vaguely associated with abortion, and mainstream doctors wanted nothing to do with it.

In her naïveté she simply disagreed with them. She defined birth control as a public health problem and undertook to persuade the medical profession that they ought to lead the fight for it. Every chance she got, she suggested to doctors that saving the lives of mothers wasn't enough when they could make the lives of these women so much better by helping them avoid unwanted pregnancies. In the end, the American Medical Association adopted her concept that family planning is a public health responsibility.

But birth control was not enough. Her work in the field convinced her that all Americans needed to know much more about their own sexuality, and they ought to learn about it at home and at school. This concept was of no interest at all to Planned Parenthood, but, as Calderone herself pointed out, it was an issue best promoted by a person who, like herself, was a grandmother, a mother, a physician, and a Quaker. In 1964 she enlisted professional colleagues. With no financial backing, they set up the Sex Information and Education Council of the U.S., popularly known as SIECUS.

SIECUS promotes "open and honest" sex education in the home and in the schools by serving as a catalyst for community action, a consultant to school boards and citizen groups, and a clearinghouse of information for parents, teachers, physicians, social workers, youth leaders, and the clergy.

She needed Quaker staying power to survive the organized opposition unleashed by conservatives. In a statement enshrined in the *Congressional Record*, the John Birch Society branded her an "aging libertine." Her speeches were picketed so nastily that she expected someone would eventually take a potshot at her. But the attention she attracted to the issue rallied financial support, and many schools requested help from SIECUS to set up trial programs.

Opponents objected that sex education belonged in the home, not the school, but even those who held this view agreed that parents couldn't teach their children about sex because they didn't know enough about it themselves. The way out of the dilemma was to educate parents. The remedy was easier to imagine than execute, but Mary Calderone did not flinch from it. In 1981 she launched a campaign to set up easily accessible centers where parents could come to learn about their children's sexuality and meet the challenge of socializing it.

At seventy-eight this "aging libertine" exults in her health and in her sexuality. "I'm so fortunate," she says. "There's absolutely nothing wrong with me. No heart disease. No arthritis. I love my three square meals a day. I bake my own bread and slather it with margarine. I sleep soundly eight hours a night. And I never have jet lag. I just get off a plane anywhere in the world and eat whatever meal is next being eaten there."

How does she do it? There is no single or exclusive secret. She uses strategies available to anyone willing to take the trouble. She boasts of her good constitution, and her father had it before her: Edward Steichen continued to be an intellectual influence at the Museum of Modern Art well into his eighties, long after he organized the ambitious international photographic exhibit "Family of Man." But as she talks about her daily life it is easy to see that she compensates for physical changes in generally available ways. The unusual thing about her is that she simply sees and uses more of the ways around a decrement than occur to most people. She does not, for instance, have time for a program of exercise, but when she moved to the city she made up for the activity she used to get from climbing stairs by running up and down the steps of the subway she had to take to work.

Another advantage is her willingness to use the help available from new technology. She admits to a lot of minor surgery for the repair of body parts showing wear and tear, such as operations for bunions, varicose veins, and cosmetic improvements. And she's willing to take trouble. Contact lenses weren't advised for older people when they first came out, but she learned how to use them because she wanted to be able to engage people eyeball-to-eyeball without any glass in between them.

All this adapting is easier because she has never had to lean on any of the conventional stereotypes. Her career bears no resemblance to any of the traditional life-stage programs. She bore four children, two in her twenties and two in her forties. Instead of a curve that peaked at childbearing years, the course of her life moved steadily up as she grew in skill, in confidence, and in the scope of her work and dreams. She doesn't count anything she did before she was fifty as work. At seventy-eight, she says, she feels no different from the way she remembers feeling at seven, but she is in a new phase of her career. In 1982 she retired from SIECUS to become adjunct professor in the Human Sexuality Program at New York University's Department of Health Education.

Like Mary Calderone, the ageless have not planned their lives or followed any pattern. They have simply responded imaginatively to the accidental situations they have encountered. They remind us that humans are not lilies or frogs, which are biologically programmed to grow on a predetermined plan that is exactly the same for every individual of the species, but self-directed individuals who deliberately adapt to the particular circumstances that happen to confront them.

This ability to adapt as individuals is the reason that human beings live longer and differ from each other more widely than individuals of other species. In his book *The Panda's Thumb*, Stephen Gould points out that we are the only animal that survives beyond the 800-millionth heartbeat, a longevity constant that relates the life span of a species to its size and consequent heart rate. (Elephants live longer than mice because their hearts beat more slowly, so 800 million heartbeats take longer. The hearts of big animals beat more slowly because it takes longer to get the blood around their bodies.)

Only humans have these extra years, and they are gloriously uncommitted. Neither nature nor culture seems to care what happens to individuals after they have reproduced. For these uniquely human years there is no agenda.

The View from the Plateau

We know very little about the potentials of these later years. On most of the standard maps they are terra incognita that is either left blank or decorated with the kind of mythical beasts early map makers sketched on parts of the globe about which they had no information. A few of every generation have spied out this unknown land and brought back curious, half-believed travelers' tales. We have to take these tales seriously now that we are all really going there.

According to one report, in later years the world begins to seem as magical as it did in childhood. For essayist Malcolm Cowley, at eighty "you can sit still and look at things." British essayist V. S. Pritchett concurs. At eighty he reported a "new sensation that living people are a wonder" and found himself "looking at places much longer and more intensely." A seventy-five-year-old sociologist friend reports that the world appears to be getting more miraculous. "I used to wonder why so many things went wrong, but now I find myself wondering how it is that they ever go right." On being asked how it felt to be old, Albert Einstein replied that he felt "neither hope nor fear, but interest in observing the universe."

What happens when you stop climbing and the view ahead is a plateau? The answer is, you feel free.

FREE FROM FAMILY OBLIGATIONS. "For true happiness, there is nothing like being a childless widow," an old Welsh woman told Anne Morrow Lindbergh. Anne Morrow Lindbergh didn't like the verdict, but she's a wise old woman herself and she didn't deny it.

FREE FROM SELF-INTEREST. "When you are sixty-five you have proved yourself already or you have not," semanticist S. I. Hayakawa pointed out. "You are no longer on the make." He was making a case for voters to send him back to the U.S. Senate, to which he had been elected after his retirement from the presidency of turbulent San Francisco State College.

FREE FROM WORRIES ABOUT WHAT PEOPLE THINK. Maggie Kuhn, the founder of the Gray Panthers, became more militant in her old age because she felt free, as she put it, "to raise hell." Old people I interviewed seldom asked that their names be withheld, even when they were candid about their personal lives. When I asked Rosser Reeves if I could use his name, he said, "Hell yes. There's nothing you can say about me that could possibly hurt me."

FREE TO HAVE FUN. Agatha Christie, the mystery writer, enjoyed a "second blooming that comes when you finish the life of the emotions and of personal relations and suddenly find—at the age of fifty, say—that a whole new life has opened before you. Picture exhibitions, concerts, the opera. It's as if a fresh sap of ideas and thoughts were rising in you."

FREE TO WORK FOR THE COMMON GOOD. Once you are on the plateau it is easier to see what is happening to the human race as a whole, and there is less to stop you from doing something about it. Eminent people have invested the precious capital of their reputations in high-risk causes. Albert Schweitzer, the doctor who won world fame for his medical missionary work, launched a campaign for world peace after he was seventy. He was joined in this effort by Linus Pauling, winner of the Nobel Prize in chemistry, who lost his passport because he insisted on publicizing the danger of testing the atom bomb. Both were depicted as doddering old crackpots who had wandered outside their fields.

Late-life altruism is more common than it at first appears. Senior business leaders are sometimes so afraid of being denigrated as do-gooders that they explain their nonprofit ventures as "just good public relations." Often this means going back to the big, simple issues with which we grappled before we started careers and families.

Unused Rooms

But the most exciting freedom of later years is the freedom to become a unique individual, different from any other on earth. To do this, you have to go back to a forgotten or undeveloped part of yourself. It may be a challenge you dared not take, a truth you could not face, a talent that you were never able to use, an opportunity you could not or would not take the first time you encountered it.

At various times in my later life I have been afflicted by a recurrent dream. I am surveying the rooms in my house, and I suddenly remember that there is another that we never use. Sometimes I am living in a cheap apartment and the extra room is full of broken-down furniture and cobwebs, opening on a tenement-style fire escape. Sometimes it's the room behind an old-fashioned apartment kitchen that architects used to squeeze in, as a sort of afterthought, for the live-in maid. At least once it was a two-story ballroom with stately pillars and elegant chandeliers wrapped up in dustcovers.

In the dream, I peek inside. It is dark, dusty, sinister, but not unfamiliar. I say to myself, "Of course! I've forgotten. There's always *that* room back there. We could use that space now." I try to remember how and when we used it and why we never go into it. It's not as bad as a nightmare, but I wake up anxious. The dream keeps coming back. The question is always the same, but each time I'm living in a different home with a different unused room.

The dreams come in bunches at times when a program of love or work is running out. The first set came after my father died. At forty-five and newly remarried, I was abruptly freed not so much from his physical care as from a relationship that had taken more out of me than I knew. The very next year, to the surprise of everyone, especially myself, I had a baby and started writing books. Another attack occurred when I had finished a book and was trying to muster the courage to attack a subject that neither I nor anyone else around me thought I could handle. Empty rooms plagued my nights again when my husband died.

The dreams are a problem-solving exercise. They are a way of scanning the attic for useful things put by, a way of saying, "Now, think, what were you doing before you got into this commitment?"

Separations are inevitable in later years. Death and divorce are traumas that visibly age the survivors. But, however painful, the experience liberates the energy that was bound in the relationship and relieves the inhibitions that made it viable.

The classic example is the flowering of Eleanor Roosevelt after FDR died. When President Truman asked her to represent the United States at the United Nations, she thought she wasn't qualified. When she finally accepted she learned how to use her name and her inside acquaintance with public affairs to advance her own ideals rather than the political interests of her husband.

At the United Nations she was able to promote international understanding between nations and policies that respected the dignity of individuals when these ideals conflicted with the dominance of the United States being sought by John Foster Dulles, our Secretary of State. The opportunity to help needy individuals all over the world was like a shot in the arm. In what are supposed to be declining years, Eleanor Roosevelt increased her output of work. Dulles opposed her appointment, but he saluted her heroic achievement in drafting the Universal Declaration of Human Rights and shepherding it through the U.N. General Assembly.

Nobody realizes how much energy a relationship impounds until it is over. For the second husband of Colette, the famous French novelist, the release was explosive. Maurice Goudeket was sixteen years younger than Colette, but he was sixty-five when she died, and at first inconsolable. Then, to his surprise, he was seized with "ungovernable fits of impatience, a kind of muscular revolt, which obliged me to stay out until dawn."

At first he thought it must be unhappiness, but later he concluded that it was an "upsurge of vitality" or an "attack of energy" that had been repressed as he became adjusted to Colette's slowing rhythm. Six years later, at seventy-one, he remarried and fathered a child; his eyesight improved so that he could read without spectacles; and a wisdom tooth started coming, "strong, firm, and powerful—a tooth, by the way, that I could very well do without."

Doing what you have always wanted to do can release enough energy to overcome physical handicaps. I. F. Stone, the iconoclastic political reporter, wanted to become a professor of philosophy but didn't do well in school and never finished college. When, late in life, he suffered a heart attack, he gave up his newsletter and sought revenge on the academics of his youth. He applied his skill at investigative reporting to the twenty-five-hundred-year-old mystery surrounding the death of Socrates and produced a plausible solution. A painstaking detail man, he learned Greek from scratch in order to study the record directly.

Some of the ambitions laid aside during middle years are easily achieved. The grandmother of a friend of mine spent all her working life at a sewing machine in New York's garment center. Her children worried about how she would keep occupied when she was retired. To their surprise, she bought a ticket to Israel with her first Social Security check and has been happy doing volunteer work there ever since. This was what she had secretly wanted to do for decades.

Other ambitions were laid aside in youth because they are hard to achieve at any age. This is particularly true of the challenge of work that is a test of talent. Like many other young people, Rosser Reeves wanted to become a serious writer, but most of his life he felt he couldn't afford the risk of trying to do it. What sidetracked him, he thinks, is a piece of advice an uncle gave him when he was only eight: "Some people lead small lives. Some people lead large lives. Lead a large life."

Rosser's father was a Southern preacher who never made more than sixty dollars a week in his life. At nineteen Rosser decided that the larger life required larger sums of money, so he spent the next thirty-six years making it.

A big man, in the 1980s he admits that he is big rich. "I sold billions of dollars of advertising," he says with professional hyperbole. "I stashed away millions of dollars, and a lot of it is in gold I bought when it could be had for fifty dollars an ounce. I wrote famous campaigns like Anacin and Kools. I replaced sponsored shows with the spot commercial. I set the tone in television advertising. I wrote a best-seller, *Reality in Advertising*. We were constantly breaking new ground, expanding the company. We had twenty-eight offices in eighteen countries. I revolved the world like a satellite. It got to be just like riding a bicycle: automatic. A treadmill. A series of repetitive motions. I realized that I couldn't lead a larger life if I continued, so on my fifty-fifth birthday I quit."

Not that he had anything against making money. With time to invest in new ventures, he actually made more than when he was working double time on the treadmill. But his goal was now to live as largely as he had earned. Instead of revolving among eighteen offices, he revolved among four palatial residences: a house on a private island in Larchmont, New York; a house in his native state of Virginia; an apartment in New York; and a "really lavish" mansion on a hundred-acre botanical garden on Montego Bay, Jamaica, with thirty-two servants.

"For a while I was a kid in a candy shop," he recalls. "Buying the places. Fixing them up. Taking care of the money. But after three years I began to feel like an old well-sweep horse put out to pasture who keeps going around in circles as if he were still hooked up to the tow. So I got rid of it all."

In the 1980s he has only one home, an apartment on Gramercy Park, but he is steadily writing books. For starters, he wrote books on his hobbies: one on backgammon, another on chess, and what he regards as the definitive handbook on pool. His novel, *Popo*, about a drunken poet in Greenwich Village, required him to write a lot of poetry. Even before it appeared, he was working on another novel set in the Players Club, a landmark near his home, and it is full of mad, creative people.

Identity Seeking

Later years are the only time when you can be sure of who you are. Only then is your track record long enough to reveal a reliable pattern. It takes a lot of living to become a unique individual. Babies look very much alike in the hospital nursery, and the pictures in a high school yearbook resemble each other more than the graduates do at reunions a decade later.

A teenager may talk about searching for her identity as if an identity were a misplaced fortune cookie secreted somewhere inside her body at birth. But identities are not found but grown over years of responding to circumstances. The pattern of our genes converts our experiences to our particular use just as it converts the food we eat to the flesh and blood of our particular body.

Only in your later years are you free to look at parts of yourself you have had to shove to the back of your mind. The insights that emerge are not always painless. Dr. Robert N. Butler, the psychiatrist now heading the Department of Geriatrics at Mount Sinai Medical Center, has urged his profession to help older people review their lives. Regret over what sometimes seems a misspent life is one of the reasons that people over sixty-five are especially vulnerable to suicide. He reports that elders experience the kind of identity crisis that we expect of teenagers, and emerge with a firmer sense of themselves. He points out that both take to gazing earnestly at themselves in the mirror. And, like teenagers, older people coping with an identity crisis can be restless, rebellious, and even impetuous. They may switch careers, move to an unexpected location, quit a marriage that has weathered many decades, fall suddenly in love, or pursue a whim that appears to others—often including their own wide-eyed children—as unrealistic, even rash.

Luckily, the life review that Dr. Butler describes need not always generate a dramatic crisis. The ageless most often come to understand themselves by a phenomenon of later years that is usually a pleasure. After middle age, memories of scenes and feelings long forgotten well up into consciousness. Insights often accompany these attacks of memory.

It rains, and I hear the sound of the drops on the window of my childhood room. I see the tar baby I stuck on the fence when I was nine, the Tutankhamen design of the slipcovers in the library. Images laid aside for fifty years pop up unbidden as I circle La Guardia, tired of my book. Why is it that I forget the name of my next-door neighbor but remember the name, the face, and even the perfume of my second-grade teacher?

Nobody seems to know why the circuitry of the brain bends back to the beginning after middle age. Folk wisdom says that old people live in the past because most of their life is over. Sociologists are kinder. They suggest that old people turn to their memories for company because young people shun them.

Brain researchers grope for analogies. Is the brain a pail that overflows when it fills? Does the device for forgetting that keeps us all from going mad peel off the most recent memories first?

Psychologists don't know how memories are packed in the brain, but they suggest that the ability to perceive and store new impressions declines with age, so that the earlier ones remain the sharpest. If a chemical fixes impressions in memory, it may weaken over the years, like a photographic fixative that gradually loses its power.

Neuropsychologists think in electrical and chemical as well as behavioral terms. At Stanford University, Dr. Karl Pribram is trying to find out whether brain waves change when a person reminisces. He points out that brain waves slow with age to the frequency characteristic of childhood, and suggests that this congruence might account for the fact that childhood memories are more easily retrieved by the elderly than events of the recent past. "Perhaps memories are frequency modulated, much as they are in FM broadcasting," he speculates. "Retrieval mechanisms must address the broadcast. This is called a context addressable memory."

Psychiatrists see these vivid childhood memories as a return of the repressed. Dr. Butler thinks it is natural for older people to stumble on their early conflicts in reviewing the course of their lives, and he thinks they are better off for dealing with them. The encounters that result are material for fiction.

Walker Percy was sixty-eight when he published *The Second Coming*, a novel about an attack of memory that solved a mystery in the early life of a sixty-six-year-old Southerner very much like himself. The memory forced his character, Will Barrett, to recognize that his father's death was not an accident but a suicide. The novel relates how this reinterpretation of the event hovered around the edge of his mind for months and finally emerged when the three-iron golf club he was swinging reminded him of a gun and hunting in the woods with his father.

"Until today, he had not thought of his father for years," Percy writes. "Now he remembered everything his father said and did, even remembered the smell of him, the catarrh-and-whiskey breath and the hot, quail reek of his hands. And strange to say, at the very moment of his remembering the distant past, the meaning of his present life became clear to him, instantly, and without the least surprise as if he had known it all along but had not until now taken the trouble to know that he knew."

The rest unfolds like a textbook psychoanalysis. Armed with the truth, Barrett untangles the knots that had kept him inactive most of his life and puts his newly released energy to work in a productive new career and marriage.

Turnarounds like this may not be as neat in actual life, but they really happen. An older person can't undo the years that may have been wasted in the past, but experience may have made her more resourceful in devising a solution. Jimmy Carter's mother is a good example. One of her early conflicts was that she wanted to support civil rights for blacks at a time when her husband, like many other Southerners, disapproved of the movement. Lillian Carter was sixty-six when her husband died, but she joined the Peace Corps, survived its rigorous training course, and learned to type so that she could qualify for it. She said she chose India for her fieldwork because, like her native Georgia, it was "a dark country with a warm climate." It was also on the other side of the world from disapproving friends and family.

Or take the late-life reversal of Benjamin Spock, the famous baby doctor. In his seventies, Dr. Spock divorced his wife of fifty years and married a nontraditional woman half his age, the kind of woman he might have married if he had been starting out in the 1970s. A psychiatrist by training, Spock explains it as a deferred rebellion against authority, particularly the authority of his mother, whom he attempted to please by pleasing the mothers of America through his writing. He does not look to his new wife for maternal support.

Why Not?

So we come back to the initial question: why are some people ageless while most of us merely grow old?

Well, for starters, the ageless are a privileged lot. All the ones we've cited seem to be rich, educated, successful, talented, or just plain lucky. But of course this doesn't really answer the question. Privilege doesn't make you ageless automatically. All rich people aren't ageless, and neither are all college professors. Talents wither, and not even all the healthy people become ageless, in the questing sense of the people we would all like to be.

Maybe the trouble is with the question. We have been asking why the ageless keep on growing as if they were in possession of some secret that we could bottle and take by the spoonful if only we could wrest it from their grasp. But maybe there isn't a secret. We just think there is because we have been asking the question the wrong way around. Instead of asking, why do some people keep growing all their lives, we should ask, what prevents the rest of us from growing? Why do we wind up old?

Our problem may be that we have been taught to underestimate ourselves, to think of ourselves as animals instead of as humans. Baby humans come into the world a bundle of options. Some keep more of these options longer than others, and as we have seen, a few succeed in going back and picking up those that seemed already lost.

So what stops growth? Every coach, parent, and teacher knows the answer. Ridicule, like the child-rearing tactics accepted when today's old people were children. Lack of challenge, like the limited, lockstep schooling and work rules that discouraged them in their youth. Lack of response, like the sexism that withered love in their youth by limiting communication between men and women. Isolation, like the social barriers that confined small-town Americans to limited relationships.

Now it is clear that we do not seem to be headed for the technological utopia touted in the 1950s, nor for the limitless growth envisaged then. But we are breaking down the obstacles that limit individuals. Consider, for instance, how many more people now can use the strategies that enabled Margaret Mead to function as she did in Houston.

Margaret Mead is a good example. Like so many of the ageless, she was a communicator, the author of dozens of books and hundreds of articles, a lecturer who established rapport with many different kinds of audiences.

An anthropologist conscious of the way that roles are used, she adapted accepted conventions to her personal needs throughout her life. She began her career by questioning the roles expected of her. At a time when women were handicapped in the professions she insisted on defining the jobs she did herself instead of following the rules laid down by an employer. She once defined a career as what you would do if you didn't have to earn a living.

She refused the restricted, repetitive labor to which women were relegated, even when they were professionally trained anthropologists. Women were not welcome on field trips when she first went to the South Pacific, but she overcame that limitation by arguing that a woman could collect material native women would never reveal to a man.

She rejected the notion, prevalent in her time, that sexual love is ugly or frivolous unless it is directed to the production of children. Convinced that she was infertile, she entered relationships with men that furthered her personal development, and left them without regret when they no longer served that purpose. When she later succeeded in having a child, she did not make her daughter the focus of her existence.

As an anthropologist she was professionally trained in flexible living arrangements. During much of her life she lived with unrelated adults who had joined together because they happened to be pursuing common goals at the time.

At the appropriate time, she drew on the role of grandmother, but characteristically broadened it beyond blood relationships to become what she was often called—grandmother to the world. Throughout her life she showed that it was possible to overcome all of the obstacles simply by not allowing roles or stages to limit her.

At the end of her life she refused to accept the role of a dying person. She may have feared that people wouldn't pay attention to what she had to say. In our society sick people are excused from their normal responsibilities and expected to concentrate on getting well. Their only real obligation is to follow the doctor's orders. But since pancreatic cancer does not respond well to chemotherapy, such a course would have wasted more than a year of her useful life.

Margaret Mead was a pioneer. In her later years she played the role of model for the thousands of women college students who thronged to hear her speak. Her example showed that individuals need not accept all the restrictions that they think society is prescribing for them. Since her death America has steadily moved in her direction, so that millions who hardly know her name are able to live by her standards.

In the following section we will see how the human use of the human years is changing the meaning of health, work, love, and what it takes to sustain a satisfying life.

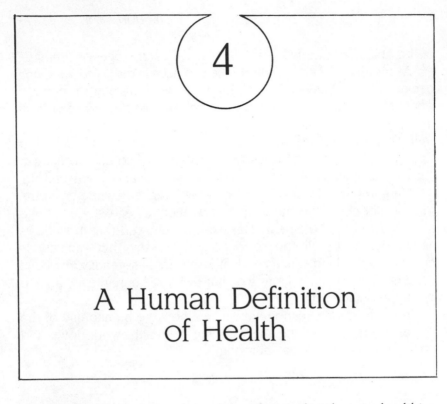

A Human Definition
of Health

The first thing you notice about the ageless is that they are healthier than we think they have a right to be.

Some of them are dismayingly vigorous. We may not be planning to run the Boston Marathon in four hours, one minute, and twenty-five seconds at the age of seventy-three, but we are glad to know that John Kelley was able to do it. We think it is fine that financier Benjamin Buttenweiser walked eighty blocks every day to his Wall Street office the year he was eighty, even if we don't expect to be like him. As a matter of fact, the main reason we hate to think of our later years is that we don't like to visualize what is going to happen to our bodies when we get to be seventy or eighty or ninety.

How long is your future?

The question is basic. It becomes more urgent as the years go by, and, barring a killer disease, much harder to answer. Agemates vary more widely in health and vigor as they grow older. At very high ages, the differences can be startling.

Most people accumulate disabilities over the course of their lives, but some individuals seem to escape all of them. It is possible to be like the wonderful one-hoss shay in the poem of that name by Oliver Wendell Holmes, which was "built in such a logical way/It ran a hundred years to the day" and then "went to pieces all at once."

Human one-hoss shays go on with their normal activities for decades after their agemates and then depart without pain or trouble. They may be sick for weeks or months, but quite often they simply die without warning in their sleep, like Lowell Thomas, the CBS newscaster, who remarried in his mid-eighties, took his bride around the world for a honeymoon, and went skiing with her in Europe at eighty-eight. He was eighty-nine when he died.

They are remarkable people. I talked with the ninety-seven-year-old Aunt Bee Bee of my high school classmate Dorothy a few weeks before her death. Blood tests had indicated cancer, but Aunt Bee Bee had no complaints, and the doctors doubted the tests because they couldn't find clinical signs. An amateur midwife, she had attended Dorothy's birth, but when I visited on the occasion of our fiftieth high school reunion, there was Aunt Bee Bee, sitting in her accustomed chair. She was so slight that a breeze might have blown her over, but it hadn't been so long ago that Dorothy had caught her lugging a heavy rug three flights down from the attic.

How do you talk to a bright-eyed, attentive little bird that is getting ready to die? The worst of it was that she sensed my embarrassment.

"Forgive me if I don't get up, I've just got myself settled," she said, by way of letting me know that she could get up if she chose.

I reminded her of the cardigan sweaters she had knitted for my friend that looked exactly like the ones that the rich girls bought in the store for eighteen dollars when we were in college during the 1930s.

"I always like to be doing something with my hands when I'm sitting," she said, almost in apology. "May be just nervousness." The petit point covers in the dining room were her work too.

"Come again soon," she said, when we left, as if she knew that I didn't know how to say good-bye. A month later she was gone, like the one-hoss shay, without complaining of a specific symptom, a classic example of the supposedly natural death that doctors used to be allowed to ascribe to old age on the death certificate.

There are likely to be more one-hoss shays in the future. Mortality rates no longer rise as steadily with every year of advancing age as they used to. The tendency is for agemates to stay alive through the middle years and die within a few years of one another in their late seventies.

This is good news for everyone over one year old. Life expectancies are usually figured from birth. In the past they rose dramatically because we were saving babies and young people. The life expectancy of people who had already survived to sixty-five rose slowly from the days when Benjamin Franklin negotiated our peace treaty with Britain in 1789 at the age of seventy-eight. But in the 1970s we made gains against every one of the killers of adults except suicide and lung cancer. As a consequence, the death rate for people over sixty-five fell 2 percent a year. In 1980 men over sixty-five could expect to live to seventy-nine and women to eighty-three, with even more years ahead for those who were college-educated, professionally employed, or lucky in their choice of ancestors.

This means that your chance of beating the life insurance tables is getting better every year. Actuaries have to base their charts on the death rates of people older than you, and since mortality is declining, the rate will be lower when it is your turn to get there. In 1980, for instance, a forty-year-old white woman was at the midpoint of her life, with forty more years to live: in 1950 her counterpart had only thirty-six.

There is reason to believe that gains will continue. Medicine will advance, of course. Improvements in living conditions will help even more. But the biggest boost will be psychological. Doctors themselves admit that health and vigor depend on how people feel about themselves and their bodies. Many of the physical ills of people born before World War II can be traced to the myths of age and the scars of the Great Depression. Finally, in an adult society we will all be more tolerant of bodies that no longer look or move like those of teenagers.

Medical Gains

Medical engineers will ease the discomforts that plague old people in the 1980s. You'll chew with your own teeth, or permanently implanted false ones. There'll be simple surgical procedures for cleaning out the calcium deposits that make a joint stiff, the way you clean the rust out of a hinge that sticks. If necessary, the entire joint can be replaced with an artificial substitute, and improvements in communications and surgical techniques will make it easier to replace failing eyes, skin, kidneys, hearts, and even brains with transplants.

There will be mechanical and chemical measures to keep your body working. Tiny computers may be implanted to regulate lagging functions, as pacemakers now control erratic heartbeat. A pea-size electronic package implanted in the mastoid bone will remedy the kind of deafness that hearing aids cannot now help. There'll be hormones to help you store items in memory and maintain your sexual responses.

You'll resist the infectious diseases that now strike older people harder and more often. To begin with, you'll be spared the complications of the childhood diseases that weakened everyone born before World War II and can cause trouble even late in life. There will be ways to keep your natural immunity from declining with age, new vaccines to protect against diseases for which we have no present remedy, including cancers.

Best of all, you won't suffer pain. One of the nicest things about the twenty-first century is that nothing that will happen to you in it is going to hurt as much as something that has probably happened to you already. By the twenty-first century we will have found a way to harness your body's natural pain-killing mechanisms.

But the biggest contributions your doctor will make will not be curing your aches and pains, but preventing them. Dr. James F. Fries of the Stanford University Medical Center in California figures that we have eliminated 80 percent of the premature deaths from disease before eighty-five that a baby born in 1900 could have expected. In the 1980s most people die of cancer, heart and artery disease, kidney failure, emphysema, adult-onset diabetes, or one of the other diseases of bodily wear and tear.

These degenerative diseases won't succumb to miracle cures or the kind of vaccine that eliminated smallpox and polio. Scientists would have to find a way to tinker with genes, trick the body into growing a new heart or kidney, or devise artificial substitutes for worn-out vital organs. The most promising medical approach is to slow the wear and tear on these vital organs, but that's not where we are spending our money. Dr. Fries figures that we spend 80 percent of our medical resources trying to treat diseases that can be eased, delayed, or prevented but not really cured by the time that they make you sick enough to go to the doctor.

Prevention is becoming the key to late-life health, and as Dr. Fries points out, it is not in the hands of doctors. The best the medical profession can do is identify the habits that ward off degenerative diseases and urge the public to adopt them. And though it has sometimes seemed like an uphill battle, there is evidence that the public is listening.

In the 1980s good health habits once regarded as effete are now the height of fashion. A glass of white wine has become more acceptable than a two-fisted shot of whiskey. Nouvelle Cuisine has substituted sauceless little vegetables for the cholesterol-heavy dishes of traditional French cooking. Racketball and yoga are replacing hearty steakhouse lunches. Mindful of burnout, employers are relaxing restrictive work rules and repudiating pressure tactics. They are beginning to provide athletic facilities that offer exercise breaks instead of coffee breaks. Ashtrays are out of style, and so are driving short distances easily walked or biked and boasting about how busy you are and how many hours a day you choose to work.

Health educators have done such a good job that they can't even measure their efforts accurately anymore. In 1981 a control group of males had cut down eating and smoking almost as much as counterparts chosen by the National Heart, Lung, and Blood Institute for intensive lifestyle reeducation.

Material Conditions

The biggest gains in life expectancy have come not from medicine, even preventive medicine, but from improvements in living standards. Remember Christmas seals? Tuberculosis was a leading killer in the childhood of many people now alive. The germs were so common that almost everyone was exposed to them, but the people who died from TB were apt to be the poor who lived crowded in airless slums and didn't get eggs or milk or meat very often. Doctors understood this, but all they could do was send those patients who could afford it to sanatoriums out in the country and feed them hearty meals. Families that were not overcrowded to begin with moved their beds out to sleeping porches during the summer, and charitable people gave a little bit of money to send poor kids to fresh air camps in the country for a week or two.

None of these measures could eradicate the pool of germs maintained in the large number of people whose living conditions lowered their resistance. But that pool of germs began to dwindle when poor people earned enough money to move out of the unimaginably fetid slums in which they had to live before World War I. The disease was declining by the time medical researchers developed drugs to combat it.

The steady improvement in food, clothing, housing, safety, and emergency medical care over the past half century will continue to increase the vigorous years Americans can expect for many decades to come. Up to now these straightforward gains have been part of every family's history. The oldest child of my grandparents was the only one to have the bowlegs of rickets, a reminder of the limited diet available in the first few winters in the wilderness. The grandfather who survived a North Atlantic shipwreck succumbed to a ruptured appendix that could have been avoided by a simple operation even then had a doctor been available. Most of our grandparents lived on farms that were not only isolated but downright dangerous. Barns were loaded with safety hazards, carcinogens, and allergen-bearing dusts that government regulators would forbid in a modern factory.

Eventually, of course, we will run out of the gains that we can expect from rises in purely material standards. They are coming more slowly already. The American diet leaves much to be desired, but junk foods simply can't be worse than the dirty, greasy food eaten by slum dwellers in the early part of the twentieth century, and relatively few Americans die today because they can't get to a doctor.

Can we expect a similar bonus of healthy years from the non-material trends we have been projecting? Will older people live longer when there are more of them and age is not made into an issue? Will health improve when robots and computers do more of the physical work? Will technological advances help us to stay well, or upset us and make us sick? Will the employment practices of a slower-growing economy reduce the stresses that many doctors think now shorten lives?

To answer these questions we need to know why some people live so much longer than others. We know very little about what prolongs the active life of seemingly ageless people, and scientists aren't even trying very hard to find out. We spend 10 percent of the Gross National Product on what we call health, but virtually all of it goes for ailments. Only a few thousand of our over 7 million health care workers and a paltry few millions of the $300 billion we spend on health is devoted to studying why some people remain healthy.

Biologically, the active old people have overcome formidable obstacles. Christine Fry, an anthropologist specializing in aging, summarizes what is happening in the body of a normally healthy sixty-year-old: "Metabolic rates decline as does cardiac function. Lungs further decline in size and ability to oxygenate the blood. Kidneys receive less blood and as membranes become less permeable, they remove fewer wastes from the blood. It takes a longer time for nerves to transmit their messages and stronger stimuli are needed to trigger sensory information."

These processes go faster in some bodies than in others. Attempts to measure biological age have considered widely diverse measures. Some are tests of physiological function, such as basal metabolism and blood pressure. Others are laboratory measures of red blood counts and urine, physical measurements such as grayness of hair or skin thickness and elasticity. Still others measure how quickly you can adjust the focus of your eyes between near and far objects or hear high pitches, or how quickly and accurately you can move a pencil between zones on a piece of paper.

One common test rates biological age on the basis of how well you can identify an incomplete picture of a common object, such as dotted lines that delineate a cat. At the National Institute of Mental Health, researchers developed a reasonably accurate predictor of longevity, which they call "organization of behavior." They found that the old people they studied who lived longest were those who planned for the widest variety of activities every day, such as watching investments, cultivating a garden, volunteering in a hospital, or refinishing furniture.

There's no use asking doctors how healthy people stave off entropy. They see fewer healthy people in the course of a day than the rest of us, and the one-hoss shays they see hardly at all. Some of the people whose secret we need to know make a point of staying away from doctors. Oliver Wendell Holmes, the nonagenarian Supreme Court justice whose father wrote the poem, used to say that it would be better for the human race if all the drugs in the pharmacopoeia were sunk to the bottom of the sea, although worse for the fishes.

There's no use asking the hardy survivors themselves. A centenarian has outlived 399 of the babies born on his birthday. Many of them express surprise that they are still alive. When asked for their secret, they tend to fall back on the values of their youth. One individual will say that he always got up early and chopped wood. Another will say that he never drank liquor, while a third will attribute his health to drinking just a drop every single day. In the sexist days of my youth, my great-grandmother's hundred years were attributed to her selfless domestic service to other members of the family.

Statistics about the characteristics of the long-lived sound more reliable, and we have a great many of them. Sex, race, heredity, education, income, marital status, and occupation are important influences, but the numbers don't interpret themselves, and they are apt to suggest theories that cannot be verified.

The Numbers

Not all of the longevity statistics can be taken seriously, but they arrest us because we can't help applying them to ourselves even when we don't quite believe them. Dr. Reubin Andres, clinical director of the National Institute on Aging, points out that if you want to live a long time you should arrange to be an easygoing, relaxed, married woman Ph.D. over sixty-five who earns less than $50,000, works on a road gang, lives in a small town, plays tennis five times a week, doesn't smoke or drink, and had four long-lived grandparents and no deaths in the family from heart disease or stroke.

The studies contradict one another because they are directed to a single factor and can't possibly hold constant all of the many other influences on longevity. Dr. Andres says that followers live longer than leaders, but you can also find a study showing that geniuses live longer than the rest of us. Are geniuses followers? Can a follower be a genius?

Generally speaking, short lives aren't very merry, even while they last. If you want to die soon, the statistical evidence suggests that you arrange to be lonely, stupid, neurotic, unhappy, unimaginative, and moody.

The surest predictors are the givens over which you have no personal control. There's nothing you can do to lengthen the lives of your parents, ensure that your mother was between eighteen and thirty-five years of age at your birth, arrange to be born white, female, and the firstborn, keep a relative from succumbing to a stroke at an early age, or avoid being born a twin. Twins have a shorter life expectancy than those born singly, and those who emphasize the roles of heredity report that identical twins die closer in age than fraternal twins, whose genes differ.

Gender makes a lot of difference. A baby girl is born to eight more years of life than a baby boy.

Race affects life expectancy, too. In the United States Orientals are not noticeably more privileged than whites, but they can expect to live from two to four years longer, while a black male baby has six years less of life to look forward to than a white baby born the same day.

We don't yet know all the ways that genes influence longevity. For instance, some people seem to be born with a natural immunity to infection. James Wylie Mahaffey was a soldier who never caught colds. During the Spanish-American War he nursed comrades dying of yellow fever without ever getting it. In the pandemic of 1918 he was the only one who didn't catch the flu. A stroke disabled him when he was over a hundred, but on his hundred and sixth birthday, in 1981, he was the country's second oldest veteran. The new biology now supports Mahaffey's claim that his resistance was hereditary. Dr. Roy Walford of the University of California at Los Angeles thinks he has located the genetic control for immunity on the sixth chromosome.

Another genetic possibility is that you may be born to live your life fast or slow. Like a crocus or a butterfly, we all come into the world with a timetable for growth, and just as long-lived species take longer to mature, so individuals who take longer to grow up may take longer to grow old, too. Swedes, for instance, are supposed to be slow to respond. Elderly Swedes look younger and Swedes in general live longer than comparable Americans.

The luck of your genes can't as yet be helped, but lives are shortened by circumstances that can be changed, if not by the individuals concerned, then by the system. We know that money, education, prestigious occupation, and, at least for men, being married are not only good in themselves but good for extra years of life.

We know that lifestyle matters. If you put data about yourself and your habits into a computer at the U.S. Public Health Service office in Atlanta, it will read out how many years you can expect to add to your life by giving up smoking, drinking, or drugs; taking off excess weight; staying with an exercise program; or fastening your seat belt every time.

Personal habits aren't entirely under personal control: it is just about as easy to relax in an organization designed to motivate by competition as it is to diet when you are required to entertain at sumptuous lunches every day. Yet health educators never tire of games that encourage you to try the statistics on yourself.

According to a "Longevity Game" distributed by the Northwest Mutual Life Insurance Company, vigorous daily exercise will add three years to your life, but if you are aggressive, ambitious, or nervous (you have sleepless nights, you bite your fingernails) subtract three years, and if you are unhappy, subtract another year. Continuing to work after sixty-five earns you three more years of life, while smoking more than two packs of cigarettes a day costs you eight. The numbers are presented as the experience and medical underwriting policy of the company. Some companies go so far as to charge nonsmokers lower premiums.

Health promotions may promise life expectancies based on nothing more solid than the habits doctors currently think are a good idea. According to a "Health Hazard Appraisal" devised by Dr. Lewis C. Robbins and Dr. Jack H. Hall of Indiana University, you can count yourself three years younger than your chronological age if you drink skim or low-fat milk, but you have to add six years to your actual age if you eat meat three times a day. Since we haven't followed people on various diets to the end of their lives, these numbers are merely guesses.

They intrigue, but it's hard to know what they mean. Intelligence and longevity seem to go together. A Metropolitan Life Insurance study shows that college students live longer than agemates with less education, and honor students live longer than classmates with average grades. But which causes which? Are naturally long-lived people smart, or do smart people use their smarts to avoid circumstances known to be life-shortening? If the old are wise, is it because age brings wisdom, or because the wise know how to live long?

To take another example, we know that men who went in for athletics during college live longer than classmates who didn't, but did athletics improve their health, or were the healthiest and potentially longest-lived students more likely to engage in athletics?

Defenders of the traditional family like to point out that married men live longer than bachelors. But does this mean that marriage prolongs a man's life, or only that men who marry are healthier than bachelors to begin with?

Take weight. We are all convinced that fat people dig their graves with their teeth. And it's easy to prove with the numbers. The grossly overweight die sooner, but does this mean that taking off weight will lengthen your life? Not always.

The very old are sometimes very thin, but there is hardly a calorie counter among them. Wispy, wiry bantams like Eubie Blake, Norman Rockwell, or Pablo Casals never seem to worry about what they eat because they never feel like eating more than their bodies need at any given time. But it isn't certain whether thinness in itself prolongs life, or the natural appetite that keeps weight low and constant. If it's the appetite regulation that counts, then it's no use starving yourself to attain low weight by a conscious effort.

If you are very heavy, you can cut the extra hazard you face from diabetes, heart disease, and other life-shortening ailments by getting rid of the excess weight that makes them more dangerous. But how much good will a diet do for your health if you're not excessively overweight? Because it was an important public health issue, Dr. Andres undertook a long-overdue review of the data, collating and in some cases recalculating all the previous studies on the hazards of overweight. He had a personal interest in the outcome because he is of the pudgy build that is always being advised to reduce.

Dr. Andres found a slight edge for those with a few more pounds than the height-weight tables proclaim ideal, and no penalty in years of life until you get to be more than 20 percent over. Most of the millions trying to reduce are less than 10 percent overweight. They may slim themselves down to fit into a smaller size. They may feel more virtuous or energetic. But they aren't necessarily adding years to their lives.

Middle-aged people say they are dieting for the sake of their health. If so, their idea of health is an artificial return to the body of their youth.

Finally, the statistics on life expectancy mean less and less the older you get. At birth, for example, a girl can expect to live eight more years than a boy, but her edge is only six when they are forty, five when they are sixty, and two when they are eighty. According to Dr. Erdman Palmore of Duke University, by the time you get to be sixty it doesn't even matter how long your parents lived. He believes that any residual genetic effects are washed out by the overwhelming weight of sixty years of environmental influence. The race gap actually reverses after sixty-five: fewer blacks than whites survive to that age, but those who do live longer. And after you get to be sixty, smoking, cholesterol, and (contrary to myth) even money no longer make a difference.

The numbers are as fascinating as horoscopes, but they are actually based on the circumstances of life in the past, some of them on circumstances more than fifty years in the past. The most sensible conclusion they suggest is that long life is not the result of any special mystical quality, but is rather due to good luck in avoiding the life-shortening accidents and insults that accumulate over the course of a lifetime.

Future gains will have to come from a broadening of the circumstances that enable the lucky to avoid these threats. For most of it we will have to look to a reduction in nonmaterial stresses and frustrations.

A New Definition of Health

Whatever their physical condition, people born after World War II are going to feel better in their later years, because an adult society will allow them to deal more realistically with changes in their bodies.

Old people of the 1980s expect to be limited. They are victims of the stereotypes of age. Like most of us, they have accepted the prevailing notion that in order to be healthy you have to be physically capable of earning the kind of living that had to be made with muscle. It is, of course, an obsolete standard.

You will be healthier in the twenty-first century because you will live in an adult society that will measure health by a more realistic standard. Instead of rating yourself on the basis of blood pressure, vision, and other absolute scores on a doctor's report, you will rate yourself on how comfortably you are able to live with your physical resources, whatever they happen to be.

Some people already define health as an adaptation between their bodies and the demands they make on them. There are many ways to achieve this adaptation. The body itself can be changed, as when a cataract is removed to improve the sight of someone whose work requires him to absorb information from books. But the same thing could be accomplished by leaning more heavily on tape recordings that deliver information through the ears rather than the eyes. Health consists not in perfect sight or perfect hearing but in how economically the individual uses all the available resources.

Adaptations differ from one individual to another and for each individual over the course of his life. Young people may draw more heavily on their bodies, older people on changing the way the task is done, or redefining their goal to substitute a different kind of task altogether. Bodies change with age, and they do not necessarily become less adaptive. The adaptation can be poor for a robust but uncoordinated teenager, but superb for a veteran adapter whose body is almost completely worn out.

By the relative standard of adaptation, Margaret Mead was healthy at Houston because she succeeded in making the speech for which she had come. She drew on a lifetime of experience in setting priorities, husbanding her strength, and adapting to the physical and social discomforts experienced by anthropologists in the field. Most of all, of course, she drew on the formidable power of the human mind to control the human body—a power that grows in the later years, in which human beings outlive animals of comparable size and heartbeat.

People who survive to the later years fight against the ageist standard as best they can. In the last National Health Survey, 85 percent of people over sixty-five said they were able to perform their major activity, and two-thirds said their health was good. These ratings are subjective. Since major activities are defined by the respondents, the question measures satisfaction with health, rather than health itself.

But very few use anything like the potential they have to achieve a comfortable fit between body and task. To assess those potentials, we have to consider the physical achievements of ageless people who for one reason or another have resisted doing what other people expect of them. Picasso said it best: "Long ago I decided I wanted to be thirty." Having made up his mind, he spent sixty-two years being thirty.

Perhaps because it is learned, the power of mind over body grows stronger in later years than in the early years of physical growth that more closely parallel the life course of animals. Some determined old people have held back entropy with words, defying physics, physiology, and even common sense. Norman Cousins, founder of the *Saturday Review*, took over from the doctors and cured himself of a usually fatal rare disease by cultivating laughter and positive thinking. As far back as history goes, some people have cured themselves by faith, but most of them haven't been intellectuals.

An interesting recent example is Eula Weaver. At seventy-seven Eula had a heart attack. Her circulation was so poor that she was wearing gloves by day and socks at night. Her doctor had her taking more than a dozen pills a day, and although he told her that her life depended on exercise, she couldn't walk fifty feet without her calf muscles cramping so painfully that she had to be carried home. At this point she met Nathan Pritikin, a friend of her grandson's, who had also had a heart attack. Pritikin told her how he had rebelled against the doctor's pills and his orders to take it easy, and urged her to put herself on the diet and exercise program he had devised that cured without resort to medicine.

Eula believed. She cut down on her pills and put herself on a fruit-and-vegetable diet. At first she couldn't walk half a block without running out of breath, but she kept on trying. At the end of the first six months she was walking seven blocks without stopping, three times a day. In eighteen months she was *running* a quarter of a mile. After two years she was jogging a mile every morning before breakfast.

Naturally wiry and tough, Eula began to look younger. At eighty-five she was bringing home gold medals for jogging in the Senior Olympics against women in their forties and fifties, and visiting the Pritikin Center in Santa Barbara to inspire newcomers to the system. As in Alcoholics Anonymous, recruiting others maintains the cure, because it lasts only as long as the faith.

At ninety-one Eula broke training She went into the hospital for elective surgery for the repair of her bladder and didn't survive it. Pritikin insists that she would have reached her goal of jogging a mile at one hundred if she had kept away from the surgeon and stayed with her diet and exercise program.

As we have seen, there is no statistical reason to believe that a program of diet and exercise can lengthen your life in your later years. And it is safe to say that even if they did, the purely physiological impact of these regimes would be minimal. Physicians look-ing at these cases usually credit the psychological boost they give people who believe in them.

People cured by faith have to keep reassuring themselves by propagating it. This is true not only of unpretentious people like Eula Weaver, but of intellectuals like Norman Cousins or Linus Paul-ing, the octogenarian Nobel Prize winner. Pauling believes he keeps infections at bay with massive doses of vitamin C, in spite of the fact that medical research has failed to establish a connection.

There isn't a doctor who denies the influence of positive think-ing even on seemingly hopeless conditions, and especially for older people, but we don't really know how it works. At the Gerontology Research Center in Baltimore, Dr. Paul T. Costa, Jr., is examining the relationship between symptom reporting and health status. Doctors know that pain is almost entirely subjective, and that objective signs, such as the spurs of arthritis on X rays, don't always result in symptoms the patient notices. Dr. Costa found that elderly men who developed signs of ischemic heart disease without complain-ing of symptoms were more stable and better adjusted, as measured by psychological tests, than those without signs who reported symptoms. It remains to be seen which group lives longer—the well-adjusted sick or the worried well.

Cheerful nonagenarians may ignore quite serious impairments. Dr. Ludwig Aschoff, the famous German pathologist, visited a ninety-seven-year-old colleague who was engaged in studying his own phenomenal health. When the man died two days later, Aschoff was so surprised that he participated in an autopsy. They found signs of lobar pneumonia and metastasis from a malignant tumor of the thyroid, which had produced no symptoms the old man could recognize, although equipped by his training to do so.

Doctors and nurses believe that many older people die because they think it's time for them to die. At the State University of New York at Geneseo, a psychologist has designed an experiment to test this theory. In 1965 Dr. Lawrence Casler began suggesting happy long life to fifteen healthy octogenarians in a New York City nursing home. So far they have lived an average of 8.1 years, compared with 1.9 for fifteen matching controls who didn't get the encourag-ing sessions, and they've had fewer illnesses.

How does it work? Human beings have bodies that learn how to do what is urgently desired of them in ways that are often difficult to understand. This, of course, is the essence of training for ballet, sports, or any other physical activity, and the reason that exhortations to do better are so big a part of physical training. Motivation is especially important in long-distance running. According to Dr. Fries, training is more important than age in running the twenty-six-mile marathon race. He finds that the best time a long-distance runner can expect to make declines only 1 percent a year.

Doctors are often amazed at the adaptations handicapped people sometimes make. In Austin, Texas, Dr. Guy Shuttlesworth plays golf with a seventy-year-old who simply refused to quit the game when he lost the use of one leg. His stance and swing are unorthodox, but they work so well that he is one of the best golfers on the links. Dr. Shuttlesworth is a gerontologist, and he thinks his friend persisted until his body developed alternative ways of hitting the ball. Retired men often play better golf than they did when they were younger and had less time for the game. They automatically adjust their swing to declining muscle strength by swinging as women golfers do.

One of the British old people Ronald Blythe interviewed for his book *The View in Winter* was a ninety-one-year-old woman who had become a Montessori teacher in her youth because the withering of an arm at eighteen months had made her especially sympathetic to children who weren't doing well in the village school. By the time Blythe visited her she couldn't move one arm at all, and could move the other only by throwing it forward and up, but here's how she cooked: "To stir something on the gas-stove, I have to throw my good arm forward to seize the saucepan, and to bring it down low on a chair or stool so that I can let my not-so-good arm hang over it." She thinks she stayed young for her age because she learned early to fight physical debilities.

Human bodies are ingenious, but so are human minds. If health is the fit between your body and the tasks you assign it, there is leeway on both sides of the equation. A horse has to be shot when it breaks a leg. The leg can be set, but you can't put a horse in a wheelchair or teach it to use a crutch. Human beings can identify the nature of a difficulty and find a way to cope with it.

Some old people are ingenious in inventing devices that compensate for a physical limitation. When he could no longer ride a regular bicycle, Laurence Olivier had a special one built for a film he was making that required it. A special scaffold enabled muralist Allyn Cox to continue painting the corridors of the House of Representatives when he was eighty-five.

Like most novelists, Eleanor Clark lives through her typewriter. When macular degeneration threatened her eyesight, she taught herself to write with felt-tip markers on a large gray drawing pad. "Try first to write a page a day, this way," she wrote on the pad's first page. "Get used to it." Her account of how she got used to it became her book *Eyes, Etc.*

Inventions are the dramatic exceptions. Most of us adapt to our decrements by changing the way we do a task that becomes difficult, just as we almost unconsciously shift a burden we are carrying from one arm to the other in order to equalize the strain. When a twisted knee doesn't heal, we give up jogging and take up swimming instead.

We greatly underestimate our ability to adapt to common decrements such as weaker muscles, slower-focusing eyes, and a tendency to miss high-pitched tones. Most of the time we counter them with one of the strategies for coping with a difficult mental or physical task that almost everyone learns over the course of a lifetime. One of them, for instance, is to cut a job that seems overwhelming into many small steps that can be taken one at a time. That's the way the old Montessori teacher succeeded in cooking with a withered arm.

The most useful all-purpose strategy, and the hardest for young people, is simply to slow down. Like bandleaders who cut time when they want a rest, veteran performers slow the rhythm of an act so cleverly that the audience seldom notices. The old ballerinas do entrechats, but fewer to the beat than when they were younger. At ninety, banjoist Paul Cadwell gave up displays of sheer speed in favor of pieces he described as "lively, but deliberately not racing."

Slower is often safer. Investigators marveled that everyone was saved when a cruise ship burned to the keel off the coast of Alaska. They decided that panic didn't develop because the passengers were retired people who had the experience to realize that their best chance for survival was to remain calm. Old people drive slowly, but they have fewer accidents per mile than teenage males, at the height of their sensory and motor acuity.

Dr. Adrian Kanaar, a rehabilitation specialist, is one of the many physicians who have chosen to practice beyond the normal age for retirement. He simply takes longer with each patient. Foot tappers unwilling to wait their turn for unhurried consultation go elsewhere, leaving him with patients close to his age, whose appreciation is more important, at this stage of his life, than the money he could make in a more intensive practice. In addition, he's probably practicing better medicine.

With experience, you can bypass many operations that are strenuous but nonessential. If you've followed Euclid's proof of the Pythagorean theorem you can use the bottom line and forget the steps that led to it. Intuition is dumping the evidence you've already examined, and people who have examined a lot of it can get away with more dumping than those to whom every proposition is new. It takes a little while for some brides to discover that nobody is going to see dirt under the bed.

Old people learn to sharpen their priorities. They get practice if only because it is harder for them to pay attention to two things at once. Smart old people keep away from cocktail parties, where several conversations compete for attention. Like eighty-year-old Bill Paley, they give parties small enough for general conversation.

But perception is so much in the mind that people with failing eyes and ears can see more than people with 20/20 vision who don't know what to look for. The neurophysiologists tell us that the brain sends as many messages to the eye as the eye to the brain, and the interpretation of these messages has to be learned by experience. Because he knew how things worked, my eighty-year-old father was always the first to see what was wrong with something around the house, even though he had to peer at it this way and that through the visual cage of his cataracts. Octogenarian tycoons notoriously doze through meetings but snap wide awake when anything unexpected happens.

The pioneers who keep up with people half their age husband their energy. John Kelley didn't learn how to ration his energy until he had run fifteen of his fifty Boston Marathons. At seventy-three he lets younger runners tire themselves racing ahead at the start, and then passes them to run his last miles faster than his first ones.

Mary Calderone boasts that she never stands when she can sit, or sits when she can lie down. President Reagan does not invite congresspeople to play tennis with him, as President Carter did, but he projects the image of outdoor vigor by riding horseback for the TV cameras. U.S. Presidents are performers with a little control over the script.

Strategies for saving personal energy are often little tricks that each person reinvents over time, for himself. Whatever your age, it's easier to push drawers shut with your foot, drain vegetables from pots with a slotted spoon instead of carrying the whole heavy thing to the sink, and finish one task before starting another.

It takes a long while to learn enough about yourself to conserve your psychic energy. Things like holding your tongue until anger recedes. Avoiding people who you know are going to make you angry, or resolving in advance that you are not going to let them do it to you.

Then there are all the useful little tricks for remembering the many things all of us are always forgetting. It takes some living to learn that the best mnemonic device of all is time itself: sit still, let your mind go blank, and wait for the elusive fish that is nibbling at your line to swim up into view.

Old copers counter forgetfulness by tacking lists of things to do on the refrigerator door and jotting down names they are afraid they will forget. If they lose the note, they calmly go down the alphabet until they strike a letter that rings a bell. *M.* Yes, it began with *M.* Ma? Me? No, it was Mi. Mirabel!

There are other memory tricks. One is called chunking. You associate the chore you think you will forget with another you are sure to do, like taking your morning pill right after washing your face—easier unless you miss the cue, as I did the morning I flew in from San Francisco on the red-eye express and didn't get to wash my face properly at all. Donald O. Hebb, the psychologist who is spending his retirement using himself as a subject for the study of aging, blocks the front door with things he is afraid he will forget to take with him when he leaves the house.

The psychologists tell us that old people can learn anything they were formerly able to learn if they are allowed to take their time and learn it their own way, instead of in classes designed for young people. It is, for instance, harder for them to learn by rote or by the manipulation of abstract systems, but if the material can be presented in words they can draw on verbal abilities that decline more slowly than memory and mathematical ability.

In the adult society of the future, a nonageist standard of health will add many years of active life now lost by people who give up activities they assume are possible or appropriate only for teenagers. But the most exciting reservoir of future gains in longevity is the long, historical trend to social equality.

The statistics of longevity suggest two life-prolonging advantages of the privileged. One is freedom from the constraints that frustrate poor, ignorant, low-status workers. The other is what blacks sometimes call "respect," by which they mean acceptance in the mainstream of society. Both are natural rights that we feel should be available to everyone.

More Freedom

One way to test the influence of freedom on the length of life is to look at the statistics we have on longevity by occupation. Professional and technical workers live longer than those who do less prestigious work, but are these brain workers saved from the noise, pollution, and dangers that wear down manual workers, or is there something positively life-prolonging about their work?

Status itself could be the protector, because the eminent professionals listed in *Who's Who in America* live even longer than their colleagues who didn't make the book. But it makes a lot of difference how they attained their status.

Presidents, who have the very highest status of all, are not so lucky. "Hail to the Chief" doesn't keep them alive. In fact, twenty-two of the thirty-five Presidents of the United States who died before 1980 were shorter-lived than their contemporaries in the general population. That means more than half, even if you leave out the three who were assassinated. And it isn't accidental.

The data suggest that they would have lived much longer if they had refused to run. Their wives have seldom been enthusiastic about having their husbands in the Oval Office, and the statistics prove that the wives have been right. According to a Metropolitan Life analysis, the lives of our Presidents have been shorter than those of the candidates they defeated, shorter than the lives of their own Vice-Presidents, men like them in every way except for the experience of the presidency itself, and shorter than the cabinet ministers, congressmen, and governors from whom presidential candidates are recruited. If Presidents are shorter-lived than presidential timber, we have to look for something that is killing about the job itself.

Awesome responsibility doesn't seem to be the lethal factor. Supreme Court Justices make decisions that compare, in historical impact, with those made by Presidents, but they outlive the average citizen instead of dying sooner. And so, as a matter of fact, do holders of every other high office, with a single exception. Like Presidents, mayors of New York fall short of their life expectancy. They are widely known to have the country's second hardest job.

Why the differential? What is the root cause? Could it be the simple privilege of deciding yourself what you are going to do in the course of the day instead of having to do what other people tell you? There is growing evidence that constraint can really shorten life. We know, for instance, that heart attacks are more likely to strike the kind of driven person who always feels pressed for time, and that he can ward off a second attack by working with a psychologist to reduce this sense of urgency.

Researchers studying the value of exercise found that rodents lived longer when provided with wheels on which they could run if they chose, but when they were *forced* to run on the wheels they died as soon as the rodents who were forced to be sedentary. The moral seems to be that jogging won't prolong your life if you have to force yourself to do it.

Active old people are seldom slaves to other people's schedules. Mary Calderone insists that she doesn't plan her busy life, she just gets up every morning and does what most needs to be done at the moment. When Hoyt Catlin was close to ninety, he used to swoop down unannounced to check up on workers at his Fertl Cube plant and take off on long trips on the spur of the moment.

The self-employed live longer than those who work for others, and the reason most often given is that they are free to plan their own work. This independence seems to be the reason that farmers live almost as long as professional men in spite of the physical hazards of farming. Supreme Court judges enjoy the same privilege. Like farmers and college professors, the Justices hold themselves to standards they set, and each one decides for himself when it's time to retire. Paul T. Costa, Jr., chief of the section on Stress and Coping at the Gerontology Research Center of NIA in Baltimore, believes that the power to determine the course of one's career affects longevity more than the actual job description.

The theory is supported by dramatic differences in the mortality of otherwise similar occupations. Take college professors and journalists. At the highest level they gather and interpret facts and present them to a particular audience. Their skills are so similar that individuals often move from one field to the other. But a *Who's Who* notable who switches from journalist to college professor is cutting his death rate from a third above the national average to at least that much below it, and women in these fields survive little longer than the men. For winners in the status race, occupation is a better predictor of life expectancy than gender.

What's the difference between the jobs? People who have done both always talk about pressure and competition. Professors make their own deadlines, while journalists compete with one another fiercely and are at the mercy of events beyond their control.

Consider, for another example, the longevity of orchestra leaders. Musicians and performing artists in general have a higher than expected death rate, although the famous outlive the obscure, but the death rate for performers who are also symphony conductors is 38 percent lower. Conductors like Toscanini, Kostelanetz, and Benny Goodman keep going as long as Supreme Court justices, although their work is considerably more physical.

What is the difference between just plain musicians and musicians who are conductors? The most striking is that conductors beat the time the musicians are constrained to follow. Swinging a baton keeps the arteries of conductors young, but so, of course, would playing the drums or cello.

Or consider, for another example, the occupation of president. Unlike Presidents of the United States, presidents of the top 500 corporations live longer than men their age in general. One reason for the difference may be that while U.S. Presidents can never at any hour of their term escape the hounding of top-flight journalists (who are cutting their own lives short in the process), the corporate presidents answer only to boards that meet infrequently and in private. In spite of the heavy load they bear, corporate presidents have fewer heart attacks than subordinates who have to punch time clocks.

Finally, increasing control of schedule may explain the rising life expectancy of doctors. When most of them made house calls and practiced alone they lived little longer than the average in spite of high income, education, and the veneration in which they were held, but they now live almost as long as business executives. Group practice, regular hours, and specialization may protect them from the constraining pressures of constant emergencies.

Stress is an occupational hazard of jobs that require instant response to ever-present but unpredictable outside threats. These are the conditions of work in city newsrooms, air control towers, rush-hour traffic, military combat, and the Oval Office of the White House.

Nothing ages as fast as a threat that leaves you helpless. Television audiences watched permanent furrows etch the face of President Carter when there was nothing he could do to secure the release of the American hostages in Iran. Like Byron's Prisoner of Chillon, your hair can turn white in a single night. It happened to an American seaman in an Arabian jail while awaiting the fate of a man he had knifed in a brawl. The man lived, so the seaman wasn't beheaded according to Arab custom, but when he was forty-two a physical anthropologist guessed his age at sixty-two. A former prisoner of war has figured that American servicemen lost four years of their life expectancy for every year of incarceration.

Luckily, as we shall see later in more detail, the long historical trend is in the direction of freedom and choice at work and at home. A slower-growing economy will discourage workaholics from

damaging their arteries and make it economic for many of the normally ambitious to take some of their pay in leisure. We may, for instance, have many more husbands and wives who elect to go part
time while rearing their single child, and many more childless
workers dropping out of the labor force for a year or two of travel
or education. And we can expect some gains in active years from
technology that will reduce the dull, dangerous, and demeaning
jobs that carry the highest death rates, and create more interesting,
freer jobs for skilled technicians.

More Respect

Finally, there is reason to believe that progress toward social equality and equal opportunity is increasing the life expectancy of
Americans.

We are the richest country of the world, but we do not lead the
world in life expectancy. According to the last United Nations report, males in Japan, Sweden, Switzerland, Denmark, Israel, Canada,
England, Wales, France, and Italy are living to be more than seventy-three, while American men are averaging only sixty-nine.

The usual explanation is that we are a big, diverse country. This
is a polite way of saying that our health statistics lump together two
very dissimilar populations, the rich and white, who live as long as
the Swedes or the Japanese; and the poor and black, whose lives
are much shorter. Although our standard of living is higher, the gap
between rich and poor is wider in the United States than in Japan,
Sweden, and most of the other developed nations of the world. If
we are going to catch up with them, we are going to have to find a
way to narrow this gap.

There is something puzzling about these statistics. It's hard to
escape the conclusion that it's not only material deprivation that is
shortening the lives of the poor and the black, but something about
the gap itself. We may be shortening the lives of our underprivileged
by the way we feel about them, or, more accurately, the way we
make them feel about themselves. We blame the poor for their
poverty. We exclude the blacks from the mainstream in pointed
ways. In Sweden and Japan the poor are not left out. They are ac-

cepted as victims of misfortune who have a right to be supported.

We know that individuals sicken and die when they believe they are worthless or that nobody wants them. Most of the old people in nursing homes are there not only because they are sick but because they have run out of family and friends. Many of them are visibly scarred by the loss of respect that they suffered in the Great Depression of the thirties. They are listless because so many options have been denied them that they can no longer imagine anything that they want to do. Some withdraw into lonely silence because they have accepted the notion that their meager earnings were a measure of their worth. Their bodies have been eroded by decades of inturned anger.

The other side of the coin is that social acceptance, involvement, and the respect of the community are literally life-prolonging. Among 268 old people followed for more than twenty years at Duke University, one of the best predictors of health, happiness, and longevity was involvement with people outside of the immediate family in clubs, churches, civic groups, unions, or other groups that required them to interact with strangers. As one eighty-year-old put it, "Eight decades after birth, the loners are all dead."

The ageless I studied were not only sociable almost to a fault, but ingenious in replacing roles that circumstances increasingly force them to relinquish. At the very end, those who find themselves older than everyone around them sometimes create a role for themselves as an example of survival. "I've asked myself a lot of times why I'm still here," Eula Weaver told an interviewer when she was eighty-seven. "The only answer I find is that maybe I can help people help themselves. Maybe I'm around so I can tell people there is a way to live well and good and useful if they would only push their plates back and get up off their seats and go out and walk and jog and exercise."

According to Jeff Beaubier, a physical anthropologist who has studied human longevity, the aged live longer in societies where they have useful social roles, such as the island of Paros in Greece, Soviet Georgia, and Swedish and Japanese villages. The Japanese, especially, venerate the elderly. They like to live and work in groups and they take great care to leave no one out, so it is probably no accident that the highest authenticated age attained by any human being was reached by a Japanese. His name is Shigechiyo Izumi, and in 1982 he was a hundred and seventeen years old.

We may never have the tightly knit society of Japan, but we are becoming a more inclusive society, and the progress shows in our vital statistics. No one contends that blacks are now fully integrated with whites, but the race gap in income and schooling has narrowed over the past generation, and so has the gap between whites and blacks in life expectancy.

We have a long way to go before the average man can expect to live as long in America as in Sweden, where social equality is a national fetish, but we are moving in that direction. In the 1960s some young blacks were escaping from the ghetto that isolated them from the mainstream of society, and deliberate discrimination against them was no longer regarded as tolerable. Conservatives may slow but cannot really stop our progress toward equality. It is down the broad highway of the American heritage. The American Dream enshrined in the Declaration of Independence means life, liberty, and the pursuit of happiness for everyone. We are not distributing years of life as equitably as we could, but we have traveled too far along the road of a single standard for all to abandon it now.

There is more life ahead. Advances in medical technology, preventive medicine, nonageist standards, more leisure, less pressure on the job, and a more just society are some of the reasons that your later years in the twenty-first century will be healthier than you now expect.

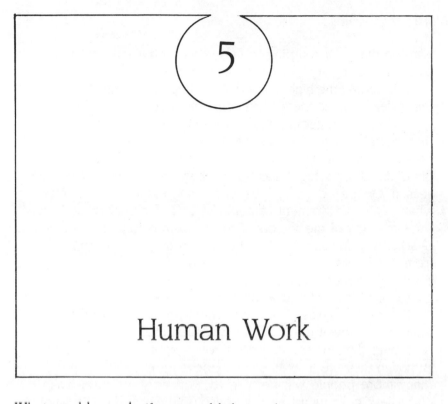

Human Work

What would you do if you could do anything you wanted?

If you are over sixty-five, the answer is supposed to be "Nothing." You hear about the fabulous people like Ronald Reagan, our fortieth President, who keep working into their seventies, but the old people you personally know are lying on the beach in Florida as happy as clams.

A retired car dealer has sat there so long in his shorts that he is tanned mahogany brown all over. "It was always a dream of mine to sit under a palm tree with a mint julep in my hand and take life easy," he says. "Now I'm doing it." He's been doing it happily for thirteen years.

The dream of leisure is compelling for people who have been working without a real break since they started out in the Great Depression. You hear about the sumptuous parties the rich old people throw at Palm Springs, where the wealthiest gather to do nothing that could be called purposeful. You see them laughing at poolside tables in television commercials for retirement communities, where life for the middle-income retired is billed as a nonstop party. Or romping from one planned activity to another in places like Sun City, Arizona, which provide recreation for every taste, including the high-minded. Or sitting on folding chairs beside the trailer, because there is no house to keep and no taxes to pay.

You see them getting off chartered buses, clutching airline bags that proclaim them members of an excursion to the Holy Land. Or being taught how to have fun in community college courses on disco dancing, a big educational draw of the 1980–81 college season. Or spaced on park benches as motionless as sea gulls on wharf posts in retirement centers like St. Petersburg or San Diego.

A majority of the seniors of the 1980s are content to lie on the beach. They consider work to be duty, drudgery, constraint. Relief from this burden is the ultimate goody of the American Dream. They collect retirement as their due when they turn sixty-five, as gluttonous for its pleasures as kids let loose in a candy store.

But for the ageless few, the never-say-retire minority, work continues to be adventure, fulfillment, self-expression. Their work is so rewarding that they would do it for nothing, and frequently do. Although they are a small minority now, they are working the way many more people will be able to work in the future, while the clams have been happy to retire because they are the victims of the working conditions of the past.

One of the ageless is Bob Myers. Bob grew up in the Depression. As a boy he hated the idea of taking the kind of job he saw the grown-ups doing. He says he was thinking of ways to retire before he even started working. At college he took the engineering course that led to a job instead of the liberal arts, but he promised himself that he'd quit as soon as he could, learn Greek, and spend the rest of his life reading Plato.

He told me this while sitting on his terrace at Santa Barbara, offering me strawberries and oranges he had grown himself. Unexpectedly thin, his long furrowed face lengthened by a pointed beard that makes him look like an El Greco, he is a vigorous man of sixty-two who retired at the age of forty-seven.

Friends couldn't understand why Bob chose to retire at the height of his powers. Strangers tended to think there was something mysteriously wrong with his health, but he always told them no, he wasn't sick, just tired of working.

And with good reason. Work had turned out to be more absorbing than he had thought and he had spent almost a decade working night and day on one project after another. World War II was breaking out when he graduated from college. Engineers were in demand. The work was a challenge. Like other bright young men, he went from one defense plant to another, taking on new responsibilities and a bigger salary at every move.

After the war the stakes were even higher. Markets and companies were changing. Bob went to work for a little toy company that was so deep in the red that the owners had to pay him in stock. After a year of working around the clock, he turned it around and made a fortune. Lush offers followed. Rather than take a job that would tie him down, he moved from company to company, solving specific problems. Work turned out to be fun, and although he was making a lot of money, he and his growing family began to live in a way that required every bit of it. Bob had married his college sweetheart, and lived the good family life of the 1950s until after the last of their four children was in high school.

Early in his forties, two things happened to Bob.

One was the Human Potential Movement. He learned about it in a weekend course in management methods. The lecturer talked about the satisfactions of achieving instead of merely getting ahead, of relating to people instead of merely using them. Bob signed up for a course on "Getting in Touch with Your Innermost Feelings," and eventually sampled the rich array of therapies and disciplines that flourished in California during the 1960s. A coeducational touch session broke up his marriage.

The other thing that happened was a windfall of time *and* money. A gadget Bob had rigged up to help his wife dispense baby oil for wiping his firstborn's bottom turned out to be the solution to a production problem on one of his jobs. He had taken out a patent on the little squirter, mainly for kicks, and because he knew how to file the application himself. But now that he had time, he began to brainstorm dozens of uses. One of them hit a market. The gadget turned out to be just what doctors needed for mass immunizations when they had to swab a succession of arms with antiseptic, so he set up a little assembly line in his garage.

Bob insists he's retired. He doesn't regard anything he does as work. It takes about a day a week to turn out all the squirters for which he has orders, and the work isn't taxing. All he does is to stand around while two part-time workers run the little assembly line he has set up in a shed on his place, or chin with the part-time bookkeeper, the sort of thing his blue-collar father called shooting the breeze, or goofing off on the job.

But that's not all Bob Myers does. In addition, he is usually working on a consulting project for a company that has a problem, but he has strict rules about the assignments he'll take. It has to be something that he likes, something that won't commit him for more than a year. Most of all, it has to be something that won't interfere with the other things he and his second wife want to do with their lives, like soaking in the solar-heated hot tub Bob designed for the garden, or camping in the High Sierras whenever the spirit moves them. When I visited, he was developing a program for motivating professional workers who were tired of working but hadn't been lucky enough to invent a squirter.

Bob and his new wife don't plan ahead. They get up every morning and do what feels right for that day. If a project appeals to them, they work. But it doesn't seem like work, because they do it at home, part time, and only when they feel like it. To a man who has spent decades in straitjacket jobs, that seems like playing.

Bob would never go back and work as hard as he did in defense plants during World War II, and he would never again consent to the terms on which he did it. Less lucky than he, most engineers—and other workers—his age have spent decades trapped in jobs that they don't like.

When you ask people in their late fifties why they want to retire, they say that it isn't the work itself that they want to quit, but the guff they have to take to do it, and they go on at length about mickey mouse rules, dumb bosses, childish competition, endless meetings, shabby politics, and the constraint of nine-to-five schedules. That's labor, the kind of drudgery you would never endure unless you were being paid for it.

Meaningful work is what everyone wants and cannot find in the 1980s. More and more people are disillusioned by the conditions of their employment. Studies find that old and young want a chance to apply their talents to worthwhile work over which they have some control. However the questions are worded, the values come through. A chance for self-expression. Work that is important in itself. A voice in how it is done. A schedule and pace of one's choosing. Congenial co-workers. In the Michigan survey of 1977, 37 percent would trade a 10 percent pay raise for a shorter workweek, and 48 percent would give it up in exchange for more paid vacations. In one survey, nearly two-thirds said they would turn down a new job that paid five thousand dollars more than they were making if it was uninteresting. Blue collar, white collar, everybody wants work instead of labor.

Professional work has always been our model of work that is worthwhile in itself, but industrial rules have succeeded in quantifying it into labor. Newspaper reporters punch time clocks. Lawyers time phone calls so that they can charge the time to the appropriate client. Some companies pay bonuses to engineers for professional activities on a system borrowed from factory piece rates: so many points for reading a paper at a professional meeting, so many points for securing a patent, so many points for an idea the committee considers patentable.

Teaching has traditionally been the most rewarding work of all, but bureaucracy has made our public schools and universities into factories where teachers and students alike are treated like laborers. Students do not learn under these conditions, and five or six years of it threatens the most dedicated teacher with the malady now called burnout. Many of them quit before society has recouped the cost of training them.

For sixty-year-old Tim Vickery, relief from teaching ninth-grade history loomed like the approaching comfort stop on a long drive. The closer he got to it, the more he could afford to recognize how badly he needed it. Like a prisoner doing time, he crossed each school day off the calendar. Classes were big, and students somehow not as responsive as they had been when he had begun his teaching career. He was tired, bone tired, and his hearing was getting so bad that he thought that the only way he could get through a class was to do all of the talking himself.

Just before Thanksgiving, a thirteen-year-old girl caught him at it. She mumbled a rude remark that he didn't quite understand, but when he tried to pass it off with a smile, the class burst out laughing, clapping, whistling, and stamping feet. Tim was shaken. Maybe after all these years he hated kids. Maybe his life had been a total failure. After a weekend of brooding he came in Monday morning and resigned, never mind the cut in pension for quitting in the middle of the year.

Retirement was a revelation. Liberated from the role of teacher, he volunteered to help excavate a Revolutionary War site near his home. The other volunteers were young people, who showed him how to use the spade and listened intently to the stories he told them about eighteenth-century life in America. He let his beard grow. He bought jeans and boots and caught the hang of the music they brought along to the dig.

His wife pointed out that he was still teaching. It wasn't kids he hated. It was school. Like many other people of his generation, he had to get rid of his job to do his work.

In the 1980s Social Security benefits, small as they are, enable people over sixty-five to hold out for the kind of work that everyone wants. A Harris poll reports that more than half of the work force hope to continue working after retirement, but in 1982 only 11.8 percent of the people over sixty-five were actually earning. Many more would work if they could find work that suited them.

People over sixty-five anticipate the way things will be for adults of every age in the twenty-first century. As retired workers they enjoy a floor of income that allows them to survive without working, and since they aren't expected to earn, they don't lose status by choosing to live in frugal idleness.

The Redefinition of Work

The ageless minority who continue to work are harbingers of work to come. As volunteers or small venturers working out of their homes, they are finding the unmet needs that will create new jobs in the future. Others are showing that traditional work can be efficiently done on flexible terms, such as part time, that give individual workers more control and leeway. They are helping to redefine the nature of work for the whole economy.

What we regard as work has been redefined in the past and will have to be redefined again and again in the future. A great deal of essential work is always done outside of the formal structure, while many jobs accomplish nothing useful at all, but the boundaries are always changing. New jobs typically grow out of work that has not been regarded as paid employment. Before the Civil War, for instance, nursing the sick was not regarded as a regular paid profession.

New jobs evolve out of the extra work that people in old ones do above and beyond the call of duty. Janice Kendall did not regard herself as a shining light of the faculty at the prestigious university where she had taught for thirty years. She was the first in her family to go to college, and at seventy is still uncomfortable when she is addressed as Dr. Kendall. Only after she retired did she find a job that recognized as work the extracurricular help she had always given to students.

When she was a girl, the idea of becoming a college teacher occurred to her while reading a book in the library called *The Idea of Progress*. It seemed an impossible ambition then, and she freely admits she wouldn't have tried if she had known what she was getting into.

As a graduate student in the Depression, she had no more money than the poor families she was studying for her doctoral dissertation in sociology. She wore a hole in her only pair of shoes walking to her classes because she didn't have carfare. She felt closer to the poor families she was studying than to some of the upper-class professors who were supervising her dissertation.

She also admits she wasn't brilliant. Analyzing the data for her thesis gave her migraine headaches. She got her first college job because as a single woman she was willing to work for less than an equally well-credentialed man.

Intellectuals on the faculty snubbed her. Her superiors praised her for her "heart," and assigned her the grubby departmental chores the stars of the department felt were beneath them. She accepted the role. She never spoke up in faculty meetings, never took sides in academic politics, and never asked for a sabbatical. After she bought a house near the department offices, she seldom ventured into the heart of the campus.

Overlooked by the faculty, Janice was popular with her students.

A gourmet cook, she liked to invite them around to her house for dinner and listen to them argue with each other or talk out their doubts about the careers they had chosen or their problems with their parents. She rarely gave advice, but sometimes referred them to a book or was reminded of an anecdote. She didn't think of these evenings at her house as work, but in later years her students remembered these sessions as the source of their real education.

Janice was one of the professors who couldn't wait to retire. She was happy to get out of faculty meetings, committee meetings, paper work, and academic politics, but she missed the students. To replace them, she signed up as a tutor with Empire State College, a statewide New York experiment in matching adult students with local tutors who help them map out an individual course of study.

The flexible arrangements appealed to Janice. No faculty meetings. No grades, no departmental chores, no rule against eating or even cooking on the job. Just students dropping around to the house to discuss their goals and map out a course of study likely to advance them. Janice felt like Monsieur Jourdain, in Moliere's *Bourgeois Gentilhomme*, who was elated to discover that he had been talking prose all his life. Her students became friends. She fed them. She knitted sweaters for them. She remembered their children's birthdays. Finally she was getting paid for the real work that she had been doing all her life.

Teaching is so underrated now that it is due for a renaissance. Schools are so bankrupt that most of the new opportunities in teaching are developing outside them. If you look at what many people in other fields actually do on the job, an increasing portion of their duties consists in learning.

Army officers and IBM managers spend a substantial part of their highly paid time keeping abreast of the state of their arts, and much of it in formal classrooms. Physicians aren't required to go back to school as a condition of their license, but the AMA and state governing bodies urge them to take advantage of a broad array of educational services designed to keep them abreast of medical advances. In the future, all of us will spend more of our paid time learning. In the process, we will make more—and perhaps more satisfying—work for teachers.

Education has always been a prolific source of new occupations, but it will generate them even faster in the information-rich future. Teachers have always done well in selling, because high-level sales has always been a form of education. And they are the primary profession for motivating people and ordering data, skills that have many applications outside the classroom. Experienced teachers can lead in creating these new occupations.

The important new work of the future has to be discovered by people experienced enough to see what needs to be done and free enough to try it. Sometimes a task just hits a retired person in the eye when she isn't expecting it. That's what happened to Jane Grossinger, a tiny, lively woman who came to this country from Russia when she was a baby. Jane had no intention of turning another tap when she retired from her job as a forelady in a garment factory on Seventh Avenue. Between Social Security, the pension her union had negotiated, and a rent-controlled apartment, she figured she could just get by.

"I've paid my dues," she said, beaming, at the party they gave her. "The rest is for me!" Next Monday morning she set the alarm clock for six o'clock for the joy of going back to sleep after turning it off. At the end of the week she drew out her savings and paid for a Caribbean cruise, her first time out of the United States since she passed through Ellis Island as a baby.

In Port-au-Prince she treated herself to a drink in the best hotel, and whom should she meet in the bar but an old boss who had moved his shirt plant to Haiti, where labor was cheap, but business wasn't thriving.

Piece rates were low, and the Haitian women he had hired were willing. Most of them had a passel of hungry kids at home. But they spoiled more shirts than they finished. He had told them that he would lose the plant if they couldn't do better. They needed those jobs and they were trying, but it didn't look good.

Jane was sure that they could learn if they really wanted to work. "That's what I used to think," he said. "But these people are different. They want the jobs, but they are afraid of the machines, and I can't make them understand." He took her through slums of naked kids to the tin shack where a dozen women were staring at as many sewing machines.

Jane couldn't stand to see them doing it wrong. She didn't speak

French, so she had to show them. "Like this," she said, and they gathered around, curious. She couldn't get away until she had sat beside every woman. Next morning she was back. The tour left without her. She and her boss became partners.

After they saved those women's jobs, they took a contract to train the work force of a plant being opened up to employ women in a village in North Africa. She complains about the flies and the heat, but she doesn't know when she'll ever get back to Brooklyn.

New work sometimes grows out of a special interest developed as a sideline to a conventional career or even a hobby that, like Chinese calligraphy, is prized not so much for what it is as for the pleasure that goes into doing it. I have a mouthful of gold because I once had a dentist who liked to make inlays so much that he used them long after gold was practical. Masterpieces of a lost art, my present dentist calls them.

He used to cast them himself in a little laboratory behind his office. He hoarded the inlays he took out of patients' mouths, and rigged up a way to retrieve the gold dust produced in the process. When he had enough on hand he would make a little gold charm. He got started on this hobby when he saw a gold amulet in the Egyptian collection of a museum and bet his wife he could copy it.

When the price of gold rose he retired and made a nice little killing at the work that he had always regarded as play.

Second careers pioneer the new work ahead, because they are undertaken for the satisfaction of doing them. Rocky Stone, the CIA officer who helped put the Shah back on the throne of Iran, has enlisted colleagues in Self Help for Hard of Hearing people, an organization that works out to the appropriate acronym SHHH.

Milton Rettenberg was surprised, toward the end of his life, to find himself in possession of knowledge so special that he was literally not allowed to retire. All his life he wanted to be a musician, but he grew up in the Depression and was afraid he wouldn't be able to make a living at it. He was a good enough pianist to stand in for George Gershwin on tour, but he played it safe and went to law school.

During most of his adult life he supplemented his law practice by playing the piano for radio shows, although sometimes it seemed to be vice versa. Since his friends were musicians, he was forced to explore the then uncharted field of musical copyright. It was hard to prove infringement and, since composers weren't organized, even harder to collect, because infringers were seldom worth suing.

Television commercials changed the picture. Sizable investments by eminently solvent companies were vulnerable to claims that the jingle promoting their product was a variant of some poor composer's copyrighted tune. Composers organized associations to defend their rights.

Rettenberg's practice thrived. Every time he tried to retire, advertising agencies raised the retainers they paid him to screen their commercials for possible lawsuits. He could have gone for the money, but he opted instead for the time. At seventy-nine, he limited his practice to mornings so that he could spend the afternoon with his ailing wife, and still made more money than he had ever made in any year before.

The paths taken by these ageless people suggest the ways we will define work in the future, but to complete the picture we also have to imagine the role work will assume in the adult society we have been projecting for the twenty-first century.

We supposed that the economy would grow more slowly, so that all but the most competitive would invest less of their energy in paid employment than made sense when rapid growth repaid that effort handsomely. Then, if we can look beyond the troubles of the 1980s, and project the long-term economic trends of the past half century, it seems clear that machines will continue to cut the human hours of effort required to put a floor of material comfort under everyone. One result will be that jobs will simply be a less important part of the lives of many people.

Visualize, if you can, a world in which work will be much less prominent a part of everyone's schedule. Everyone won't be following the same career pathway. You'll cut back on work during periods when you want to spend more time on family, friends, hobbies, sports, or other interests that in our work absorption we now call "outside." And though most people will work on and off throughout their lives and into their later decades, they will spend fewer hours of their lives in paid employment.

In the twenty-first century it will be hard to say whether or not someone is retired. The word itself will sound old-fashioned.

If asked, you might say, "Yes, I retired last year, but I'm the only maintenance man who knows how to stoke the old coal-fired furnace they had to put back in service for six months, so I'm back on a six-month contract to keep it going. It's easy work, because all I have to do is to check it out every day to be sure the regular maintenance force is carrying out my instructions."

Or you might answer, "No, I won't retire for five more years, but I'm not working now because I've taken leave with pay for a couple of months to try out living on the farm we bought long ago in Oregon."

So much future work will be swapped and shared that the explanation might have to be much more complicated. You might have to say, "Yes, I left the company completely a year ago, but I'm sitting in today for the man I trained to do my job. He wanted some time off, and he's agreed to pay me back by helping me with my garden this summer."

However you try to define your status, chances are that you'll go on earning after sixty-five. It will be much easier to work part time on terms of your choosing. Jobs are steadily being created in hospitals, restaurants, travel, recreation, and other services that need more workers during the few hours of heavy demand, as well as in professional services that can't be counted in hours and don't have to be done at any particular time or in any particular place.

According to Peter Drucker, a management consultant and economist, employers are going to have to learn to use full-time people and part-time people, people past retirement age, and people who are willing only to work at a special skill and then move on to a different employer once they have finished the assignment for which they were hired. Very few people will work for the same company all their lives.

All of these trends are leading to the kind of work that is now in most demand. You'll have more control over the work itself, and especially when, where, and with whom you do it. Like the bosses of the 1980s, you'll be paid for results instead of hours, so you'll come to work when you are needed instead of by the clock. Technology will make it possible for us all to work less and enjoy our work more.

Computers and robots will eventually force employers to treat everyone on the payroll the way they now treat managers. There will be fewer levels of supervision, less routine, and greater chance for self-expression. More work will be done in small organizations or freelanced out to individuals. Fewer will work making tangible products, and more will work in services.

Jobs will be flexiplace as well as flexitime. Most work will eventually be done in places that don't look like offices at all. The growing army of workers employed to deal with the mountains of data produced every day will take their work wherever they wish, plugging in their terminals.

Some workplaces may look like vending-machine canteens, just rows of terminals with people drifting in and out. Others will look like hotel lobbies; services such as job training and advice on health may be provided in lounges where advisers will be on hand, conceivably around the clock. But a great deal of the work of the future will be done in people's homes.

Machines won't eliminate all the scut work. Garbage may still have to be collected by hand. But if wages for dull and dead-end work continue to rise, we'll learn to get by with less of it, just as we have already learned to get by with fewer grocery clerks and waitresses.

Finally, you may go on working after sixty-five because by that time you will be your own boss. This is going to be easier in the future, because the new work of the future will be in services that can be launched on a small scale with little capital investment. You'll farm out what you can't do yourself to another small business, and with a minicomputer you can start it at home.

The trend has begun already. During the 1970s people disenchanted with their jobs began taking early retirement to go into business for themselves. Blue-collar workers bought little tractors and set up to plow out the driveways of their neighbors. Accountants found they could make their former salaries more comfortably doing the books of a few local merchants. High-powered executives passed over for promotion quit to carve out some part of the business for themselves, or to try their hand at something quite different.

New work begins with a dream. Fifty years ago the seminal dreams were big: small-town boys dreamed of sitting in a mahogany-paneled office on Wall Street; of heads turning in elegant restaurants; of being called "sir." In the 1980s the seminal dreams are dreams of personal liberation.

An engineer who works for IBM dreams of opening up a consulting hardware store within an hour's drive of the mountains. During the long meetings he has to sit through, he counts up the tools, the screws, the hasps, the hinges, and the electronic devices he will stock. Sometimes he pictures himself sitting on a keg of nails and sketching, on the back of an envelope, the devices a farmer could rig up to open his barn door from the house. When he has loaded the gear on the farmer's truck, he locks up the store, throws his backpack into the back of his car, and sets off for the hills. A few more years at IBM and he'll be able to retire with enough money to swing it.

A librarian I know dreams of making house calls to care for other people's plants. When it gets stuffy at her desk and the politics are intolerable, she pastes on a smile and imagines herself driving a little truck with gardening tools and supplies from one client to another. And she's saving up for it. She's tired of being a librarian, just as she was tired of teaching school, and she says she was tired of both jobs before she ever began them. When she got out of the Sioux Falls high school her mother took her to the local college, where they offered her a scholarship if she promised to work in the local library. As she recalls the scene, they then asked her what she wanted to study, and her mother answered, "Early childhood education." People railroaded into careers they hate are using retirement years to go into work that they would have liked better.

With modern machinery, a half dozen part-time people can operate the kind of small-scale enterprise that Adam Smith had in mind when he argued that business should be free from government regulation. A perfect example is the squirter-production business that Bob Myers set up in his garage. New jobs are more apt to be created as a result of a new idea tried out in the inventor's garage than from projects funded by well-established big corporations. This is especially true of the services that will be the new work of the future. Instead of Adam Smith's pin factory and the cotton mills of his time, the innovators will be firms that find new ways to meet the need for bicycle repair, computer software design, health services, sports coaching, protection from crime; operations such as adult camps, new food services, barter exchanges, housemate finders, and other services that big companies can't provide well or cheaply.

Even now, enterprises so small that they escape official notice may be growing faster than we know. The underground economy of transactions that avoid taxes has been estimated at from 10 to 20 percent of the Gross National Product, and the Internal Revenue Service thinks that it is growing. This growth may be the reason that the high unemployment of the 1980s has been bearable.

But the most compelling reason that people will continue to work past sixty-five is that older people will be needed. The work that machines create and leave behind is the human work that requires understanding acquired slowly over years of living.

This is a major break with the past. For two hundred years industrial progress has favored the young. Industrial work was quantifiable: so many nuts screwed on bolts, so many papers filed. Anyone could do it, and the younger and spryer, the faster. We applied the material work standard wherever we could make it fit, so we paid people on the basis of hours, even lawyers and doctors. Mandatory retirement became popular in big corporations when they found it profitable to replace older workers proficient at obsolete skills with cheap and supposedly more teachable youngsters willing to learn the new ones.

Now this is changing. The skills in demand cannot be taught in six weeks of intensive training. Time and quantity are not the best way to measure the work the machines leave behind them. High-salaried executives admit to each other that they earn their enormous pay by making one or two decisions a year that may take two or three minutes apiece. In the arts the most valuable work may be just a flash of insight. In business the most valuable work may be the ability to match people to a task, especially when two or three have to be put together to accomplish more than any of them could achieve alone. In management the most valuable work is seeing the needed tasks that no one is doing.

This is the sort of work that cannot be learned in a hurry, even at the Harvard Business School. According to Professor James O'Toole of the Center for Futures Research at the University of Southern California, we are going to need "humane individuals, with analytical and entrepreneurial skills, who know how to work in groups, and who know how to solve problems." This is our old friend experience.

Young people are good at unearthing facts. They have the physical stamina for digging up information. But information is precisely what is going to be cheap. According to the Diebold Group, a management consulting firm, future executives are going to have to know how to make effective use of data, "picking out what is relevant from a great mass of available material." This is our old friend judgment.

Experience and judgment develop slowly, over decades of trial and error. They were always valued in slow-growing, traditional societies where skills stayed the same, and they will be valued again in the postindustrial, data-rich economy of the twenty-first century.

What kinds of jobs will emerge that are specially suited to older people? Not only the jobs listed in the present *Dictionary of Occupational Titles*. Baseball players can become coaches. Policemen can become night watchmen. Writers can become teachers and teachers can become writers. Politicians are retired by the voters to the practice of the law. Those job titles describe the work that has been recognized in the present, or more often, the work of the past. In order to find the jobs of the future we are going to have to think more basically about what is going to be needed in the world we have been projecting.

It is easy to think of needs now being met outside of the formal work structure that could be professionalized in the future. At present, for instance, ordinary citizens need to know how to choose and use a primary physician, but they don't know where to turn to get competent, candid advice.

Everyone has been frustrated by bureaucratic rules, but big corporations, government agencies, and universities are just beginning to hire ombudsmen to defend, on a formal basis, the interests of customers, citizens, students, or employees affected by the organization's policies. Some ombudsmen receive and act on the complaints of individuals shortchanged by the rules of the bureaucracy, but others act as advocates for an entire group of individuals. A university ombudsman, for instance, might make a formal complaint about a cost-cutting decision to limit the hours the library is open. A corporate ombudsman might argue that the labeling of the company's products should give consumers more information.

Our present system holds together because the missing work is done informally. We find a doctor by asking our friends. When frustrated by a bureaucracy, we seek out some member of it who is amiable enough to go out of his way to help us. For this help we turn to people with years of life experience.

People past middle age are already bearing more than their share of the extracurricular, unnamed work that keeps the system running. They shrug off what they do under the general rubric of helping. When "help" is professionalized, it will bear precise occupational titles, such as Medical Services Locator or Environmental Protector.

There are as yet no formal names for the new work that will grow out of the informal help we are getting from older people, but we can begin the process of professionalization by giving names to the general areas of the services they are rendering that are becoming more important. People over sixty-five are the leaders in services that we are going to label Experience Sharing, Conserving, Systems Patching, Matchmaking, and Whistleblowing.

Experience Sharing

Experiences, good or bad, are improved when they are shared. Family and friends now meet this need informally, but they may not be as available to all individuals in an adult world of changing relationships.

Old people have a lot to offer the specialized courses, therapies, and self-help networks springing up to cope with every conceivable life situation. The very survival of old people gives them special credibility in organizations of those who share a medical experience, like Mended Hearts, for survivors of heart attacks, or Make Today Count, the network for patients with life-threatening diseases such as cancer.

An elderly survivor of a mastectomy is more reassuring to a woman who has just had a breast removed than one who hasn't yet lived out the five years that is supposed to constitute cure. At eighty-two Fanny Rosenau, co-founder of Reach to Recovery, was able to tell a woman who was still in the hospital that she herself had been scared to death that her husband would leave when her breast was removed thirty-three years ago—and that she's still scared when the doctor examines her other breast every six months.

At sixty-four Anne Oliver Bassage, a college classmate of mine who reads Spenser while making popovers and lets her wild white hair blow out of control, has made a profession out of sharing the relief she experienced from biofeedback.

"I felt I sank through layers of relaxation, as though I moved with the same freedom I had in deep water...like a trout lazing in a pool," she wrote. "I had sensations of music felt in the body—nebulous sounds, soft, rhythmic, odd modalities I'd never experienced before....There was a flowing in all my limbs, liquid, tingling, like champagne bubbles coursing in the blood....I felt I touched the reality of the inner me for the first time. I had known it was there, but it was sleeping, covered, hidden even from my deepest self."

A former professor of zoology, Anne had always been interested in medicine and had tried biofeedback to control her blood pressure. When she experienced unexpected surges of strength racing through her body she threw her newfound energy into teaching the method. Some of her students come for relief of intractable conditions such as high blood pressure and migraines, some to improve their professional creativity, and others to experience the tingle of blood she describes.

Sharing benefits the giver as well as the receiver. A senior who has organized this benefit to himself is none other than Arthur Murray, the founder of the chain of dance studios that dot the land, who is now living in Hawaii. In his eighties, he has created a way to share not money itself, as rich men often do, but the experience of making it. An avid student of corporate take-overs, he found himself taking pleasure in giving advice on stocks he expected to rise.

He was right so often that he was deluged by unpaid clients, so when he was eighty-two he simplified his life by consolidating the scores of portfolios he found himself trading into an investment club, which he managed for free. Three years later, he had tripled the money of his first nonpaying clients, a particularly heady experience for those of moderate means. And Murray found it so much more fun to watch the little nesteggs grow that when he was eighty-five he restricted new members to small investors.

Conserving

Conserving the values of the past is an important service to people buffeted by the technological advances that can change lifestyles without notice. For security we turn to the people who link us to the safer world we imagine existed in the past.

No matter that Hildegarde wears white gloves over her elbows when she sings in nightclubs. Or that Robert Frost almost forgot the poem he had written for the inaugural of President Kennedy when the wind blew it out of his hand. As public figures, the golden oldies know that we need them the way we need grandparents at weddings and they make themselves into very employable symbols of continuity. In the troubling 1980s we not only elected a President whose grandfatherly style was reassuring, we also spent our recreation dollars escaping into the past. In the 1980s new works are losing out to classics, nostalgic country music, biographies of the golden oldies, and revivals of last generation's Broadway musicals.

In personal crises we look to surrogate parents older than we are who appear to have weathered the storm themselves. Doctors, lawyers, accountants, therapists, and other people-servers retire late if at all because so many of their younger clients continue to need them. Personal reassurance is rapidly becoming part of the occupational system, and gray hairs are an advantage for many of the jobs being created in specialized forms of counseling, supporting, and advising.

Sometimes it helps to label yourself a conserver. Change creates new work in the world it is creating, but it also identifies the need for a special effort to conserve some threatened values. It was natural for women's colleges to be administered by women, but when these colleges became coeducational, trustees wanted to replace at least some of the female administrators with males.

The beleaguered female administrators reacted in several ways. Some took early retirement. Others quit in a huff. Those who needed their jobs agreed to train a younger man and then step down to work under his direction. One woman facing demotion was smart enough to label herself a conserver. Instead of taking orders from the younger man hired to attract endowment from males, she proposed a program for winning back the female alumnae who had withdrawn their support when the college went coeducational. And instead of taking the cut in pay the college had proposed, she cut her time to fit the lower salary offered her. Set up with a title and office of her own, she conserved invaluable alumnae goodwill, as well as a bequest to the college one of them had considered revoking.

Change creates work in conserving endangered skills as well as endangered values. Young maintenance men are not apt to know the ins and outs of the steam-fired boilers still being used. When the Pentagon considered reopening an iron mine in the Catskills during World War II, my former father-in-law, close to retirement then, was the only man the New York Central Railroad employed who had ever located a railroad line through a wilderness.

Young people trying to live off the land can't find what they need to know in libraries. A group in Josephine County, Oregon, discovered that none of them knew how to churn the milk of their cows into butter, but when they visited a senior citizens center to explain what they were trying to do several farm wives volunteered to show them. Conservers have been retrieving endangered skills still practiced in Appalachian villages, so if you want to know how to dress a hog or build a log cabin, you can now find directions in *The Foxfire Book*, the first of a series of books by that name that record such matters.

In many communities ageless individuals are devoting their later years to the conservation of wildlife, scenery, rivers, wilderness, historical landmarks, and institutions whose value cannot be readily measured in dollars. They are the natural defenders of the amenities they grew up enjoying. And they are often the only people in the community who can do it. Retired professionals have the time to attend legislative sessions, speak up at open meetings, testify before commissions, bring citizens' suits, raise money, and write letters to the editor.

Lettie Gay Carson has spent decades of retirement life defending commuter rail lines. Lettie and her husband, Gerald, were writers who in their fifties decided to leave New York City and live year-round in the Harlem Valley, a milk-producing area several hours by rail north of New York City. The Carsons lived in a house on a mountainside overlooking a valley of dairy farms that looked as if it had been designed by a nineteenth-century landscape painter, but the rail line serving the valley was failing. Relying wholly on automobiles would require the building of roads that would change the character of the valley.

For twenty years Lettie fought to save the railroad. When Penn Central tried to abandon the line, she brought a lawsuit that kept it going. Told that the railroad needed freight revenues to support its declining passenger traffic, she asked herself what Harlem Valley farmers needed that New York City couldn't find room for, and came up with an Oriental answer: human waste. Research into disposal problems convinced her that New York City sewage disposal plants could ship their sludge to the Harlem Valley, compost it, and sell it as fertilizer. Five local towns agreed to the plan, but New York City preferred to continue dumping sewage into the ocean, because it was cheaper.

But Lettie didn't give up. With other conservation-minded citizens she organized a statewide lobby to support rail service and prevent the expansion of highway building that threatened small rural communities. Her network helped to prevent an ambitious plan to build a bridge across Long Island Sound that would have suburbanized square miles of open country, and limited extensions of highways that threatened wildlife and the delicate sand dune environment of eastern Long Island.

Lettie was seventy-nine when the Harlem line near her home was finally abandoned. She lost a rearguard fight to prevent the railroad from selling the tracks for junk on the ground that the railroad would be needed again in the future. A few years later the Carsons decided that they could no longer live with the increasingly frequent power failures, which Lettie ascribed to maintenance cuts by Central Hudson, so they moved to Pennswood Village, a community designed for older people on the campus of the George School, a Quaker institution in Bucks County, Pennsylvania.

But a conserver never runs out of work. The Carsons were no sooner settled than they discovered that the local rail line in Newtown was in danger. At eighty-one, Lettie organized her new community to save a line that is badly needed to serve the congested suburban area northeast of Philadelphia. As of 1983, Lettie's Newtown Area Rail Action organization has kept that railroad running.

In the future, technology will continue to threaten values and institutions. Ageless advocates are needed to detect these threats and see that customs, principles, skills, and even railroads are not abandoned without a hearing.

Systems Patching

As the world gets more complicated, we need more people whose business it is to hold it together. Sometimes individuals are caught between organizations that make conflicting demands. Other individuals are left without recourse because the organizations that would normally serve them have bylaws that exclude them. This often happens to welfare clients who move to another state in search of work and find they do not qualify for welfare there when they cannot get a job. When these problems recur on a regular basis, the systems involved need patching, and the people best suited to do this patching are seniors who have spent a couple of decades working inside one of these systems.

Our medical system needs patching. It is far from comprehensive. Patients who are hard to care for are sometimes left with no place to go. Alzheimer's disease is a disability of older people that can leave them without adult control over their bodies and their emotions. They are so hard to manage that nursing homes won't take them, yet hospitals will not admit them because the disease is chronic. This means that someone has to persuade one institution or the other to bend its rules, or find an alternative way of caring for the patient.

Children with learning disabilities may find themselves similarly deserted. One of my college classmates quit the best job she ever had to go into the business of rescuing them. At our forty-sixth college reunion she told me she was letting her hair stay gray because she thought it gave her clout with the establishments she has to bend in the interests of her clients. She doesn't think she would ever have been able to do it, or even to see the problem, if she had not had years of experience in both the public and private school systems.

As she explained it, children who have trouble learning can be trained to learn like other children if their difficulty is diagnosed and treatment is started before they are nine, but our educational system isn't set up to do it. Public schools have the specialists trained in diagnosis, but they can't change classroom routines to let handicapped children learn through their strengths. Private schools can give these children individual attention, but they don't have access to state-supported diagnosticians, and some of them won't accept a child who looks as if he is going to be a problem.

The way the world is set up, nobody is on the side of these children. Pediatricians are supposed to help, but they don't have the neurological training to diagnose lags in coordination between eye and hand that make it hard for some children to distinguish letters and reproduce them. Mary, my classmate, is bitter about what she calls the ''aw-shucks'' type of doctor, who gets rid of the problem by assuring parents the child will grow out of it. Parents add to the problem by letting the children know how disappointed they are and goading them to try harder.

In her mainstream days Mary had been the kind of headmistress who worried about bright children who weren't doing well in their classwork, but the board that hired her wanted her to concentrate on raising academic standards. When she refused to give letter grades, they fired her. At the age of sixty she spent the severance pay she received on a master's degree in learning disabilities.

At sixty-one Mary set herself up as an independent advocate of learning-disabled children, collecting fees sometimes from schools and sometimes from parents. Since parents can't pay much, she earns about half as much as she used to earn in salary, but she has control over when, where, and with whom she works, and the satisfaction of giving children with learning disabilities the diagnostic services available only in public schools and the flexible programs that only private schools can handle.

In the service economy ahead, nonprofit organizations devoted to such concerns as health and education are likely to grow faster than enterprises organized for profit along manufacturing lines. But hospitals, universities, museums, and foundations attract idealistic people, who often slight the financial side of the operation. Richard Nolte is a former foundation director who knows the problem firsthand, because he began his career as part of it. A Rhodes scholar, he was early involved in a variety of international causes with high-sounding names, but he soon discovered that much of the actual work was finding money and making it meet his budget. After his initial dismay, he buckled down to the task and got to be very good at it. By a series of imaginative maneuvers he saved the American Geographical Society and its library from bankruptcy. As director of the Institute of Current World Affairs, he spent years conserving its dwindling assets, and finally discovered a legal way to rescue it from the bank, which in a moment of despair he calculated had been losing the capital entrusted to it at the rate of 1.8 percent a year.

When he retired as director Nolte went into the business of watching, examining, and, if necessary, replacing the people who manage the money of nonprofit organizations. And, as he adds cheerfully, he does it for profit.

As organizations serving people grow in scale and complexity, more people will be involved in seeing that they cover all cases without conflicting with each other.

Matchmaking

Matchmaking is an essential function that is only occasionally recognized as work. Most people have met their business or marital partners and found their jobs through mutual friends, and many houses continue to be sold without the intervention of real estate brokers. But as Vance Packard, the author, complained, we are becoming a nation of strangers. Relocations are now so frequent that they can no longer be made informally. Placement agencies and brokers of various kinds are already springing up to help people make these connections.

More will be needed in the future. In the adult society ahead, unattached individuals will be free to change their jobs, homes, mates, and lifestyles even more frequently than they do now. Older people are usually good enough judges of human nature to help individuals choose among the connections available to them.

Matchmakers are people watchers with a purpose, and they get better at it as they get older. They may be career consultants, guidance counselors, investment bankers who put people with business ideas in touch with investors, or brokers of everything from real estate to less-than-carload lots of chemicals. Like novelists, they scan every personal encounter for data that might come in handy later. They pursue stray remarks of no interest to anyone else, and cock their heads to one side to listen harder to people who impress everyone as bores. Years later they will fit that person's interest or skill into somebody else's need as neatly as if it were the missing piece in a jigsaw puzzle.

There will be new, unsuspected interests to mesh in the fast-moving, information-rich world of the future. A foreign-service officer who was born on a farm thought he had no skills for a second career in business when it came time for him to retire, but he did have hundreds of affluent friends all over the world who wanted to invest their money in America. So many of them asked him about American crops and farmland that he decided to become an international real estate broker specializing in agriculture.

Matchmakers constantly add to their mental files, but they file selectively, as experience has taught them whom and what they no longer have to remember. At eighty-two Armand Hammer was flying around the world making breathtaking deals in the international oil business, because he personally knew so many of the people involved in it. Seeing the mutual interests of your acquaintance gets easier in later years for everybody.

Whistleblowing

Technology of all kinds raises public issues that can no longer be handled in secret. Blowing the whistle on public officials who overstep their powers is a form of public service that is becoming more urgent, and older people have the perspective as well as the freedom to do it. Many of them have no inhibitions about raising hell with the establishment. Even when they are wrong they improve the dialogue, because they have nothing to lose by speaking out and nothing to gain by keeping quiet. And sometimes they are awesomely right.

At seventy-five, Irma Thomas of St. George, Utah, has shown that a single individual can define an issue of national and international importance. She is generally credited with launching the campaign that is forcing the government of the United States to confront the possibility that the fallout from the radiation of atom bomb tests may have injured the health of the civilian population.

Irma has neither powerful friends nor scientific credentials. An amateur potter, she is an ordinary housewife and the mother of seven in St. George, a small town that had only five thousand souls in 1951, when the atomic bomb was tested 145 miles away at Yucca Flats. Government officials have steadfastly insisted that the fallout from bomb tests could not hurt anyone in the town, but strange things began to happen to Irma and her neighbors.

Irma's husband came down with cancer. A brother, a sister, two sisters-in-law, and a brother-in-law were similarly stricken. Four of Irma's daughters suffered such medical problems as muscle damage, stillbirth, and ovarian cyst, and they weren't the only ones. Young women were having trouble conceiving and carrying their babies to term, and many of the babies were born with defects.

Irma wrote letters to everyone in authority, but the potential danger of the bomb test was a state secret no government official was willing to discuss in public. Furious at the brush-off, Irma began to assemble statistics. By 1982 she had the names of two hundred people in town whom she thought were victims. She counted thirty-six people within one block of her home who had contracted cancer or leukemia, fourteen of whom had died. When authorities denied the validity of her evidence she told her story to anyone who would listen. Reporters came not only from the American press, but from Germany, Japan, England, Scotland, Sweden, Holland, and Brazil. To charges that she was provoking mass hysteria she made the tart retort that mass hysteria was reasonable under the circumstances.

Irma organized a Committee of Survivors to carry on the fight against the government. In 1978, 1,500 people in Utah, Arizona, and Nevada were suing the government for damages due to cancer or leukemia contracted as a result of fallout from atom bomb tests at Yucca Flats. Ten lawyers in three law firms were investing all their time on fallout cases, on a contingency basis. A joint suit of twenty-four representative plaintiffs was tried in the District Court of Utah in the fall of 1982, but the potential conflict between the rights of individual citizens and national security is so fundamental that the issue will eventually have to go to the Supreme Court.

One of the most celebrated recent whistleblowers is Howard Jarvis, a cantankerous businessman from California who is generally credited with launching the tax revolt that is changing the basis of American politics in the 1980s. At sixty Jarvis retired from the prosperous manufacturing business he had founded during World War II, and although he had dabbled in politics all his life, he had little influence until he was seventy-five.

Politicians had always written Howard Jarvis off as a crackpot. All through the free-spending 1960s he continued to talk like Herbert Hoover, whom he had once served as a press officer. At the Los Angeles City Hall, no one paid any attention to his tirades against the extravagance of the "liars" and "popcorn balls" spending the people's money in the legislature. A political outcast, he couldn't get elected to public office, but he kept insisting that the people wanted less government and lower taxes.

In 1976 Jarvis decided to go over the heads of the incumbent politicians, directly to the people. The following year, with the help of Paul Gann, a retired real estate salesman, he gathered the 500,000 signatures required to put a constitutional amendment on the ballot. He proposed that the Constitution of the State of California limit by more than half the amount of property taxes that local governments could levy and the services they could provide.

To the surprise and dismay of mainstream politicians, the rebels succeeded not only in getting the amendment on the ballot—where it became Proposition 13—but in mobilizing the votes to pass it. Lids on local government spending followed in other states, and politicians began to campaign on the basis of economy rather than on an increase of government services.

Whistleblowers keep big organizations accountable. In Washington, an informal network of former defense officials quietly funnels information on misuse of the huge military budget that is easy to conceal because it can be classified as secret. These informants have been called "closet patriots." Oversight of this kind is so valuable that both the federal government and big corporations are setting up channels through which employees can report the misdeeds of their associates without risk of personal reprisal. The job is best done by individuals who understand the system but no longer depend on it for their livelihood—in other words, the retired.

Utopia?

Experience Sharing, Conserving, Systems Patching, Matchmaking, Whistleblowing. These are the names of some of the essential but undefined services that are generally now being done outside the established occupational structure. Many of them are the favors adults expect to do for each other as a normal part of everyday living. They are the sort of helping services that were commonly left to women before women expected to work for pay. But in the 1980s the only adults free to do undefined work are those who have retired from the mainstream of economic activity, and as we have seen, their years of experience give them a natural advantage in doing it.

The work of these ageless pioneers benefits everyone who expects to live in the steady-state, adult world of the twenty-first century. It foreshadows the kinds of services and the flexible terms of employment that will characterize new jobs in the future.

Services are the only direction in which our economy can now be expected to go. By 2020 computers, robots, and improvements of various kinds will have reduced the hours of work it will take to put a rising floor of material comfort under every American. Workers freed from production jobs will be available to work at providing the services that people want when their material needs are met. This sounds utopian only because it hasn't happened. But it is beginning to happen. My grandfather would never have believed that 3 percent of American workers could feed the American population and much of the rest of the world as well, or that we would ever have more teachers than farmers.

Technology promises a rising standard of living with less distasteful labor, but it is not yet clear what political upheavals we are going to have to go through to get to it. In the beginning, people will be thrown out of work by machines. This has happened before, of course, but this time we won't be displacing farmhands, factory operatives, and inarticulate dock workers, but aspiring first-generation college graduates cheated out of the middle-management status to which they think their education entitles them.

In the 1980s young college graduates are following the conservative political line of the corporations they hope will employ them, but if middle-management jobs dry up for several years, they may feel shortchanged through no fault of their own and demand the kind of income supports the Reagan Administration has tried to take back—only bigger and better than the modest welfare supports of the Great Society of the 1960s. Welfare for college graduates will come higher than welfare for unemployed high school dropouts in our central cities.

One way or another, jobless prosperity will mean that entitlement programs will have to grow. Government will have to tax the profits the technology reaps and distribute it to the consumers. Business enterprises that control the new labor-saving technology will discover that they cannot reap the profits it promises unless consumers have the money to buy its products. If unemployment cuts their sales, they will turn to the government for help, just as farmers promoted food stamps for the poor in order to sell their surplus crops, and builders promoted publicly funded housing when millions of poor people couldn't afford private housing.

One way or another, more of your income in the future will come directly from the government, some of it in the form of publicly funded schooling, housing, and medical care; some in greatly expanded unemployment benefits; and some of it in programs for supporting students, artists, veterans, scientists, or people engaged in some socially useful activity that doesn't provide enough money to support them at a socially acceptable level.

When subsidy programs multiply, some conservative reformer will discover that it is cheaper to consolidate all our income transfers. Instead of Social Security, veterans' benefits, Medicare, scholarships, sick pay, unemployment insurance, food stamps, rent subsidies, and all the rest, we will one day have to have a comprehensive social security system. Your Social Security pension could easily become just the last of a series of income supplements that began with the tuition grants that saw you through college in the 1960s.

In the past, moneymaking has organized life in America. In the high-technology service society ahead, work will be more rewarding and less confining than it is in the 1980s.

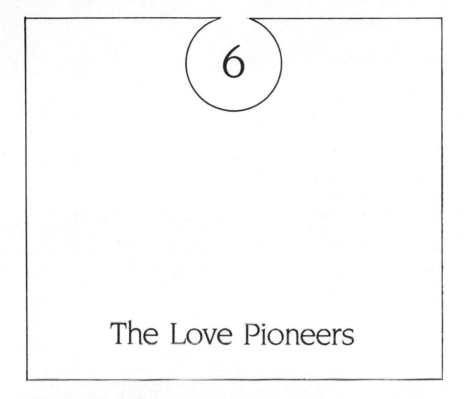

6

The Love Pioneers

Love never dies, but it changes its face. In the 1980s even the ageless are not prepared for the love life that awaits them in their later years.

Many years ago I had a boyfriend who said he was looking forward to getting old enough so that sex wouldn't get him into trouble anymore. It was only half a joke. At the time, both of us believed that love was your body's way of trapping you into having children, that you couldn't control it, and that it would be all over when you got to be, well, say, thirty.

All dead wrong.

Love is something your mind instructs your body to do, and it doesn't end when you are through making babies. It's a silly mistake, but almost all of us make it.

We believe advertisements implying that sex is impossible for people who don't look stunning in bathing suits. Dyeing your hair improves your love life only if it changes what goes on in your head. Starving yourself into the clothes that you wore as a girl won't do. (If you do fall in love, you are apt to start cooking and eating and gain it all back.) Love improves with practice. It gives you the springy feeling you may associate with youth, but it cannot be induced by arresting the natural course of your human development.

We get the idea that love is only for the young because the old people you see around you don't seem to be thinking sex, or you imagine they aren't because they remind you of your parents, whose sexual relations are, of course, unthinkable.

Most people born before World War II were brought up to think that sex was something they could expect to outgrow, and that's exactly what happened to those who continued to think so. As we shall see, even Kinsey didn't realize the impact of this destructive notion on the libido of his older subjects.

The good news is that you don't have to be like these sad old folks. If sex is reasonably good right now, it's likely to continue to be good in the future. You can get an idea of what's ahead from the pioneers of independent mind who never bought the notions that inhibited most of their contemporaries.

The testimony of these pioneers is surprising. In later years the important thing about sex is the closeness of being together, the thrill of touching and stroking, and the warmth of a friendly body in bed. A classmate of mine was so happy to be back with a man she had passionately loved in her youth that it would have been enough, she said, just to lie in his arms for hours on end.

Couples whose love for each other has developed over decades can express themselves physically even with severely limited bodies. When she still had her paralyzed, dying husband at home, Gerda Lerner dismissed the night nurse one hour before the day nurse arrived so that they could make love. In her book *A Death of One's Own*, she describes how she managed to get her husband into their big double bed the last time they knew they would ever again be alone together:

> The bed was far too low for easy transfer and I was sure I would not be able to get him out of it once I had him in it. Anyway, I managed. I settled him in comfortably, raising up his head with propped pillows, secured him against falling out and rolling off. Then I slipped in beside him on his "good" side. I held his hand. Eyes closed, it felt normal, right. It felt like the

hundreds of nights we had lain together side by side. Thirty-three years. A whole lifetime.

We made love that morning. It was sad and sweet and tender. He did what he could and gave me all his gentle love, his strength and secure trust in himself and in both of us, despite his helpless and crippled body. Amazingly, he spoke to me with his body the way he had always spoken.

The Lerners weren't the first and won't be the last couple to triumph over the decline of their bodies. A generation earlier, Lael Wertenbaker reported that the night her husband learned of his cancer they made love that was simple, mutual, and profound. To protect his tender abdomen, he had been sleeping with his back to her instead of in her arms, as they usually did, but "that night, adjusting to fit after each turning, we were more than usually close together, the full length of our bodies."

Some of these love pioneers are people who defied the conventions from the very beginning. Others joined the sexual revolution of the 1960s in their later years, sometimes along with their adult children. In the 1980s liberated old people are beginning to come out of the closet, and they sometimes speak up with remarkable candor.

"Everyone tells me about companionship," a recently remarried old man stood up to say in the question period after a lecture on sex. "It gets me mad. Sure, I want companionship, but I also got married for sex. I always had an active sex life and still do, and I'm eighty-two years old." All eighty-two-year-olds may not be so lucky, but he's not unusual.

In spite of the sexually stunted youth we all survived, some old people have succeeded in liberating themselves from traditional hang-ups. Surprisingly liberal attitudes were reported by eight hundred Americans over sixty queried by Bernard Starr, a research associate of the Center for Gerontological Studies at the Graduate Center of the City University of New York, and Marcella Weiner, adjunct professor of psychology/gerontology at the City University of New York. They found, for instance, that nearly two-thirds had nothing against homosexuals, although very few had any desire to try it themselves. Four-fifths approved of masturbation, and nearly half admitted to doing it. This is progress toward tolerance for people who grew up at a time when the only respectable sexual experience was intercourse between married people, the husband on top of the wife in the classic, or missionary, position.

But they didn't stop with accepting the sexual behavior of others. Nearly 40 percent of them said they wanted to try new sexual techniques themselves. A seventy-one-year-old woman thought she ought to experience "female-female" but would have to locate a partner. A widow her age confessed that oral sex was "not as bad as I thought it would be," and another recommended it "to add excitement." Quite a few reported that they didn't think there was anything left for them to try. A sixty-year-old widow wrote in that she had tried everything but "swinging, group and communal sex, homosexuality, sex with animals, and anal sex," while others made no exemptions.

These people were clearly experimental, and it seems to have paid off for them. A third of the Starr-Weiner men and women said that sex was not merely as good as it had ever been, but actually better. And they weren't sentimental about what they meant by good. When given a choice, 43 percent said orgasm was the most important thing about the sex act, 26 percent said foreplay, 16 percent voted for love, but only 8 percent chose intercourse, the respectable sexual outlet.

"What does this mean?" I asked a woman the age of the Starr-Weiner subjects.

"Finger fucking," she said, without a trace of embarrassment. A widow's response was a little more delicate: "There are other forms of stimulation, and I am open to experimentation."

There are a number of reasons that nontraditional sources of orgasm may be especially important to maintaining the sex life of older people. Alternatives such as oral sex are one of the ways that couples maintain sexual contact when one of the partners is ill or unready, and these occasions are more frequent in later life.

Then, too, alternatives help a couple maintain a satisfying relationship during later years, when her need for sexual satisfaction may be more urgent than his. When a man slows down, or has trouble maintaining a hard erection, he may be more willing to stimulate a woman's clitoris directly, so that she has an orgasm every time.

In doing so, he may find himself taking the kind of pleasure in her satisfaction that she took in satisfying him when his haste short-changed her. This adaptation may explain why 41 percent of women said sex was better than when they were younger, compared with only 27 percent of the men.

There's no physical reason that your sex life should satisfy you less as you get older. Social scientists unwittingly perpetuate the notion of inevitable decline by promoting sex for older people as if it were a difficult ideal, and while they have always declared that sex is *possible* and even common after sixty—after all, a lot of them are over sixty themselves—ageist assumptions in research design have led them to underestimate it.

In the beginning of sex research they were misled by cross-sectional data. In the 1940s, when Kinsey began collecting the first scientific information on the frequency of sexual intercourse in males, he found that the old men he interviewed had sex fewer times a week than the young men. This sounded like proof that the frequency of sex in males declines with advancing years. Actually, of course, it proves only that men who were old in the 1940s had sex less often than men who were young in the 1940s. It didn't account for the fact that the old and the young were of different generations.

They were further misled by their own ageist assumptions. Researchers didn't find sex in the lives of older people because they didn't think it was worth the effort to look for it. They simply assumed old people were as far beyond sexual feelings as they imagined their parents to be, and wouldn't want to be asked about something they had lost.

"Why sex?" a young professional asked when she heard about the Starr-Weiner inquiry. "Older people need so many things—more money, better housing, ways of combating cancer and heart disease." Researchers would much rather spend their time on problems that can be solved by programs taxpayers can be persuaded to fund.

Old people didn't go out of the way to correct the omission. They had been reared not to talk about sex, especially with authorities like researchers gathering data. The result was an age distortion. In early studies of sexual attitudes young people brought up to frankness were in favor of more liberal sex for the old than were the old people themselves.

For a time, researchers and subjects were trapped in self-confirming silence. Sociologists assumed that widowed old people wanted their old roles back: old men remarried primarily for domestic care, old women for the chance to give it. And since old people were brought up with the same assumptions, they simply restated these conventions to the few researchers who bothered to ask them about their feelings.

These assumptions were very important, because the appetite for sex is not a constant like height or weight that can be accurately counted in numbers, but a fragile emotion that can be aroused or destroyed by expectations. Early generations of Americans grew up in societies that carefully limited sexual satisfaction.

Luckily, of course, the conventions did not succeed in repressing everybody. In every generation some individuals have been able to preserve their sexuality or to renew it. Starr and Weiner found many people over sixty-five who were responding to the sexual revolution that began in the 1960s. But the love pioneers who give us a glimpse of our future selves remain a heroic minority. They strike us as odd precisely because most people their age are sexually stunted.

It is difficult to convey to people born after World War II what sex was like in the 1930s. Extramarital sex was elaborately clandestine and either expensive or an awkward transaction in the back seat of a car. Masturbation, the last resort, was widely believed a risk to sanity that manifested itself in pimples, and then as now, a lot of young people had pimples. "We were both virgins when we married," a ninety-year-old told me, "but she got pregnant on our wedding night, the very first time we tried it. Neither one of us was really ever comfortable doing it again."

Birth control and abortion were uncertain, inconvenient, illegal, and, for practicing Catholics, a sin against their religion. During the Depression devout young couples wrestled with their natural urges. An Irish neighbor who had a baby the age of mine confided that her husband was so afraid of making her pregnant that he was sleeping on the couch in the living room. She complained to me that she might just as well not be married at all.

We are just beginning to appreciate how much of the sexual potential of later years has been concealed by the way we have attempted to measure it. Researchers are becoming more careful about drawing conclusions based on differences between the old and young of any one time, and about asking questions that project their own assumptions onto their respondents.

Kinsey's first subjects are now in their later years, and while these particular individuals haven't been found and interviewed again, others their age are doing better than the older men who were interviewed in the 1940s. In 1980 Starr-Weiner's eight hundred adults over sixty had sex on an average of 1.4 times a week, about what Kinsey found for his forty-year-olds back when Starr-Weiner's subjects were forty, too. And while Kinsey reported that a quarter of his seventy-year-olds were impotent, two-thirds of the Starr-Weiner men said that sex was at least as good as it had ever been.

There are a number of reasons that adults born after World War II will be having more sex in their later years than they now expect. First, no one need fear that his sexual activity will decline by the difference Kinsey found between old and young. Sexual activity wanes with age, but much more slowly.

Second, sexual activity has been steadily rising in America, so that if individuals taper off in their later years, each successive generation cuts down from a higher level of activity. Many future old people will undoubtedly remain as active as yesterday's young people.

Finally, there is evidence that more young people are practicing oral sex and other alternatives to intercourse as part of their sexual repertoire from the very beginning. They will have no hang-ups about drawing more heavily on them in later years when these alternatives become more convenient.

A New Kind of Love

Sexually liberated old people are exceptions to their generation, but they are not mere curiosities. They are pioneers exploring the kinds of love available only in the postreproductive years. The relationships they form in their later years can tell us what lies ahead for adults who grew up in the 1960s. They are our only clue to the sexual future of the first generation of adults who were not expected to commit themselves for life to a sexual partner or to conceal their sexual lives as somehow indecent.

Their experience tells us about a whole new country of love that unexpectedly opens up in later years. Old loves aren't a faded carbon copy of earlier relationships. Judging from their experiences, you can expect a rewarding personal life in the twenty-first century. You will continue to improve your sexual skills. You will be more impulsive and more romantic. You may go back to a long-lost love of your youth, or you may experiment with relationships you now regard as inappropriate.

Better Sex

Sex will continue to be an important part of your life in your later years, and since it is a learned art, you can expect to get better and better at it. Old couples may be more matter-of-fact about sex because it doesn't carry the possibility of pregnancy, but they know more about the resources of their bodies for pleasure. The experienced also have the advantage of knowing more about human as well as explicitly sexual responses. They have learned that sexual satisfaction depends on the quality of a relationship rather than on images of glamour.

These possibilities can come as a shock to an older person's middle-aged children. Jane couldn't imagine her mother having a serious suitor, so when Jim proposed marriage she thought at first that he was making a bad joke at Mother's expense. She was suspicious. What could Jim possibly want from Mother? After all, Mother was no beauty: frankly fat and accustomed to ruling her roost, she was seventy-one and looked every year of it.

More to the point, neither Jane nor her brother could see what possible good the match could do for Mother. She had too many friends in the church to be lonely. She had a comfortable, paid-up house, and she lived the way she liked. She had been a widow for twenty-four years, so she wasn't one of those women who can't live without a husband. She had turned down earlier offers of marriage.

So why rush into one at seventy-one? And so suddenly! Even their mother usually suspected such haste. But Jane held her tongue when her mother started talking about the wedding. She was obviously serious about it, and as fluttery and coy as a young pink-and-greenie.

What, Jane asked her brother, would they do about sex? Maybe they would just ignore it. But it was pretty hard to ignore what was supposed to follow a wedding, even if you were in your seventies. Maybe they had an agreement about it, but neither Jane nor her brother could imagine their mother talking about it.

Besides, Jim was a few years younger than Mother, and at sixty-nine he was clearly still interested. Jane had caught him putting his hand on her mother's knee. Mother hadn't resisted, but how would she feel about actually going to bed with a man after all those years? Jane was sure that her mother wouldn't sleep with any man who wasn't her lawfully wedded husband. Mother had always had strong fundamentalist scruples against even such mild forms of sin as drinking and smoking, so you couldn't expect her to start committing the sin of fornication in her seventies.

Jane tried to find a tactful way to talk about sex with her mother, but when she attempted to bring up the subject Mother insisted on talking about the wedding. It was originally planned as a family affair, but the guest list kept growing. Jane and her brother were so afraid that Mother was in for a rude awakening of some kind that they insisted on taking her out to dinner the night before the wedding to find out what was really going on.

They soon discovered that Mother didn't need any moral support. She was still her old practical self. Now that all the children were in town, she and Jim had decided to postpone their honeymoon so that everybody would have a chance to get better acquainted. When they protested that this wasn't the idea of a honeymoon, she just beamed. The evening degenerated into a sort of family-style bachelor party, with Jane and her brother drinking too much without any protest from their teetotaling mother. At the end, they gave her a box marked "For your wedding night." After a great deal of debate, they had bought her a filmy black nightgown and peignoir, as a change from the flannel sleepwear she had always worn.

The newlyweds weren't shy. At midnight after the wedding, the bride phoned her daughter to thank her for the nightgown, and late next morning they invited themselves to brunch.

Had they or hadn't they?

The children debated the issue together and decided that somehow or other they had.

New Romance

In your later years you will be freer not only to experiment sexually but to pursue romantic impulses that you would have shrugged off with a smile in your middle years of adult career and family responsibility. The love pioneers are showing us that it is possible not only to love but to fall in love at a very late age.

Moralists distinguish between two kinds of love: the first is a deep understanding and concern for the welfare of the beloved; the other, more dubious variety is the psychological state of bewitchment with the idea of a relationship with the beloved. The two are so different that a psychologist has coined a special name for the kind of love that people are said to fall into. Dorothy Tennov calls it "limerence." Her book *Love and Limerence* explores the difference. Songs exalt the limerent variety of love as a phenomenon of youth that cannot last because it is based on innocence and inexperience.

The songs are wrong. Age is no protection. Limerence strikes the elderly without warning, and it strikes at elderly men with special force.

For Quint and Martha it happened in Las Vegas.

Las Vegas is open all 365 days of the year. At Christmas the lights, crowds, action, and glitter are especially attractive to people who can't expect happy surprises at home.

The day after is a letdown. Martha had flown in from California on Christmas Eve, but she lost the fifty dollars she had budgeted for the slots. There was no place she particularly wanted to be, so on December 26, 1979, she decided to take the slow and the cheap way home.

When she got on the bus, all the window seats were taken by people who looked broke, dejected, or otherwise unsavory. But the man close up behind the driver was clean-cut and cheerful. She liked his neat plaid jacket, the brisk way he turned his head and said no, the seat beside him wasn't taken. Her first impression was of a man who cared about his appearance.

Quint thinks the first thing he noticed about Martha was that her eyes were violet-blue. And then, of course, he noticed her figure. He guessed—and, from long practice, correctly—that she was five foot two and 125 pounds. Not bad. He opened up with the weather, but soon they were talking about themselves.

No, he hadn't come to gamble. His wife of sixty years had died a little more than a year before, so he had come to Las Vegas to spend Christmas with his daughter, who lived there. Now he was going back to his semidetached house in a retirement community in Riverside. Lovely house. Nice neighbors. She should see for herself.

Martha explained that she had never had children. Four years ago she had been widowed for the second time. She was on her way to her flat in San Diego. They talked about Vegas, about the bus, about food, about their ages. His was ninety, hers eighty-nine.

Something thickened between them quick as pudding on the fire. Forty minutes out of Vegas Quint heard himself saying, out loud, "I think I am falling in love with you." And he proposed, right there on the bus, for all to hear. The bus driver turned his head, then looked back to the road.

They didn't say much after that, but they took each other's name and phone number. He got off at Riverside and let her ride on to San Diego alone, but the next day he called her and invited her to visit him.

Martha hadn't expected to marry again, but Quint wooed her. He arranged for a neighbor woman to put her up, all very proper. He took her to dinner with his daughters and their husbands, and she liked them. On Sunday he took her to church. The minister was for it.

Why not? And why wait? On Monday she said yes. Quint's daughter put on a wedding for them in Las Vegas. Twelve days after they met, they took the same bus for their honeymoon. A regular who had overheard the proposal wanted to know if they were married, and they nodded happily.

Newspapers wrote them up cute. Two weeks after they were

married they were on the *Today* show, along with Dr. Gerald Hodan, a psychologist who declared them not only sane but actually in love. Old people, he added, were less bashful about what he called "PDA" (public displays of affection).

Quint says he has always been a fast worker. He fell in love with his first wife as soon as he saw her, but it was World War I, so he couldn't marry her until he got out of the army. But he's not the only old man to fall in love at first sight. A few months after the McCoys were on television, another old couple met on a bus. Less alert than Quint, the man didn't get the woman's phone number, but he put an ad in the paper of the town where she got off, and they married shortly after she answered it.

The logistics of late-life marriage are simpler. A widow remarrying after sixty can keep the Social Security benefits she already has if they are higher than what she would get as a dependent of her new husband. And the problem is not how to set up housekeeping but what to do with the extra set of gear.

Speed makes sense, but grown children regard it as unseemly. "Who is this man?" a middle-aged son exclaimed when he learned that his mother was going to get married. She cringed. Old lovers are as uneasy about what their children will think as they were about what their parents thought of their very first sweethearts.

One seventy-year-old was so afraid that he would be considered a fortune hunter that he insisted on disclosing his financial assets to the forty-five-year-old son of his intended, and all but formally asked him for his mother's hand in marriage. But, as she had predicted, the son was worried less about losing an inheritance than that she was foolish to do "a thing like that at her age."

Rather than face him, they eloped. Furious, the son informed her that henceforth he considered their relationship "residual." She wept, for all the world like an errant daughter turned out in the snow by an unforgiving father in a nineteenth-century melodrama.

Her son, of course, was an old-fashioned exception. Few middle-aged children are openly hostile, but they may have trouble sorting out their feelings. "I'm glad for her," a daughter said of her seventy-one-year-old mother's marriage. "I'm really glad for her," she repeated, as if she had reason not to be. "All I care about is the way he treats her," she added in a burst of generosity, and then, more candidly, "I guess I really feel relieved, like a mother who has married off her daughter."

Dr. Gerald Hodan says frankly that he doesn't understand why old people marry on impulse, but he's seen them do it. He told me about a widower who, on the very day his wife died, phoned a sixty-year-old widow who had moved away to Florida to tell her that he had been in love with her for forty years. All that time they had been married neighbors who played bridge every week and spent their vacations together without so much as an innocent flirtatious remark. Yet when he called, she took the next plane north, and in no time at all they were living together and considering marriage.

You are especially vulnerable to limerence when you have just lost a person around whom you have organized your life. In the past, widows and widowers have been made to feel that they could not or should not expect another love, but in the freer environment ahead a person who loses a mate will be expected to find another. Love pioneers who remarry late in life are already making this healthy response to bereavement.

It is not at all clear what happens inside when you lose a partner who has shared your life for decades. It may be that you lose the switch that turns off sexual responses to other potential partners. At the same time, you can be overwhelmed by the return of the energy that for years has been impounded in a deep relationship. The liberation can be explosive.

One newly widowed woman was surprised to find herself remembering the long-forgotten songs she had liked and the clothes she had worn thirty years ago, before her marriage. Her explanation was that those younger years came welling up in her mind when she asked herself how she was going to live as a single person.

Long-Lost Loves

What might have been is the stuff of which dreams are made, and the longer you live, the stronger the pull to try the other road. Love pioneers are romantic enough to marry a star-crossed love of their youth. It is sometimes easier, late in life, to realize the nature of an early relationship.

A seventy-year-old woman told her daughter about running into the boy from a neighboring farm with whom she had been forced to drive to high school every day. Both of them hated it because they were ashamed to explain why they always arrived together. There was no school bus in those days, so her father had lent his father the money to buy a car on the understanding that his daughter would always be able to ride to school in it. "He didn't attract me then," she told her daughter with what sounded like teenage vehemence, "and he doesn't attract me now." Yet after twenty-two years as a widow, she married him three months later.

Sometimes a love pioneer is attracted to the boy or girl who was merely part of the scene when they were forming their first attachments. At sixty-seven, Muriel Humphrey, widow of the Vice-President, went back to the town where they both grew up to dedicate its new Hubert Humphrey Airport. Someone told her that one of her high school classmates had just lost his wife. She hadn't seen him for fifty years, but on the spur of the moment she dashed off a note to tell him she was sorry. Lunch followed. Little more than a year later, they married.

A surprising number of love pioneers go back, in their later years, to a childhood sweetheart forgotten during childbearing years, or separated by accident, war, or quarrel. Like many another doughboy, Roswell Barrett came back from World War I to find the girl he had left behind was married to someone else. Time healed the wound, but when he was eighty-eight she turned up as the grandmother of the bride at a wedding he attended. The situation was so evocative that after the shortest possible decent interval the octogenarians followed suit in the same church.

Some of the reunions are too farfetched for even the boldest fiction. At eighty-one Isaac Corkland decided to write his autobiography. For help, he enrolled in a creative writing class. As an example, one student brought in the galleys of a book she described as an account of the life of one of the first women to graduate from M.I.T.

"Was her name Martha?" he asked. Sure enough, the author was the girl he had fallen in love with when his transport to France was delayed at Camp Mills on Long Island in 1918. Under a program for entertaining the troops, the local YMCA had assigned her to take him to the theater in New York. Their letters went astray in the war, and both eventually married and reared children. He had heard she had gone to M.I.T., but never succeeded in getting in touch with her.

Neither can now remember whether they actually kissed good-bye in 1918. Martha thinks not. At eighteen she wouldn't have kissed a man before accepting his formal proposal of marriage. But in 1980 they are living together happily in sin, because Martha no longer believes in marriage. *Full Circle* is the title of her autobiography.

More of these reunions are ahead. Lovers separated by World War II are just beginning to find each other. In the next few decades some of the couples who separated during the 1960s and 1970s will find that they still have limerent feelings for each other and decide to try it again, in the hope that what they have learned during the years apart will make it possible for them to finally get it right. People born after World War II will be more apt to continue to seek romance in their later years, because they grew up expecting more out of love and marriage than the comfortable trade of sex and support that satisfied their parents. If one relationship failed to provide emotional support and stimulation, they did not hesitate to look for these intangibles in another. Those who have had a series of partners know how to start a new relationship.

But romance is not a constant. Your idea of it changes with your attempts to attain it. Young lovers expect to share every thought and feeling, but they soon discover that this is impossible. Those who have accepted the image of romance depicted in June/moon popular songs conclude that love is reserved for the very young and give up the attempt to pursue it. This is what happened to the ageist people born before World War II who are old in the 1980s.

The ageless respond in a different way. They accept the insight and build on it. They give up the futile attempt to understand what can't be shared, and keep the relationship fresh by deepening the mutuality of whatever it is that the partners have in common.

The art of partial relationships is not learned quickly or easily, but it has an unanticipated advantage. Those who know how to bypass areas of difference can develop satisfying relationships on the basis of very narrow common ground. Armed with this skill, they are able to replace the loss of a partner in later years, when the number of potential partners dwindles.

More Space

Ageless lovers give each other space even when they are incurably romantic. According to Dr. Hodan, Martha and Quint didn't cling to each other in the television studio, as younger newlyweds do in a new and potentially threatening situation. This didn't mean that they avoided physical expressions of their affection. They held hands when they were beside each other, but felt free to wander away from each other to talk to other people in the studio or visit the coffee urn.

Dr. Hodan's comment reminded me how bereft I felt the first time my husband left me alone long enough to buy a pack of cigarettes when I was a bride of nineteen. I was hurt, but also astounded. How could he walk out the door without me? We had spent the first two days of our marriage almost literally hand-in-hand, and it hadn't occurred to me that it would ever be otherwise.

But every relationship changes. Even the most devoted couples don't go through life holding hands. According to Dr. Ida Davidoff, a Connecticut marriage counselor who has continued to practice into her seventies, older people need to feel that they can withdraw at least temporarily from even the closest marriage relationship. Individuals become authentic by accumulating experiences peculiar to them alone, including a growing set that they cannot share with even the closest partner. The young ideal of sharing everything would stunt both partners and threaten the marriage. Usually, partners adjust to each other's growing need for privacy.

Ageless love pioneers give each other lots of space. They may not even attempt to share a bedroom. Instead of reforming a messy mate, it's easier to give him a room where his possessions can be undisturbed. Even those who are married may spend weeks or months apart. A relative of mine gave up trying to get his wife to spend the summers with him on their farm. In their later years she used that time for travel to places he didn't like and visits to people she liked more than he did. Some couples who meet in their later years make no change in their living arrangements. They maintain their former homes and take turns visiting each other. Married or single, older lovers do not expect to go everywhere as a couple.

Two-career couples are learning young to give each other the space that they will need to keep love green in their later years. Owls and larks no longer worry because they can't share breakfast. In metropolitan areas, pace-setting young professional couples no longer expect to have dinner together every night at the same fixed time, but plan their time together on the basis of what each has to do. They find that they don't have enough time together to keep each other fully informed about their working lives. Many of them outlaw business entirely and spend their time together on common concerns that have nothing to do with either career. Those who have to live away from each other for business reasons learn the art of spending their precious time together on what unites them instead of on what divides them.

The Shifting Balance

The dependence of lovers on each other is never exactly reciprocal. Love has been described as a relationship between one who loves and another who condescends to be loved. If so, the balance is never constant. Although the direction of dependence can shift in the twinkling of an eye, the balance tends to shift with the passing years. During their childbearing years women are the dependents, but in later years men increasingly lean on their wives for every kind of emotional support.

A bride will try hard to understand what her husband sees in baseball. She may go along to parties that bore her in order to remain part of his scene. When we were discussing how our marriages had changed, a college classmate said that she didn't make the effort to go on pack trips with her husband anymore, because she was allergic to horses. She did not say whether the allergy was something new or she had ignored it when as a bride she had made a point of going with him.

These shifts are a natural part of the life cycle of men and women. As Gail Sheehy has pointed out in her book *Passages*, women defer all other interests while their children are young. The result is that they are ready for the wider world just when their husbands have had their fill of it and need the support and warmth of closer personal relationships.

The late-life independence of women causes problems for traditional couples. Homemaking wives dread the retirement of their husbands from business. What happened when ''we'' retired was a major topic of conversation at my forty-seventh college reunion. The problem was lunch. Some boasted that their husbands had learned to get their own or were considerate enough to get out of the house on bridge club days. Other women were cutting down on volunteer work just when they were beginning to pack a little clout.

''It's just not polite to go out of the house in the morning and leave him to his own devices all day,'' a resignee contended, and she didn't take it kindly when somebody suggested that she was talking about her husband as if he were a child.

The rising dominance of the wife creates another kind of problem for two-career couples. Usually the man is older, so he reaches retirement age first. In the past women quit when their husbands did, as a matter of course. Social Security recognized this custom by allowing women to retire earlier than men. Most of the time they were eager to get out of the dead-end jobs they had been doing.

Now this is changing. In the 1980s many women want to work longer than their husbands. Most of the time, they simply need the money. Women are healthier in their later years, so in many families the wife is better able to continue earning. Increasingly, however, she wants to continue because she is genuinely absorbed in her job. Since affirmative action, dedicated older women have been belatedly promoted to positions of real authority at the end of their working lives, and they don't want to miss the chance to prove their ability.

This natural shift in the balance of dependence between the sexes will be more obvious in the adult world of the future, and as they adapt to it men and women will become more comfortable with each other. Although they fly in the face of traditional roles, love pioneers are already demonstrating that it is perfectly possible for a man to respond to a woman who is investing less of her ener-gy in her relationship with him by investing more of his energy in his relationship with her.

For me the transition was so natural that I didn't realize it was happening. My husband, Tom, was a talented publicist with friends in the media. He always seemed to have clips about me in his pocket to produce at the slightest excuse. But though feminists sometimes admired the support that he gave me, he couldn't possibly qualify as a liberated man.

Tom was a Texan both of whose grandfathers had served in the Confederate Army. He always took out the garbage, but his solu-tion to a wife who couldn't get off the phone to cook dinner was to pass me a note suggesting that we go out to eat. If I shook my head, he took his newspaper to the table and waited patiently for dinner to appear. When it came, long habit required him to rise to seat me, even when I simply didn't have time to sit down.

I met Tom in 1948, when he wrote me one of the thousands of encouraging notes he was always dispatching to fledgling writers. He claimed he had been a writer on *Fortune* when I was a researcher, and he had an office phone list to prove it. Both of us had been fired from *Fortune* after the war, he because he couldn't rise above the lack of facts to do a story on what would happen to Japan if the emperor abdicated, and I because my research reports were pep-pered with the kinds of ideas that only writers were supposed to have. In those days a *Fortune* writer was supposed to be an imagi-native male kept in order by a fact-minded female researcher. Both of us were crushed that we couldn't do what was expected of us.

Tom set out to help me become a writer. He introduced me to editors. He took me to meetings. He thought of places to send my rejected manuscripts. A researcher at heart, he dug up facts and books for me. By the time he was sixty-five and I was fifty-five I had become the writer and he the researcher, and I think we both agreed that the marriage got better as we went along.

The change in the needs men and women have for each other is more dramatic for those who are single. It is fortunate that single old women greatly outnumber the supply of available men their age, because they are generally less eager than men to marry.

Women in retirement communities tell you that they like men for companions but they don't want to become some old man's maid.

The Sex Gap

The shifting balance affects a couple's sex life. In their later years women become more interested in sex, but, at least in the past, the interest of their older partners has remained the same or slowly declined. In the past couples simply ignored this shift as an embarrassment, but the sexually liberated adults born after World War II will deal with it openly in their later years. The sexual mismatch can be bridged by alternatives to intercourse practiced by the people interviewed by Starr and Weiner, but the social mismatch requires more heroic remedies.

Some of the love pioneers of the 1980s are women who were brought up to expect that sex would be the least of their late-life problems. One of them is a woman we'll call Janet.

Friends noticed that Janet was becoming more lively in her seventies. She began to wear provocative clothes, things like an impressive hat with a curved feather framing her face. She went to everything, spoke up in town meetings, got herself elected to the school board, and began to build herself a political base. The late-life transformation puzzled the neighbors, but Janet never explained. The explanation she gave me would have shocked them.

"I used to have a courtly, sexy husband," she told me. "Now he's a wizened little man with a charming sense of humor. Sex got to be such an effort—and for my sake, he made it—that I tried not to bother him. I guess I made up for it, though, by saying yes to all the community organizations for which I had never had time."

But it wasn't easy. Politics is notoriously sexy. After an especially lively caucus, one of the younger men found a chance to pat her knee. She smilingly withdrew, of course, but thinking about him on the way home, she had an orgasm and nearly drove off the road.

Old women may be ambivalent about taking on a husband, but they feel very keenly their lack of a man. "I want sex," said a widow in her sixties, "but where are the men?" The answer is, taken: at every age after sixty-five, there are five times as many widows as widowers.

The deprivation is brutal. Thirty percent of the women surveyed by Starr-Weiner had no sex life, though most of them wanted it. The obvious solution is for old women to get together with younger men, and a surprising four out of five of the Starr-Weiner people approved of exactly this.

Sexually, younger men are a better match for older women than the men their age. And it's not a one-sided bargain. Benjamin Franklin, who was always something of a ladies' man himself, wrote movingly of older women, who in addition to being safe from pregnancy could be counted on to be knowledgeable, discreet, undemanding, and grateful.

Stan was a public health officer trying to organize a new kind of child health clinic. Bella was a pediatrician in the county's most prestigious medical group. He admired her style when he heard her argue the unpopular side of a wrangle at the local medical association, so he asked her to serve on his advisory board.

They were polar opposites. At thirty-three, he was idealistic, uncertain, bland, poor, handsome, and ambitious. At sixty-one, she was worldly, confident, rich, wrinkled, and sharp. Because she thought she was ugly, she had taught herself to be witty. She's too snobbish to use the title to which she was born in Central Europe, but not too snobbish to mention the offbeat parts of the world she knows, or to slip easily into the mother tongue of any foreigner to whom she is introduced. A gourmet cook, and just divorced from a leading local judge, she gave elegant parties. Her vibes were too strong, her wit was too sharp, but everyone knew her and everyone always came.

Stan and Bella met when both of them were running away. Stan, from a passive, doll-like girl whom he recognized, in the nick of time, as a dieted-down edition of the mother who had tethered his father to a dull but steady job. Bella, from her latest attempt to cure the spastic colon she contracted when her son was expelled from school. She was practicing meditation to calm her nerves, but the thoughts that welled up were all about sex and Stan. In no time at all she couldn't think very long about anything but seeing him, touching him, sleeping with him, cooking for him, watching him, thinking up ways to make him smile. She made no demands, but she managed her schedule so that she was always free whenever he could get off for lunch.

Stan was enchanted. He felt he had been translated instantly into the magic world on the other side of the peephole. Her parties aroused him sexually. The wine, the talk, the names of the men and the clothes of the women went to his groin. He accused her of putting an aphrodisiac into the drinks, and could hardly wait for the last guest to leave.

There was no concealing it. They were both so happy that anyone looking at them instantly knew. Something tight inside Stan snapped. He talked his way to a grant for the clinic.

She took off weight, swam extra laps, bought new clothes, gentled her wit. She had always been too tired for sex with the judge, but she was ready for Stan whenever he wanted her.

It lasted three years, but it couldn't last forever. Rather than let it end badly, Bella watched for a graceful chance to end it herself. When she saw her daughter's roommate was attracted to Stan, she passed the word that he was available. A few Sundays later the younger woman rang Bella for the recipe of the quiche Bella used to make him for breakfast.

Stan married the younger woman. Until she became pregnant, they biked to Bella's house and played tennis on her court. Was Stan a cad? Bella shrugs. Stan got a wife from the bargain. As for Bella, somewhere along the line her colon subsided and never caused trouble again.

There's no set pattern for older women and younger men, but there are more of these couples around than you'd think. One old woman got rid of her double bed so that the neighbors would think her young friend was sleeping in the guest room when he stayed over. She figured that they would never believe the two of them slept together on a cot.

At seventy-five, one world-famous woman had two young lovers among the many men she frequently saw in her business. One lived on the East Coast, the other in California. By careful attention to her travel schedule she managed to spend a day or two and sometimes a week with each in the course of a month. She says she wouldn't have wanted to marry either of them, even if they had been available. Both wives knew about her, and neither objected.

Open marriage is the ideal solution for the sex gap of later years. When children are not involved, the compact between the partners is personal rather than social. No great harm is done to third parties if the compact is broken, and if it is limited, several mates are not only thinkable but satisfying.

Tolstoy said that happy families are all alike, and so is the baby-making mode of love on which they used to be based. The limitless alternatives came to grief in czarist Russia, but they are faring better now in the sexually liberated society of the United States.

There are many patterns of love, and there is no reason to believe that all of the most rewarding have been invented. Women and men born after World War II were freer than their parents to explore the possibilities during the all-too-short years before they settled down to making babies. Many more of them will explore the possibilities in a more leisurely way during the decades of active adult life available to them after their baby-making days are over.

In the adult society of the twenty-first century you will no longer suppress the surge of sexuality that comes after childbearing years. Postmenopausal women will be sexually more venturesome than their husbands, and better prepared for the years they will have to spend alone at the end of their lives. Future widows will have had the experience of supporting themselves and, since most of them will have had more than one serious relationship, the experience of surviving separation. More orgasmic than their early-twentieth-century counterparts, they will look for new ways to express their late-life sexuality.

In the twenty-first century you will be more physical in expressing love of every kind. You'll kiss and caress your acquaintances more freely, and you won't be disturbed if these casual contacts occasionally stimulate you to orgasm. And because you will be more spontaneous, you won't force yourself into sex when you don't really want it. You'll expect dry spells that last for weeks or even months. Then the barometer falls or a crocus appears and boom! you're off.

You'll be sexually active all your life, although not necessarily always with a partner of the opposite sex in the missionary position. The chances are good that you will try forms of loving now rejected as pornographic: erotic massage, a vibrator, oral or manual techniques—even something as innocent as running around the house without clothes. Before you are through, you may be in for swinging, group sex, or a homosexual relationship.

In the 1960s the first sexual revolution asserted the right of unmarried men and women to make love solely for their personal pleasure. In the twenty-first century the second revolution will recognize the nongenital forms of loving that enter, to some degree, into every kind of human relationship.

7

Lifestyle

The steady state adult society of the future will offer everyone many choices of lifestyle. In the 1980s ageless pioneers are using the freedom of their later years to explore the choices available to vigorous adults no longer tied down by jobs or children.

Some of them choose adventure. I literally ran into one who had made this choice when we both dived for the same cab at the Houston airport and shared it on the long ride into town. He had the weatherbeaten face of a man who has worked all his life outdoors. A wildcatter?

"Close." He laughed.

He looked grizzled and self-assured enough to be the retired captain of a freighter, but he shook his head.

"You'd never guess it, but my game is buried treasure. For the next three months, that is," he added, as if in fear of being typed.

Peter Armstrong is a retired derrick rigger who was spending the winter exploring a Spanish galleon sunk in the Caribbean in the seventeenth century with a million dollars' worth of gold. The professor of Spanish colonial history who had located it had spent his summers researching old charts and records in Madrid. The Caribbean is loaded with wrecked ships, but the professor was reasonably certain he had identified the one that was supposed to have the gold. An admiralty lawyer who was going to spend the winter on his yacht in the Caribbean anyway was contributing his boat and the equipment they would need; if they didn't strike gold, he would simply write his vacation off as a tax deduction.

It sounded like a harebrained scheme cooked up by adventure-happy youngsters, but the divers were the only ones under sixty, and except for the admiralty lawyer, none of them was rich. Word of the expedition had attracted volunteers with skills to offer. An expert rigger, Peter was their all-around mechanic. A doctor who had a house on one of the little islands nearby had offered it as a base for the expedition, and he also was giving advice based on his familiarity with the ocean currents in the area. The marine biologist was taking her husband along because he was a buried-treasure buff and willing to keep the records, a secretarial chore that nobody wanted. All of the other spouses were staying at home.

Peter's wife, Manya, a retired librarian, was spending the winter with a college classmate whose husband had died, leaving her with a big old house full of books, some of which might be valuable. Manya enjoyed being with her old friend and was helping her list the books and offer them for sale. Manya had no interest in buried treasure, hated the heat of the tropics, and loved the ambience of Boston. It would be good for both of them, he thought, to spend this winter apart.

Luckily, they could afford it. Neither had ever made a lot of money, but they had earned enough to collect the highest Social Security benefit, and each had a decent private pension, too. In addition, their home was paid up, and they had been able to rent it for a fabulous sum for the winter because housing in Houston was short.

If the gold materialized, they were going to spend their share of the treasure redoing the house. If it didn't, they would do it themselves, with help from a college student or a mechanic willing to trade skilled work for the extra room and bath they no longer needed.

Ageless pioneers like the Armstrongs are exploring new ways of living with a freedom that in the 1980s is otherwise permitted to adults only when they are in college. The analogies between college and retirement are striking. Both are periods of transition during which individuals are free to experiment with new priorities.

College students and the retired share many privileges. Both are excused from the responsibility for supporting others, and they are not even expected to fully support themselves. Grocery money comes as a gift from another generation; in later life it is Social Security instead of a check from parents. Some comes from savings or a little nestegg of securities, perhaps, instead of the money a student saves from a summer job. And some of it comes from any kind of work available. Neither students nor the retired take their status from their jobs. A student can work at a blue-collar job without dropping out of the middle class, and so can a retired office worker.

Like college students, the retired are free to move to a different part of the country if they want to, just to try it, but mid-life adults have to stay where they work or their children go to school. The Armstrongs welcomed the chance to get out of Houston, at least for a while. Students often choose a college that gives them a chance to try a new environment. City kids think it's romantic to go to a country college, while country kids often head for universities in big cities.

At college a student can choose to live in a dormitory, share an apartment or a house with one or more others of either sex, live alone, or vary the above. The Armstrongs lived in all of these ways the winter Peter spent hunting for sunken treasure. A student can join other students in cooking and eating formal meals, eat standing up alone whenever he feels hungry, or in a cafeteria alone or with others—options available to older people, too.

It's the same with clothes. Students and retired people can dress to suit themselves. They are not expected to give formal parties to return invitations to affairs of this kind extended to them. And both are free to move in and out of living arrangements. The Armstrongs parted company for the winter because each wanted to spend some months with people in whom the other had little interest. Small children and parents are committed to live together, but childless adults are free to please themselves.

The comparison shows that it's not your age that determines

your lifestyle, as the life-course theorists imply, but the demands that your circumstances make upon you. Freedom from jobs and children gives adults a second, late-life chance to put their lifestyle ahead of their responsibilities.

In the adult society ahead, more people will be able to put their lifestyle ahead of their work from the very beginning. This, of course, is exactly the reverse of the way most people born before World War II set up their daily lives. In the 1980s the exceptions have become models of ideal later life.

I learned of one of these exceptions through Marjorie Fiske, the life-cycle sociologist at the University of California at San Francisco. When we talked about the dreary later years to which the Depression of the thirties had doomed our contemporaries, she agreed that we might have something to learn from the exceptions, like Richard Ohmes, a man she had known since they had worked together in New York in the 1930s.

At seventy Dick Ohmes has the easy stride and straightforward manner of a skilled blue-collar craftsman. All his life he has followed his nose from one occupation to another, but he has always maintained a mix between indoor and outdoor work. At the moment he and his wife, Frances, are living a very simple life in a small house in the woods on the Hood Canal, just a ferry ride across the bay from Seattle.

As he always has, he spends half of each day in strenuous physical activity. On the Hood Canal, he is clearing brush, splitting logs, growing and raising most of what he and Frances eat, and running three miles even on days when his back is bothering him. He conducts no-smoking clinics for the American Cancer Society, but spends most of his time painting, sculpting, reading, and learning. He teaches a course in retirement living at the local community college, and if he wished, he could tell the class that he has spent fifty years researching the subject.

Dick Ohmes is one of the few Americans his age who was as free in his college days as young adults have been since the 1960s. During his college years he went to the University of Vienna, where students lived as independent adults, without parietal rules, and were free to follow the courses that struck their fancy. The rate of exchange made living in Vienna so cheap for an American that Dick was not pushed to come home and find a job in New York, and the longer he stayed, the less willing he was to tie himself down to one. When he finally came home he worked for a while for the University of Newark Research Center, in market research, a field pioneered by Viennese sociologists.

As he reviews his life, Dick Ohmes is able to see that his important decisions have always been made on impulse. He moved to Florida, he claims, out of sheer perversity: he defended the South as a place to live against the annoying cliches of a New Englander he met on a train, and ended by convincing himself to settle there. Once in Florida, he undertook a series of ventures, some more successful than others, but all of which seemed like a good idea at the time.

He found cheap Florida land and planted it with tung-oil trees. Tung oil is an ingredient in lacquers and waterproofing materials that comes from the nuts of the tree, which previously had been grown only in China. World War II cut off the supply. American farmers were not eager to try a new crop that would not bear fruit for at least five years, but Dick was intrigued by the challenge and succeeded in the risky venture.

While waiting for the tung-oil trees to mature, he raised cattle and wrote for the local paper. When a paleontologist told him there were fossils in the Florida rivers, he learned to scuba dive and spent fifteen years exploring them. The cattle supported his growing family, but when he tired of the work, he sold them and moved the longest distance possible inside the continental United States, to the state of Washington.

In the 1980s Dick is an exception among his contemporaries, but if he is a model of later years he may also be an example of what is in store for the mobile experience-collectors who graduated from American colleges in the 1960s.

Ageist Retirement

In the 1980s very few people think of their later years as a time of adventure. Many of them have resisted their impulses so long that they are panicked by the very idea of freedom. They are even

ashamed to loaf. When I asked my high school classmates what
they were doing, they scribbled things like "leading a life of self-
indulgence in Florida since retiring from the full, hectic, and
scheduled life we were leading on Long Island." Some old people
feel guilty every time they cash a Social Security check.

People approaching retirement are urged to prepare for leisure
as if it were a threat to life and health. A small industry of advisers
has emerged to help them bear its burdens. An affluent Midwestern
lawyer I interviewed is bracing for the structureless days ahead by
drawing up a series of lists of things he could do to fill them: "self-
improvement programs, house repairs, community chores, books
to read, people to cultivate, hobbies, places to visit."

If you were born after World War II you put off thinking about
your later years, because so few of the old people you see are doing anything that looks like fun to you. You riffle through the images
that come to mind and discard every one of them.

You could never lie for months on a crowded beach in Florida.
Or eat carrot cake with a plastic fork in a "senior citizens center"
as a change from sitting on a folding chair in the lot where your trailer is parked. Or cram yourself and all your possessions into one of
the motellike rooms opening on the long corridors of retirement
communities around Tucson, Arizona, dreary in spite of irrigated
greenery and the reliable desert sun. And while some of your older
friends may enjoy them, you do not see yourself warming to the
organized activities of luxury retirement communities—a suburban
home minus the care of the lawn and plus a doctor in atten-
dance—even if you could afford them.

Retirement communities are promoted as a total lifestyle.
Glossy literature and television commercials portray a whirlwind of
sports, parties, and pleasures in a closed community where every
need is anticipated and, as one press release puts it, "folks keep
busy from morning to night and don't take time to think about their
age or worry about their health." If your idea of fun is to interest
yourself in the community, volunteer work is available, too.

Basically, of course, retirement housing projects are real estate
promotions. They are organized by entrepreneurs who sell a
package of housing and services to older people. Older people are
able to afford surprisingly stiff down payments on entry into these

communities. Even if their earnings have always been modest, most of them can make a one-time killing on selling the homes that they own outright. They are better off than other home sellers, because people over sixty-five do not have to pay tax on this capital gain. Monthly payments thereafter cover a variety of services, some of them medical, for the rest of the purchaser's life.

Opinion is sharply divided about these communities. Since each community is designed for a narrow income group, it brings together people similar not only in age but also in education, income, and tastes. They are perfect settings for people who are comfortable only with others reliably like themselves. Although there is a retirement community somewhere for almost every income and taste, there is something artificial about all of them that makes the visitor eager to escape from even the most luxurious. Unlike colleges or even prisons, they are institutions without a purpose. The residents may be comfortable and even as active as the literature says, but they are sad because a value they hold dear is being cheapened.

The value the retirement communities debase is the Dream of Home.

No one born before World War II can quite escape the notion that there is only one really right way to live and that is in a single-family house with family related by blood and marriage. It is a notion embedded not only in our laws and taxes, but in our songs and stories. Mid pleasures and palaces, there is no place like the Little Gray Home in the West.

Home, Sweet Home

The Home, Sweet Home of tradition was a comprehensive institution. It provided everything needed for daily life: food, shelter, sex, clean clothes, support both emotional and financial. It determined not only where and with whom but especially when you could eat and sleep. It soaked up all a family's capital. The needs of the house were the beginning of all those budgets that told you how much you could afford to spend for food, clothes, fun, or anything else, and for the women of the family at least, the needs of the house prescribed how they spent their time as well.

For people born before World War II, not only was home the source of everything needed for life but owning your own was the very object of life itself. And to a remarkable degree, people born before World War II achieved that goal. According to a study made for the 1981 White House Conference on Aging, an incredible two-thirds of Americans more than sixty-five years old are living in homes of their own, and 84 percent of them have paid up the mortgage.

If more than half the elderly population own their homes free and clear, it is not because it was so much easier to buy a house thirty years ago, but mainly because they were willing to make bigger sacrifices to buy it. They were willing, for instance, to forgo the expense of travel and spend their vacations fixing the house.

Now their homes own them. People over sixty-five are drowning in space. Tax breaks and government programs have subsidized home ownership so heavily that there is little financial incentive to sell the big old house and move into smaller rented quarters. In the 1980s less than 10 percent of people over sixty-five live in houses built since 1970. Nearly half of them are living in housing built before World War II, on incomes that have not risen with plumbers' wages.

Home may not be sad, but it is often uncomfortable and dangerous. Many old people live all alone in housing that is not equipped with grab bars, nonskid floors, electrical outlets eighteen inches or higher above the floor, banisters on steps, handrails on walls, adequately lighted hallways, or doors that accommodate wheelchairs. Only 18 percent at last count lived with grown children, who could lend a hand with ailing pipes and wires. Many eat lonely meals and sometimes forget to make any.

These old people are victims of an obsolete dream that refuses to fade. Like the retirement "homes" and communities, their aging suburban homes are not the original Home, Sweet Home, but facsimiles of an earlier model. The original Home, Sweet Home was a multigenerational Homestead.

The suburban homes in which so many old people are rattling around have false fronts that make them look like Homesteads, but inside they were engineered for the rearing of children. When the children grew up and moved away, they left empty spaces behind them. But the concept of Homestead is so strong that in some suburban homes the bedrooms of the departed are kept untouched for their very occasional visits.

The multigenerational Homestead is obsolete, but we need to examine it more closely because it is the origin of the one right way to live that is causing us so much trouble. Genuine Homesteads were imposing buildings. They were typically square, as grand as the purse of the founder could buy, and designed to last forever.

What went on inside is haunting us still, and the best that can be said for it is that it was awkward even when it worked. My father grew up in a nineteenth-century household of four generations. I have a picture of the entire household ranged by the photographer on the lawn by status, each in his or her best clothes, the grand-mothers on chairs, the children in front, sitting crosslegged on the grass, Mother and Father Bird standing, flanked by the adult children with their spouses beside or behind them.

How did they manage under one roof? By dint of daily acts of heroic patience and forbearance. Three grandmothers managed to stay out of one another's way in the kitchen. Everybody had chores. When he was a boy, my father's chore was to build a fire in the oldest grandmother's room, and his instructions made such an impression on him that fifty years later he could recall being told to lay the wood down gently.

There is no recollection of any complaint, but scraps of family lore floating down the generations suggest the kind of discipline that must have been required. Breakfast was strictly at eight, and woe betide the tardy. When my aunt was late, my grandfather ostentatiously consulted his watch and announced the minutes of her delinquency. But there were rules for him, too. The only place in the house he was allowed to smoke was in the ground-floor den, which was off limits to females.

Appalling as it sounds, this was supposed to be an enlightened establishment. When family meals were the only source of nourishment, they were often eaten in total silence. In many instances this silence may have been a precaution against physical violence. We know that a great deal of violence begins with family quarrels, and emotions must have run higher when there was no escaping the family table. Since home was sacred, it was sealed against the reach of the law, so we have no way of knowing how many children, spouses, and grandmothers were battered, but the toll must have been at least as high as it is now that domestic crimes are beginning to come out of the closet.

Nobody who grew up in one of these multigenerational homes wanted to stay the course, but few of them could imagine organizing daily life on any other basis. Single people had to live in other people's homes, which was at best an uncomfortable temporary arrangement. Hotels were for the rich, who could afford to travel.

Before World War II young people left home by marrying and setting up homes of their own. Since then the trend-setting young become adult when they go away to college. "Getting away from home" and "living on my own" rank high on the list of reasons high school graduates give for wanting to go to college, and these reasons are also cited when alumni are asked to describe what they got out of their college experience.

College was never designed to be an alternative to home. It was supposed to be a temporary way station on the road to a bigger and better one. But what it actually did was give young people years of adult life in a community that played down money and status, encouraged the consumption of intangible experiences, and expected individuals to live by and for themselves. In addition to their academics, students learned that you could be nourished in a cafeteria, sleep wherever there was space for a bedroll, wash your jeans in a coin-operated laundromat, and find sex and emotional support without committing the rest of your life.

The Dream of Self-Fulfillment

College replaced the dream of home with the headier ambition to become, as the army recruiting poster puts it, "all that you can be." People who went to college in the 1960s haven't been as willing to sacrifice options in order to maintain the facsimile of a Homestead. They will welcome their later years as a time of freedom to try new ways of living.

Among the pioneers who are using their later years this way are some who are capturing the opportunities for changing the direction of their lives by actually going to college. In 1981 I talked with a dozen undergraduates at the Bridge Project for students over fifty-five at Fairhaven College, a division of Western Washington University in Bellingham, Washington. The lounge in which we met was furnished like a cheery public room in a retirement project, but the spirit of the people in it was unmistakably different.

None of the score or more of undergraduates who had gathered for coffee and talk were sitting on the floor. They were gray. They didn't wiggle. But their concerns were surprisingly like those of the teenage students in other Western Washington dormitories. They were people going through a personal transition. They glowed with the possibilities unfolding before them, and because they had come expecting change, they were unusually open to new relationships. Several couples had already fallen in love and married.

They talked very freely about why they had come to college and what they hoped it would do for them. Like teenage freshmen, some of them had come to liberate themselves from the constraints of home.

A heavy woman sitting on a hassock had come to escape an incompatible husband. "All our married life I lived his style of life, and it wasn't my style of life," she explained. "As long as I had a non-home life I could take it, but when it came time for me to retire I knew I couldn't stay at home, so I just left and came here."

Others hoped that college would launch them into exciting careers. A former matron in an institution for delinquent girls was taking a creative writing course. She had sold a story about one of her charges to *True Confessions*. Now she was trying to get out of the pulps.

Some who had come for fun were becoming more serious. "What I've learned here is that you can't be happy without a goal," another woman reported. "I always took courses, but in things like handwriting analysis, for my own amusement. But now I want to do something." Like what? "Like start a senior citizens center, maybe."

"You don't always have to have a reason for learning something," a retired college president retorted. "What's wrong with learning for learning's sake?'' He was back in college to take a course in zoology he was never able to fit in when he was getting his B.A.

And just like younger students, some of them were there primarily to get the degree. This was especially true of women who had dropped out to marry and rear children.

"No, I don't want a job, or anything like that. I just felt I wanted to go back and finish something I had started." Neat polyester, every blue hair in place, hands folded, legs crossed, the speaker looked as if she ought to be watering plants or dusting dozens of precisely placed little figurines instead of attending college.

Some of her fellow students thought her a bit compulsive. "I'd never take a course I didn't like just for a piece of paper," a Swedish-born carpenter huffed. "It's got to mean something to me."

But the biggest attraction of the Bridge was the opportunity to learn new things, which is strong in younger students too. Older students were taking everything in the curriculum except math and astronomy, but they were especially interested in courses that promised some help in understanding themselves, like "T'ai Chi" and "Self-Awareness." They had requested and been given a course in which they reported and discussed their dreams with a psychologist. One woman dreamed about rearranging the cars at the funeral of her husband. What did it mean? Like teenagers who major in psychology, they hoped that college would help them understand themselves. The problems change over the course of life, but for the ageless the impulse for self-analysis remains.

Since the Bridge experiment, postsecondary institutions ranging from Harvard to community colleges have been appealing to adults of every age. Many graduating classes now include people in their seventies and eighties. We think of them as unusual because we think of college as an investment in future earnings. But the value of the liberal arts cannot be measured in the number of years over which an economic payout can be expected. For the individual concerned, life is worth enhancing at any age.

Family Demystified

In the twenty-first century women and men in middle life won't face the agonizing choice of sharing their busy homes with their elderly parents or consigning them to the retirement communities and nursing "homes" that have been the stopgap solutions during the transition to the adult society. Their parents—and with longer active lives, perhaps their grandparents, too—will be on the move between different settings.

Your seventy-year-old mother, for instance, might spend the summer at a camp devoted to the culture of yoga. She might then go on to work for a while as a resident teacher in a school for learning-disabled children. She might visit for a few days to confer with you about whether to take a course in a college where she could stay for a semester in college housing, or go on an architectural tour of nineteenth-century Southern courthouses. If she owns real estate, it won't be a big fake Homestead, but a ski lodge in Aspen that she is thinking of swapping, at least for a year, for a condominium on the beach in Panama City, Florida.

You won't worry that she won't be able to manage getting around in these settings, even if she isn't as spry as she used to be. In the twenty-first century it won't be necessary to confine people with physical problems in a nursing home or segregate them in housing for the aged for the convenience of doctors. Bodily functions will be monitored by telephone. Paging devices will soon be nationwide.

In the summer of 1982 television audiences watched one-legged Don Bennett hop his way to the top of Mount Rainier in Washington to plant flags in the name of the handicapped. His feat was not only an inspiration to the disabled, but a demonstration of the extent to which medical engineering can overcome physical limitations. Medical engineers will improve life expectancies and the quality of life by developing artificial replacements for failing organs, limbs, and body parts, while rehabilitation engineers solve the more mundane problems of getting people up and down stairs and in and out of chairs, and keeping them in constant touch with their medical advisers. In an adult society the technology developed for war and space will be diverted to making all environments safe and accessible even for the frailest.

In the twenty-first century you won't be haunted by the fear that you are neglecting your elderly parents. They'll be emotionally, as well as financially, independent. Adult children and their parents will be freed from a sense of obligation and able to explore their common ground and psychological history. Many of them will develop a relationship that helps both generations understand themselves better.

In the past, self-development has meant liberation from the obligations of the Homestead. "We never got the good of him," my oldest aunt once remarked of a brother who she felt had deserted the farm when it needed his labor. The economic basis of family ties is no longer stated so baldly, but it is what conservatives have in mind when they worry about the dissolution of the family.

The economic work of women in traditional households is the principal reason employers have been able to pay women less than men. Especially in Eastern Europe, early textile mills found that they could lure young mothers to work at wages that would not support the cost of child care because the child's grandmother was free to care for the baby while the nimble young mother was away from home. The system is breaking down because grandmothers are out earning money, too, but it works a little better for employers of blacks. Blacks are more apt to be unemployed or underemployed than whites, so most black families have someone available to care for the children of any parent lucky enough to find employment.

Homestead values benefit taxpayers because they require families to care for members handicapped in a way that would otherwise make them public charges. Professional services can greatly improve the lives of frail older people or children with learning disabilities, but these services cost so much that families can't afford them. As we say in chapter 5, this is the undone work that will provide new jobs in the future.

When conservatives talk of the breakup of the family, they are talking about the decline of these economic advantages for employers and taxpayers. What concerns them is the declining size of households, which leaves nobody to do the unpaid work of caring for the young, the old, and the sick at home. This decline is dramatic. According to the Census, household size is dwindling toward the irreducible minimum.

At last count, for instance, the most common household on the crowded island of Manhattan consisted of a single person living alone. The most visible of these single-person households are ambitious young people beginning careers in New York, but a great many of them are older people who, with the help of Social Security benefits, are able to maintain residences separate from those of their children. As recently as a generation ago nearly half the population over sixty-five lived with their families. Now it is only one in five. Household size is declining because of Social Security and jobs for women that permit them to support themselves and their children, and conservatives marshal every conceivable objection to both.

Conservatives see only loneliness in these figures, but families are not deserting their older members emotionally. "Near, but not with" is the growing pattern for adult children and parents. According to a study cited by the 1981 White House Conference, more than half of the noninstitutionalized women over sixty-five had seen one of their children on the day before they were interviewed.

Lonely? Three of the people in those Manhattan figures are women I have known for more than thirty years. One of them is now a successful physician with an office on Park Avenue. Her sister runs the business side of her practice and maintains an apartment near the apartment of their eighty-year-old mother. Although they help each other whenever they can, each likes the privacy of a place of her own. To me, at least, it seems that they get along better than they did when they all lived together in an extra bedroom my parents rented them during the housing shortage of World War II.

The family as an economic unit may be breaking down, but the affectionate, caring family is alive and well, and functioning in many ways better than it did when family members had no choice but to live together. But because it no longer requires a common residence, the new family tie gives all adults the leeway to live with people who are not related by blood or marriage. Young adults claim this freedom when they go away to college, begin careers in a new community, or join to take a trip or to start a little home-based business. Ageless pioneers are forming nonfamily households for all of these reasons, too.

A few years ago a widowed grandmother I shall call Annabelle shocked her son by asking him to drive her to a motel where she was planning to stay with a man. When he complained that he had never imagined he'd be driving his mother to an assignation, she told him she had learned how to do it from him.

The man she was going to meet was James, a general officer in the armed forces then still on active duty, and she tells the story in the comfortable apartment she is sharing with him now. It is crammed with the mementos of two eventful but separate life histories: carved ivory elephants, ceremonial swords, Asian figurines, portraits of mustachioed ancestors, framed letters of commendation, shaky antique chairs, an extra bedroom full of rare books on military history, awaiting perusal, and, perhaps because both of them are Southerners, two refrigerators full of provisions for ritual hospitality.

There is no subterfuge about how they are living. They are not married. Both their names are on the apartment door. It's a big leap for two religious people who were brought up in small towns, and Annabelle is still a little surprised at herself.

Her story is a Southern classic. She married—for love—had three babies in rapid succession, and was leading the sheltered life of a lady in a small Mississippi community when her husband was killed in an accident. She moved back into the big old family house with her mother and became a schoolteacher. She attended a lot of church suppers and enjoyed the moral support of her small community. Then, when her sons were grown, she moved to Washington and used her political connections and teaching experience to get a job as a civilian specialist in the branch of the air force that organizes specialized training courses for servicemen. Eventually she wangled overseas assignments in Southeast Asia and other interesting parts of the world.

Back in Washington after her tour of duty, she met James, then a dashing bachelor who, after an early, brief, and unhappy marriage, had courted ladies on every continent without ever being caught. The son of a small-town Southern preacher, James talked her language. They were a perfect match, politically, socially, and even financially: between his pay and her salary they could afford a place in Washington big enough for the sideboards, sofas, oil portraits, and bulky family heirlooms stored in Annabelle's house in Mississippi, as well as the thousands of books that the general had acquired in his travels. They saw eye-to-eye on the significant conventions of living: Annabelle knew how to cook and James knew how to carve.

Eye-to-eye on everything, that is, except marriage. James was against it. On principle. As only a Southern gentleman can stand on principle. And as long as James was a general on active duty, the alternative of living in sin with a member of the opposite sex was as unthinkable to him as it was to her. For years the furniture gathered dust in the attic in Mississippi and the books remained in the packing crates.

Then, when James retired, it occurred to Annabelle that neither of them had anything to lose by moving in together.

So many people are living together in various relationships that these days the Census has trouble defining the term "family." At the beginning of the 1980s one in four households was labeled "nonfamily" because it consisted of unrelated adults or a single person living alone. Not all of the unrelated adults are of opposite sexes, and the Census has no way of knowing how many of the unmarried coed households are sexual relationships, but, like old-fashioned economic marriage, many of them must combine both sex and convenience.

Roommate-matching services find that many adults, both old and young, prefer to live with a member of the opposite sex, and get along better, too, once they make it clear that no sexual intimacy is intended. Conventional old ladies are shy about admitting that they miss having a man around the house to lift things. Older men like the arrangement because they say that the presence of a woman makes the house a little more homey.

Domestic roles may be only part of this story. A man who is not having sex with a woman is less of a threat to her privacy than a member of her own sex who naturally empathizes with her. There are many reasons that people prefer to keep their sex lives out of the house. One or both partners may fear that moving in implies too big a commitment, or merely that the relationship itself is too fragile to survive household intimacy. Some romantic relationships are based on a single interest, such as music, that has nothing to do with compatibility in daily living.

Pegi Kish demands a great deal of personal information from the clients who register with Room Mater, a referral service she runs in Dutchess County, New York. They have to say how they feel about smoking, pets, children, race, religion, liquor, parties, marijuana, and sexual preference. Somewhat to her surprise, she has found that many older people are not only willing to tell the truth about these personal habits but are surprisingly open-minded about living with people whose values and backgrounds differ from their own if the parties can help each other. She has, for instance, matched a white schoolteacher with a black woman on welfare, and a carless young driver with a nondriving widow left stranded with her husband's automobile.

Human beings are social animals and they need to live in small groups, but these groups may have many different bases. In the 1980s a Homestead partnership in rearing children is no longer the only respectable basis for a home. In the adult society ahead, adults of every age will enter temporary or partial living relationships based on programs of study, career, adventure, or mutual interests that meet the needs of the adults involved at the time.

Money Demystified

College is a place where you learn that significant experiences don't have to cost a lot of money. You may have had the time of your life on an income that qualified you for food stamps. You wore old clothes and drove an old car without apology. You swapped. You shared. You went short on food to buy a record. You saved on essentials to splurge on luxuries. As a student you got breaks on everything from tuition to airline tickets.

This is the way you are going to be able to live your later years in the twenty-first century. You'll spend money on experiences you can enjoy today instead of on the possessions that symbolize the higher standard of living you hope to enjoy in the future. Even if you are a materialist at heart, the economy ahead will encourage spending on experiences that improve the quality of your daily life.

Americans have been too busy acquiring possessions to cultivate the European arts of enjoying each day as it comes, but the steady-state economy of the 1980s is beginning to teach us how to enjoy ourselves without spending money. New Yorkers are supposed to be chronically pressed for time, but they seem as willing as Parisians to sit for hours in the sidewalk cafés that are springing up all over Manhattan, and the high price of Broadway shows has nudged even affluent professional couples into visiting art galleries and parks, where entertainment is cheap or free. Like Europeans, you may discover that you can have a good time playing chess or nursing a drink while you talk with friends.

The most important change in daily life is the lowered cost of the information that heightens the pleasure of just this sort of human interaction. The technology ahead will lower the cost of access to images and ideas, and of opportunities to stay in touch with many more people. You can get an idea of what lies ahead by imagining for a moment what you would do if you could talk to anyone anywhere for the price of a local phone call.

Your standard of living is going to respond to a new set of price tags. You won't be able to afford amenities, such as waiter-served meals or garments altered to fit, that require labor nobody wants to do. Flavorful, hand-harvested tomatoes will be so expensive that you'll grow your own or do without them. And you won't be able to get anyone to wrestle your garbage cans up a hill at any price.

You'll shift from money-intensive pleasures such as travel and collecting possessions to activities costing little or nothing, such as rubdowns exchanged between mates, bird-watching, stargazing, virtuoso lovemaking, jogging, video games, and the reciprocal joys of learning and teaching.

You'll do things yourself for which you now rely on high-priced professionals. You may want to bake your own bread or grow your own vegetables. If you're stuck in the middle of reupholstering the sofa, an expert can look at what you've done and advise you by two-way video. Barbers will charge so much that you'll cut your own hair, swap haircuts with a neighbor who has a steadier hand (maybe in exchange for mowing his lawn), or just let your hair grow.

The other side of the coin is that products people like to make will be available on a nonprofit basis. So many people will be able to indulge their interest in cultural activities such as making documentary films, producing little theater, and playing in orchestras that they will become more available than they are now. As their numbers increase, therapists, counselors, and tennis coaches may have to charge relatively less than they do in the 1980s.

The printed word will be a special bargain. Editorial costs will drop because authors and editors will be more willing than now to work for psychic pay, and electronic delivery of much of the print in which we wallow will cut the production costs that are the real reason printed material has become expensive.

But as you did in college, you'll be so much more interested in experiences than in things that you will find ways to afford them. Older people are already beginning to do it. Some of the most inventive are women rebelling against the Dream of Home that impounded their mid-life energy. One of them recently took a symbolic step in this direction.

Twenty years ago, when I first met Jane, she was a model *Ladies' Home Journal* wife and mother of four. The last time I saw her she was explaining how glad she was that she would never again have all that silver to clean. When her twelve-place set of solid silver was stolen, she used the insurance money to buy a sailboat.

Sailing was something Jane had always wanted to do, and when the insurance money came she figured she had better learn while her knees were still limber enough to cope with a heaving deck. She carries a picture of her twenty-three-foot sloop to show her friends, the way she carries pictures of her grandchild.

The silver money bought the boat, but to maintain it Jane has acquired a whole new set of friends who like to sail too. Every weekend and after hours in the summer they gather to scrape, paint, tinker, and talk. Fixing the little boat is almost as much fun as sailing it.

She is more lively than I remember her in her family days, which is probably why she seems to be slimmer and younger. She thinks that her life began to get better when she gave up trying to remarry and began to explore what a single woman could do to make herself comfortable. She used to dread coming home to an empty house, but now she and four other single women who like to cook take turns making dinner and keeping up with each other's lives. Cooking once a week is more fun than cooking a big dinner every night, and five professionally employed women have more interesting things to say to each other than do a family of growing children.

Swapping skills, swapping things—there's no end once you get started. Now that Jane is sailing, she has become interested in pollution on Long Island Sound. The task force to which she belongs is trying to raise money to put out a brochure. Jane points out that the Pan Am pilot in the group has lobsters that cost him nothing because he fishes for sport and swaps his catch with a commercial lobsterman. So far, she has found an artist to do the paste-ups for the brochure in return for lobsters, clams, and mussels. The barter feasts have been deliciously successful.

In the 1980s barter has become a big new business. By one estimate, almost half of American enterprises belong to one of the hundreds of barter clubs whose members trade excess capacity or unsalable inventory with each other. A resort hotel wants to trade its rooms for twelve new mattresses. The mattress maker can't use the rooms, but his wife wants a blue fox coat which the furrier is willing to trade for a stay at the resort. If they all belong to the same barter club, the hotel can pay for the mattresses in credits that the mattress maker uses to pay the furrier, who presents them to the hotel in payment of his bill.

Rising prices and a shortage of cash are making these deals attractive, but the system itself is costly. Barter clubs charge stiff entrance fees and discourage individual consumers who do not have a skill their members need. Individuals find swaps through bulletin boards in supermarkets and local organizations, such as the YMCA, and in informal exchanges supported by churches and local social agencies.

Some of these individual barters are ingenious. "Six 14-inch tires with chrome reverse rims are yours if you can offer Dave new frames for his glasses or a nice six-string guitar." This item is from the "Swap Talk" column run by Steve Van Hook, a social worker in Grants Pass, a small town in Oregon. The chances are that Dave will dispose of his tires for something other than what he originally wanted. For a growing number of individuals, swapping has become a hobby.

Are you wondering what you will do with all the stuff you own if you ever have to move? Fear not. In another ten years computer systems will turn the whole country into a gigantic, nonstop tag sale. You'll be able to sell junk you now consider rubbish, such as parts for obsolete machines, out-of-print books, or orphans from your set of antique Haviland china.

Personal computers are extending to individual consumers the sophisticated matching that is now economic only for businesses. If you want to turn your cello in for a flute, a computer network will find you someone who wants to exchange a flute for a cello. Computers will widen the market for swapping vacation homes. If you are tired of your beach house in Florida and would like to ski this winter instead, all you have to do is to find someone who is tired of his ski lodge in Aspen and wants a winter vacation in Florida. Swaps like these are often arranged through the bulletin boards or employee publications of organizations with people in many parts of the world, such as IBM or Time Inc., but computer networks are already extending the possibilities for satisfying matches.

In 1982 owners of home computers were offered a wide variety of swap opportunities through a facility provided by The Source, a library of data banks that describes itself as "America's Leading Information Utility." On the day I scanned the offerings I learned that Barter Worldwide, Inc. was offering airline tickets to Europe in exchange for a computer-system printer, the swap to be made at the exact trade value of the items in dollars. A few scrolls down on the screen the holder of a private pilot's license offered "a complete package including ground school, books and supplies in a condensed, two-week program in beautiful, sunny, warm Scottsdale, Arizona" worth $2,200, and was willing to take in payment "furniture, sailboat, video-taping equipment, stereo system, Drexel furniture or better, Panasonic video equipment."

The most rewarding barters need not rely on sophisticated bookkeeping or swell the revenues of little barter companies. They arise in a natural way whenever people with skills and possessions have the time and need to trade with them. My husband's dentist

talked so much about the book he was trying to write that Tom finally undertook to edit it in exchange for the new set of teeth he needed. I no longer feel like keeping the kitchen garden, but I can still go
out and pick a ripe tomato off the vine, because a young neighbor
couple make their garden on my land in exchange for letting me
pick whatever I actually want to eat from it.

Swaps are a way of relating to other people that is important for
everyone, but especially for elderly people who spend a great deal
of time at home alone. Some of the most valuable services are rendered without thought of reciprocity or pay, as a matter of simple
neighborliness.

One of my retired neighbors has a cat that is always running
away and being retrieved by the man next door. "He doesn't get
enough exercise at home," she apologized when he brought the
animal back. "The living room is too small for him."

The man had an idea. He rigged up a carpet-covered pipe with a
platform at the top. The cat seemed to understand it was for him, because he sprang to the perch as soon as it was set up, and spends
a lot of time leaping up and down it. My neighbor knew that the
man would not take pay for his time, or even for the materials that
he had bought, but she told him she hoped that she could find
something to do for him that would please him half as much as the
perch he had built pleased her cat, and he understood her feeling.

"Knit me a sweater, then," he said, knowing that she would like
to do it.

"What color?" she asked, delighted at the thought of the
project.

"Why, cat color, of course!" he replied.

So she took the cat to the yarn shop to find a tweedy yarn that
exactly matched the beautiful grays and blacks of his coat.

Good for the man, good for the woman, good for the cat, and
good for controlling inflation.

The Country

The chances are good that you will be spending more of your later
years in the country. For one thing, advances in technology are
steadily reducing the isolation of rural regions. Roads, satellite

transmission of television programs, and the computerized data that come over telephone wires make it possible to enjoy the stimulation of the city at a distance. And as opportunities for advancement decline, even ambitious young people are less willing to endure noise, dirt, crime, and crowding for the sake of career advancement. Pleasant surroundings free of strain are especially attractive to older people, so there is reason to believe that the trend will continue in the adult society of the twenty-first century.

Many of these younger people are already deserting the city and migrating to the sun belt in search of work in a pleasant climate. Some of them fell in love with the beach or the colors of the desert or the air of the Rockies when they were in college and were willing to do almost any kind of menial job in order to be able to stay. Others are trading income for the seascape along the coast of Maine or the noble vistas of the St. Lawrence River.

This concern for pleasant surroundings and scenery is new in America. When the country was growing, Americans traditionally moved wherever they could make a better living, even when it meant spending the winter in a mud hut on the desolate plains of South Dakota or living in a slum so crowded that beds were rented out on an hourly basis.

Historically, as a nation, we have never liked them. In our two-hundred-year public record it is hard to find a good word for cities. Noisome, dangerous, immoral, expensive, unhealthy, they have routinely been described as good only for making money. But that was apparently enough. In the past Americans were so eager to improve their incomes that every Census between 1820 and 1980 reported a net migration of people from rural areas to cities.

But in the 1970s this historic migration began to slow, and the Census of 1980 found that it had virtually stopped. In 1980, 26.3 percent of us were rural, up only a tenth of a percent from 1970, but demographers warned that so many people had moved into areas that the Census classified as rural that the old definitions no longer held.

The newcomers weren't bumpkins. According to the Census, they were city people working in offices, factories, and service jobs. They were people who liked the country so much better than the suburbs that they were willing to drive hours to live there, or find ways to take their city jobs and amenities to the country with them. "Countrified city" is the term J. D. Doherty of the Department of Agriculture coined to describe the way they were living.

It's hard to say who is going back to the land and what they are doing there. Drive through Columbia County, Tennessee, and you pass deserted farmhouses sagging in fields full of weeds, but they all belong to someone. A local preacher says that city people are buying them, although he is not sure just why. One old place went to a college professor interested in wildlife, who camps in the tumble-down house. Other farms have been cut up into five- and ten-acre plots and sold to city people who like to drive out on summer weekends or after work to grow a garden. Some of them talk of putting up a little house so that they can stay overnight, or even of retiring there.

The wide-open spaces are filling up with people of all ages who describe themselves as "retired," although in census terms their occupational status is often unclear. A middle-aged broker of syndicated television shows moved his business from Beverly Hills to Montana because he liked to look at the mountains. He makes fewer deals and his income is lower, but his wife finds work that she likes, part time, in a nearby furniture factory, so they manage to make ends meet.

Neither of them misses the city. In Montana the scenery is inspiring, the air is clear, the neighbors are friendly, and housing is cheap. "Put it this way," he says. "In my business I spend most of my working hours on the telephone. Here in Montana I can watch a deer out the window while I'm phoning. In Los Angeles I'd be looking at a traffic jam or a wall."

New homes are being built in the country. According to the Census, rural homes increased 40 percent during the 1970s. Two hours outside of New York City the countryside is dotted with professional workers who think they are taking it easy. Some of them moved there by degrees. A Wall Street lawyer bought a farm in Dutchess County in the Hudson River Valley and found himself doing more of his work with managers of national companies who also had places there. He found that these clients were easier to reach while supposedly relaxing in the country, so he began to take work to the farm and to stay there extra days. Eventually he gave up his city office altogether.

These days he works in a neat white office and library that he has built closer to the road than his house. It looks like an overgrown gatehouse to an old-fashioned big estate. Most of his business is done on the phone, but the local airport is only a short drive away, and from it he can get to Washington or Boston in two hours, about the same time it takes him to drive to New York.

Some of the people brought up on farms are going back to them. There's even a relative living on the farm in Wisconsin my grandfather founded before the Civil War. A generation of tenants had run the Brattrud farm so far down that none of us thought my cousin, a prosperous businessman, really intended to live on it when he bought it from my aunt's estate.

Not that he's farming it. Wally knows how, but he is through with getting up early to milk the cows. The only animals left are pets and the palomino horses he breeds for a hobby. In one of the buildings of the farm his daughter and her husband process corn into War-farin, a rat bait product that nets him twenty-five dollars for every bushel of corn he grows. The product is based on a formula devised by the Wisconsin Agricultural Research Foundation, for which it is named, and packed on an automatic packaging line installed in one of the farm buildings. They also do the physical work around the place. The whole operation is managed without hired help. In the 1980s the farm is still a Homestead.

Wally always liked the farm, and as he points out, everything he wants is right on the place or easily accessible. The friend of my grandmother's who in 1860 so desperately wanted to go to town and buy new clothes could find all the clothes a woman could want only half an hour's drive away. Before the road was built, the only way to get the milk to town was to process it into cheese. Today the cheese factory my Grandfather Ole helped to build is the stylish home of a university professor who teaches in Madison.

Roads and cars and phones make the Homestead style of life a viable possibility, and it has always attracted romantics. Ever since the Depression, intellectuals have talked about making a living on the land. Some of them have even done it. Scott and Helen Nearing

have made the money they need by writing about subsistence farming ever since they fled to an old farmhouse in the Green Mountains
in 1932. People read the books, but most of them only dream of
following suit. Over the decades, the number of family farms has
steadily declined. Then, in 1978, for the first time in forty years,
farms smaller than fifty acres began to increase. Like the contemporary Brattrud farm, many of these combine some other source of
income with farming.

In the 1980s the Homestead style of life is only one of many
alternatives. Farms were originally founded by pioneers who hoped
the land would make them rich. Those who return to the farm are
looking for a pleasant life that they know will never make them
money.

The Dream of Home as the one right way has been fading slowly
over the past fifty years. In the twenty-first century adults won't go
to live in retirement communities in their later years, or struggle to
maintain the houses that they acquired when they were rearing
children. Like college students of the 1980s, they will find that they
can do most of the things they want to do without spending a lot of
money.

In the adult society ahead, age will not determine how people
live. We will be free to use our vigorous later years to pursue individual agendas that may take us into living arrangements with
people of any age who happen to share our interests at the time.

III

Dreams and Nightmares

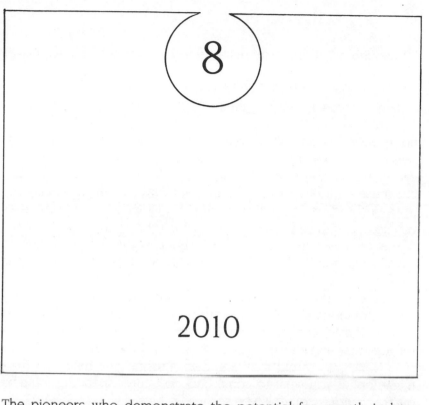

8

2010

The pioneers who demonstrate the potential for growth in later years are lucky exceptions to the times in which they live. Like the pioneer blacks and women who demonstrated that race and sex are not bars to achievement in the learned professions, they have had a somewhat different experience from that of counterparts who will follow in their footsteps after the barriers are broken. It is not enough to imagine what life in the 1980s would be like if we merely exploded the myths of age, because other things will be changing too.

To find out what your own later years will actually be like you have to imagine what you will do when present long-term trends have had twenty or thirty more years to run. This is at best a tendentious enterprise. Forecasts usually tell more about the forecaster than they tell about the future. When material standards of living were rising, we projected the ultimate in material ease by the year 2000. We put "the year" in front of it because it sounded better that way, but also to make a nice round number, a milestone far enough off in the misty distance to give science time to deliver all the things that we have always wanted.

Things like hypnotically induced time travel. Fresh water from icebergs towed from the Antarctic. Power from garbage. Or liberation from minor annoyances, like a device that automatically hoists your loaded backpack to your shoulders, or motorized flippers for underwater fish-watching. Things you could do without, like self-igniting cigarettes and invisible warplanes. As well as things you could use right now, like a private pension you can carry with you from one job to another, a phone that goes with you wherever you go, a cheap and available television tube so thin you can hang the set on a wall, like a picture, or a reducing pill that allows you to eat all you want. By the 1970s the milestone was so close that it was crowding science.

In the 1980s social and cultural trends have been attracting as much attention as future hardware. To these we must now add the new emphasis on preventive health, flexible working and living arrangements, and the flowering of nonreproductive love relationships. One way to put it all together is to imagine how New York might look if you were to come back to it after spending the next quarter century someplace else.

New York Revisited

Let's suppose that it's 2010 and you are flying in to New York from the West Coast. You are curious about what has happened to the place since you left for California in the 1970s.

From the air the country looks much the same. In the Southwest there's a new kind of ghost town: deserted retirement communities. Some were forced out of business by damages awarded to customers who charged that their advertising was misleading, while others simply failed to attract enough people who thought of themselves as old or retired.

There are no new interstate highways, no new skyscrapers to change the skylines of major cities, very few new houses, and very little need for them. Devastated areas in central cities, such as the South Bronx, were never rebuilt. There are only 14 percent more people in the nation, but they are so well distributed over the wide-open spaces that they haven't affected the scene from the air.

When your plane lands at La Guardia Airport you notice that there's nobody in the green-glassed tower; in 2010 air traffic is controlled entirely by machine. The airport itself is so deserted that at first you think it must be shut down. But then you recall that so many of the airport services have been mechanized that the only people in sight are passengers.

You carry your bag, and so does everyone else; you don't need many changes of clothing, and even warm jackets are light enough to roll into the kind of backpack you got used to carrying when you were hosteling as a teenager. On your way out you identify a badly plastered section of wall as the place where the luggage conveyor used to come out. It reminds you of the aggravation you suffered when baggage was so bulky that airlines had to take responsibility for checking it.

Coin-operated computer terminals are rowed up back-to-back in what used to be the baggage claim area. Passengers rush for them when they get off the plane the way they used to race each other for possession of a phone booth. Instead of phoning the person who you think may have the specific information you need, you dial in your personal number and pick up messages left for you by the people to whom you have given it. You can also call up whatever ongoing data you normally follow, such as the weather at your country place, the price of a stock you are thinking of buying, the latest batting average of a favorite baseball player, or the most recent figures from one of the thousands of surveys constantly being made on everything from consumer preferences in toothpastes to the percentage of people of various incomes who recognize the name of a candidate for public office.

Instead of the dimes and later the quarters you used to keep on hand for the phones, you carry a stack of coins that are worth a dollar. You need them for phones and food machines as well as for computers, and for most of the nation's subways and buses.

The dollar coins have an interesting history. They still honor Susan B. Anthony, the suffragist, but in 2010 they are made of an amalgam that is durable enough for vending although it is 20 percent pure gold. Like the silver in dimes of the 1980s, the gold has no monetary value. It was added as a concession to right-wing conservatives who demanded a return to the gold standard in the economically troubled 1980s. When a larger-denomination coin was needed, the Department of Commerce tried to capture the sentiment attached to the yellow metal by creating a gold dollar.

On the street, there's no longer a taxi queue. As you step out on the sidewalk, a driverless bus labeled MANHATTAN glides up to the curb. It's free, so instead of paying your fare as you enter, you punch your destination into a little keyboard that releases the turnstile when it registers where you are going. As soon as the bus is full, or five minutes have elapsed, a computer works out the most economical route for delivering the passengers who have boarded, the doors close automatically, and you are on your way. It's as simple as a self-service elevator.

The trip into town is quick and quiet. Traffic is light. There is no chatty cabdriver. No rattling manhole covers. No clangorous buses. No impatient honking of horns. Your bus drives slowly, but gets there soon because it does not have to stop for a single red light. In cities like New York vehicles are individually guided by computers to avoid one another. There is very little pollution from automobile emissions, and none, of course, from dogs.

You expected to see fewer people on the street than you remember. The Census of 2000 counted 10 percent fewer New Yorkers than in 1980, and the experts think the trend has continued down. But you are surprised that New Yorkers seem to have forgotten how to hurry. Midtown Manhattan looks the way it used to be on Sunday, when the only people in sight were tourists and couples peering into shopwindows to kill time.

The aging skyscrapers no longer house the thousands of office workers who used to flood in and out of them every day. Many of the suites are empty now, and as you look up, the wall of glass is pocked by unwashed panes. It is no longer economic to look for ways to mechanize the washing of skyscraper windows, and the Mexicans imported to do hand labor refuse to work on them because they believe that the empty floors are haunted by hostile ghosts. They slip over the border to do these tasks because they can make more money here than at home, even though there is no longer the opportunity to rise into the middle class that encouraged early-twentieth-century immigrants to forsake their native culture.

Downtown New York has been rebuilt to human scale. The big landmark buildings you remember are still in place, but the junky smaller buildings that used to clutter the spaces between them have been replaced by one- and two-story structures, each with an ambience of its own. Many of them are decorated with bas-relief sculpture, hand-carved doors, murals inside and out, and frescoes contributed by amateur artists from the community. One crowd scene has the faces of people who paid to be included and signed their names to their portraits.

It's hard to tell which buildings are residential and which are commercial. The office of the law firm for which you used to work is open twenty-four hours a day, but the atmosphere is relaxed. The professional staff are free to make their own hours, or work at home, a privilege most of them found well worth the trouble of learning how to use the machines that replaced the supporting staff of workers once required to type, file, and relay messages. The atmosphere reminds you of the times when you used to come back after hours to finish a task you couldn't get done while the phones were ringing.

You are visiting in the late afternoon, and you find some people who seem to be loitering. Actually, they are dropping in to work at specific tasks or keep appointments made by the portable phones through which people who have business to transact can always locate each other. One of the lounges is full of a dozen noisy people who look as if they are having a party but are actually briefing each other on alternative strategies for a major lawsuit they have been assigned to develop on an individual basis. They are chatting heatedly because each member of the strategy team is trying to defend his or her alternative.

The bustle on the streets you remember is gone, because there is no reason for crowds. There are no rush hours at nine and five. The low, inviting buildings look out on neat little parks with benches and fountains. There are no graffiti, and there is not as much rubbish to cart away as there was when the skyscrapers were filled with clerical workers keeping records on paper.

Buildings designed to handle large numbers of people have been converted to other uses. The bank where you used to stand in line to deposit your paycheck and draw enough cash for the weekend has become a health spa. Paychecks and payments go through the General Information Utility, through whose terminal in your home you bank, shop, correspond, and call up news, information, reading, and entertainment. GIU automatically deducts the charges for these services from your bank account. No waiting, no stamp licking, no check writing, no hassles.

The young of 2010 simply don't know what it means to stand in line—a good thing, too, you reflect. At this point you'd hate to have to fight a kid to a book in the New York Public Library, the way you did when you tried to get some studying done there during a school vacation.

The weather is nice, so some of the strollers are sitting at café tables in the little parks. It's hard to place them on the basis of age, sex, education, or income. Most people are wearing unisex clothing. The fashion in New York at the moment is one of the perennial variations on the loose-fitting two-piece Chinese worksuit. You adopted it with relief in your forties, when the jeans you always used to wear began to bind.

An occasional child, playing checkers with an adult, reminds you of the grown-up children of Europe in the 1980s. By 2010 only children are the rule in the United States, too. They act like little adults, and they are so rare and well behaved that their parents take them everywhere.

The eerie part of New York is that the outside has changed very little. The stone lions, Patience and Fortitude, are a bit more weathered, but they still guard the Public Library on Fifth Avenue. All the millions of books of the greatest collection in the world are still in the cavity of the nineteenth-century reservoir under Bryant Park. The general public isn't allowed to handle them physically anymore, but any book you want to consult will come to you on the screen in your home. When you call up a book, GIU automatically credits part of the fee to the author and publisher.

Rents are still high, but the housing shortage is not as acute as it was in 1980. There are fewer people to house, and more of them are singles and childless couples, who do not always want to invest time and money in a place to live. Even in the suburbs most people are living in apartments or sharing quarters with others.

There are few new single houses in the suburb where you grew up, and they are so odd that they look as if they had been designed by architects for wealthy eccentrics. Construction costs have been so high that the public buildings you remember have not been replaced, but converted to other uses. The town hall is a preventive health care clinic. Your old grade school has become a restaurant, your high school is now a prison, and the local college has been absorbed into the town: the student union has become a motel, and the playing fields and libraries are community facilities.

The college itself went out of business for lack of students, but the campus is there, and it still has a college flavor. The dormitory rooms have been rented out to single adults. They are popular with former students who think of college as the best years of their lives. Classrooms and laboratories are being used by government agencies and private enterprises for the training programs that take up more and more of the time of the people on their payrolls.

But the biggest shock is your old neighborhood. It has become a slum. The comfortable three- and four-bedroom ranch houses you knew so well have been cut up into apartments. The backyard pool that was such a thrill when you were a child was so much work to maintain that the people who bought the house filled it in and use the space to grow a kitchen garden. When they feel like getting into water, they loll in a moderately priced little soaking tub imported from Japan.

Other houses have been altered to accommodate cottage industries. One has a sign, LAWNMOWERS SHARPENED. Another, SWEDISH MASSAGE, HERE OR IN YOUR OWN HOME.

The industrial salesman you knew is still living in the house next door, but he closed his office and works these days at home. He does his paper work and books on the home computer, with some help from a neighbor who is learning the business, and he keeps the hardware working by renting one of his bedrooms to a computer mechanic in exchange for repairs. He tells you that one of his neighbors rents extra rooms to tennis players so that he can always be sure of a game, and a widow rents her basement cheap to a young man whose presence helps protect the house against burglars.

Most of the people who used to live on your street are gone.

The parents of the boy in your class sold the house when their children left and moved into a trailer so that they could afford to travel a few weeks every year. Another couple became college bums: the wife went back to college, then the husband started taking courses, and now they both live in a dormitory room.

A shock. But then, your own life hasn't turned out the way you expected, either. When your company moved you to California you talked about retiring early and taking your wife for a trip around the world. But that was before you joined the Sierra Club. Who would have thought that at sixty-three you would be teaching at the University of Alaska, tracking caribou in arctic weather, and getting a license to fly, while your wife, who doesn't share your taste for the great outdoors, makes money in the real estate business in San Diego? You expect to have a lot of new things to tell each other as well as the rest of the family when you spend a week at the home of a daughter who is hostess, this year, to the reunion of all the relatives who bear your name.

Wild Cards

This is, of course, only one scenario for New York in 2010. The future is exciting because it always deals out wild cards no one could have predicted. Who would have imagined that a crowd of Moslem fanatics would hold our diplomats hostage in Iran and help elect a U.S. President dedicated to increasing American power in world affairs? Who would have foreseen that one court would hold the telephone company in violation of the antitrust laws while another would leave IBM in virtual control of the computer industry?

Wild cards are shocking by definition, but never entirely pointless. The following are offered as a limbering exercise to prepare us for the wonderful and terrible things that can happen when older people will be more numerous, more vigorous, and more influential; and when technological advances now in sight will have changed not only our daily lives but the way we think about the economy.

The humane and civilized future ahead will not be attained

without a price that will seem much higher to some than to others. Some of our dreams will sound like nightmares to those still grounded in the competitive, traditional ethic. But if we are right about the long historical perspective, we are not going to have our druthers. As we have done in the past, we are again going to have to modify the property rights of some individuals in order to keep the economy not only just but viable.

The following sections deal with nightmares and dreams that could grow out of the long-term trends in the economy, the demography, and the technology.

Economy

The way you will live in the twenty-first century depends on the kind of economy we will have, so we have to consider first what is likely to happen on this front. Whatever their views, economists agree that a fundamental change of policy can't be postponed very long. In 1982 it became increasingly clear that there was no acceptable trade-off between controlling inflation and unemployment, or between controlling the budget deficit and making enough money available to keep major industries solvent.

The dilemma can't last. And since the only way out of a dilemma is to give up one or more of the premises that define it, the breakout is sure to cause shock and pain. It's easy enough to see what we have to do. We need to direct investment to long-term, social goals, narrow the gap between rich and poor, and distribute the fruits of the new technology to those whose jobs it displaces. The problem is not that we don't know how to do these things, but that the political machinery required to do them is temporarily out of political fashion.

It may take a crash as violent as the one we had in 1929 to jolt us out of ideology and into reality, and during 1982 a great many very sober people thought that it was going to happen. A collapse of the economy would be a nightmare at first, but once we cleared the ground, the problems created by the dilemma would disappear, and all sorts of wonderful dreams would become not only possible but so logical that they would be likely.

It is the nature of a dilemma that breaking out of it requires something unthinkable—in other words, a wild card. The following are offered as heuristic fables, some of them frankly designed to shock.

U.S. GOVERNMENT STOCK. We could balance the budget and have money left over for urgent needs if we could only get out from under the national debt.

There is a simple way, and it is called repudiation. It is so frightening that the word is hardly ever mentioned in print, but it has been done many times before without ending civilization, most recently after World War II. Drastic restructuring of their national debts was one of the reasons that Germany and Japan were able to make economic recoveries so handily after they lost World War II.

Who would suffer if the United States of America repudiated its long-term bonds? In 1990 a top-secret inquiry ordered by the President found that our national debt was more closely held than we had imagined. More than 90 percent of it was in the hands of the five thousand individuals and organizations that held more than $100,000 apiece, and after some sneaking around Swiss banks, the CIA concluded that we owed about a quarter of our national debt to members of the Saudi family.

The President and the Federal Reserve made their plans in secret. In a surprise move, the Federal Reserve suspended all trade in U.S. obligations. Holders were allowed to keep $100,000 worth of government securities, but those who held more were required to exchange the excess for a new Treasury issue called Stock in America, redeemable in the year of the maturity of the obligation it replaced out of a percentage of the gross tax receipts of that year, the percentage to be determined annually by Congress.

LONG-TERM RESEARCH TAX CREDITS. We would all benefit if we could think of a way to encourage research that had some chance of adding to our stock of scientific knowledge and discourage wasting our scientists on projects aimed at transferring money from one investor to another, as is the case when a drug company undertakes research intended to alter an existing remedy in a trivial but patentable way so that the company can get a share of a competitor's market.

We could set up tax credits for research approved by a public panel through which the interests of workers, consumers, and the general public would be represented. Few nations as advanced as the United States leave these crucial decisions entirely to private enterprise, and we may very shortly be forced to set up central planning machinery of our own in order to compete with them.

TECHNOLOGICAL UNEMPLOYMENT COMPENSATION. We might find a way to limit the damage caused by laborsaving inventions that are clearly in the public interest.

We could set up a fund for pensioning workers displaced by technologies that have been judged necessary by a review board of citizens representing consumers, workers, industry, and science. Half the money would come from taxes assessed against companies that have already profited by laborsaving technology, and half from the taxpayers.

THE TENFOLD INCOME GAP. We might find a better way to harness ambition for personal gain to the national interest.

We could amend the income tax to limit the individual reward of an innovator to sums of money that could be actually spent by an individual or his heirs. We couldn't compensate someone like Thomas Edison for his service to the economy in inventing the electric light, but we could ensure that he had as much of anything material as he could personally consume.

We might adopt, as a rule of thumb, that nobody should have more than ten times as much money to spend in a year as the minimum income we feel should be provided, if need be at public expense, for everyone in the country. The redistribution could be simply accomplished by designing an income tax form that would have to be filled out by rich and poor alike. Individuals whose income fell below the designated floor would get a check for the difference, while those who earned more than the ceiling would have to pay the excess in taxes.

CONSPICUOUS DISPLAYS. We might invent more interesting ways to compete with each other than on the basis of income and the status symbols on which we rely to proclaim it.

In the twenty-first century, older people led the way in popularizing a whole array of interesting outlets for the human urge for individual distinction. In their later years, when their need for earnings was less, some took to priding themselves on their weight, their blood pressure, the size of their biceps, or how far they could swim. Others prided themselves on how little money they needed, with highest honors going to those who managed to feed themselves in the woods with no more than an ax and a gun, or to live in the wilderness without disturbing so much as a single wild flower.

Austerity games were developed that set people competing on how many miles per gallon they could coax from their cars; how low they could keep the thermostat in the house through the winter; how much they could save by growing and canning the vegetables they would otherwise have had to buy.

FREEBIES. We might be able to find a better way to ensure the continuance of railroad, mail, and urban transit services that everyone feels are desirable even though they are not profitable.

We could simplify our bookkeeping and clarify our thinking by giving up the attempt to get individual users to pay for services that benefit everyone. We would rip the fare boxes out of buses and subways and support them by taxes on local property owners, arguing that local property owners benefit even when they do not ride.

We have a formidable precedent for the extension of freebies. In the nineteenth century many respectable individuals thought it was confiscation of private property to require childless taxpayers to support the education of other people's children. In the twentieth century everyone pays for the schools and no one denies that everyone benefits.

Demography

Lower birthrates and longer lives will change the basis of twenty-first-century politics, both domestic and foreign. Old people, women, and children will be the winners at home, and expanding

Third World nations will have more bargaining power in their relationships with other countries.

Small shifts now will blow up into unsuspected problems and opportunities a few decades down the road. Older people will have the education, the political savvy, and the sheer numbers to be a bigger political force than any previous older generation. This could result in the nightmare of an age war, or the dream of a society in which the age of an adult would be truly irrelevant.

The declining birthrate means that more women will spend enough childfree years to become financially independent of men and compete on more nearly equal terms for the policy-making posts in private and public hierarchies. By the twenty-first century young women starting up the ladder now will have risen high enough to modify the macho atmosphere of our corporate culture. This prospect is a nightmare for conservatives, a dream for feminists.

Children will be fewer but more highly prized when almost all of them are born only if and when they are actively wanted. Taxpayers and parents will be able and willing to spend more money on them. So many couples would like to have a baby—or more than one—if they felt they could afford it that programs will soon be offered to help them. A law protecting the job of a parent who takes time out to care for a child under six would be politically popular with women. Conservatives would favor it because hawks are already worried about the impact of a stationary population on our influence in world affairs.

The prospect of fewer Americans in the future will change the balance of international power. This is not a distant problem, but one that we are already facing close to home. The birthrate of English-speaking, native-born Americans is one of the lowest in the world, while the Mexican birthrate is one of the highest. According to a projection prepared for President Carter, the population of Mexico City will nearly triple in twenty-five years, from 11 million in 1975 to 32 million in the year 2000.

These projections raise the possibility of the ultimate moral nightmare. If the income gap between our two countries widens, we might not be able to control the flow of job-hungry Mexicans across our porous southern border. Even worse, their eagerness for the higher wages we could afford to pay would tempt some industries to exploit a seemingly limitless supply of frightened and obsequious labor.

Some of the new demographic wild cards seem so implausible that our first reaction is that they couldn't possibly happen. That is the way that most of us feel about the prospect of an age war that would pit one generation against another.

SENIOR POWER. When Social Security checks were delayed in 2020, Senior Power organized a march on Washington so impressive that Congress never allowed the checks to be delayed again.

Senior Power had started as an organization for combating age discrimination. Denouncing ''age chauvinism'' in tones reminiscent of the women's movement of the early 1970s, it had secured the enactment of laws against discrimination on the basis of age not only in employment and housing but in education, the arts, and the image of seniors on television; Social Security benefits replacing 100 percent of earnings for everyone over sixty-two; and the defeat of proposals to raise the age of retirement for the growing proportion of seniors able to continue earning.

Senior Power was loaded with members wise in the ways of Washington. The national board included veterans of the civil rights movement, the peace movement, the student rights movement, the consumer rights movement, and the handicapped rights movement. Senior Power attracted seniors who already knew how to picket, parade, thrust placards in front of television cameras, clap or shout on cue, feed horror stories to reporters, and mobilize computerized mailing lists and platoons of volunteers to work the phones. Their militancy laid to rest the sentimental notion that age mellows youthful radicals.

In Washington, the discipline of the old people assembling on the Mall was more impressive even than their numbers or the speed with which they had been mobilized. They traveled like an army, bringing their canteen and toilet facilities with them, billeting at night by prearrangement with suburban churches, Y's, and schools. They left not so much as a paper napkin behind them, and waited patiently to get a permit before marching down Pennsylvania Avenue.

Everyone knew why they had come, so their leaders didn't have to make speeches. The message was in the banners: WE HAVE NO TIME TO WAIT, one said. CUT RED TAPE, said another. And in the largest letters of all, the two words CHECKS NOW!

Nobody wanted to see them stand for long in the summer sun. Congress rushed an emergency relief bill through the legislative machinery. Before the end of the day, a greeting committee announced the new provisions: in the event of a shortfall of payroll taxes, the U.S. Treasury is empowered to pay Social Security checks out of funds intended for the federal payroll.

The assembly sang "The Star-Spangled Banner" and marched back to their buses as quietly as they had come.

AGE PRIDE. Towards the end of the century, sweatshirts saying OLD AND PROUD OF IT began to appear in places like Detroit, where displaced factory workers continued to live on their pensions. The town that raised the drinking age to thirty was played in the media for laughs, but reverse ageism soon ceased to be funny. A school board voted to dissolve and bus the children elsewhere. One municipality barred children from public pools because old people complained that they got in the way of slower swimmers. A mayor who denied public housing to applicants under sixty became a national hero because he defied a court order declaring his rule illegal. When courts struck down these ageist rules, leaders of the age pride movement called for changing state constitutions to raise the voting age to forty. . . .

But age hostility isn't inevitable. With a little bit of luck, the preponderance of childless adults could reduce the difference between old and young and liberate both from stereotypes of age. Age liberation could change our values as decisively as the movements for civil rights and sex equality before it. Some demographic wild cards could be dreams. One of the most utopian is a new concern for the needs of children.

PARENT'S BILL OF RIGHTS. The falling birthrate had been welcomed in the 1960s and 1970s, but it became a cause for alarm when the native-born population began to shrink. Most young couples wanted children, but felt they couldn't afford them. Housing suitable for rearing children was scarce and expensive, and so were child-care services that would have enabled both of the parents to earn the money that rearing a child required. Late in the twentieth century enlightened employers began to attract top talent by offering highly motivated young husbands and wives the option of a child-rearing break of four or five years without prejudice to their career progression, but it wasn't until 2020, when the population had actually begun to decline, that Congress adopted a national policy on the rearing of children.

In 2021 Congress enacted a series of laws and regulations that came to be known as the Parents' Bill of Rights. It protected the jobs of mothers and fathers who took up to five years off for the purpose of caring for children under the age of six, and provided education and career training for the parent taking the break so that he or she would not lose out on account of it. Parents were given preference in civil service examinations. Child-care services, including counseling for parents, was subsidized. The most popular part of the program was a subsidized housing program for families with little children.

After years of study, a team of architects and child-development specialists designed and built a series of Family Villages where children could be reared under ideal circumstances. Each village was planned for no more than a hundred families and was heavily fenced and guarded by security police so that even a very small child would be safe wherever he wandered in it. Inside, children were free to visit one another, walk to the village school, use the supervised playgrounds, and camp out in the wooded area set up for that purpose.

Admission was limited to families with at least one child under six, so the population of the villages turned over almost as fast as the population of an undergraduate college, and since courses in psychology and child development were offered free of charge, many young parents thought of their stay at the Family village as a postgraduate degree in parenting.

In the residential section of the village families lived in town houses, each of which had a backyard that could be surveyed from a kitchen window. A short walk away, in the business section, adults could find part-time, full-time, or occasional employment in shops and offices rented out to light manufacturing enterprises, mail-order houses, word-processing centers, biological laboratories, and other industries that needed the kind of work that young parents were able to do.

An educational section of the village looked like a college campus. In addition to the courses designed for parents, the curriculum included training programs offered by companies whose employees were on parental leave in the village, courses specially designed to keep parents in touch with their career interests or prepare them for a career change when they and their children were ready to leave the Family Village.

NONAGEIST LANGUAGE. In 1988 amendments to the Age Discrimination in Employment Act provided heavy penalties for violations. Regulations made it illegal for an employer to ask an applicant his age; to discourage older applicants with code words for the stereotypes, such as "energetic," "lively office," or "fun place to work"; to rate them on the speed with which they completed an employment test for a job unless the employer could prove that speed was essential to doing it; or to assign them to training on the basis of the number of years they could be expected to continue to work. Even medical schools weren't allowed to consider the work-life expectancies of candidates for admission.

Training programs for beginners were rewritten to avoid breezy, teenage phrases or patronizing instructions that assumed the beginner was a child who had never worked at an adult task before. White hair, shaking hands, cracking voices, and failing memories were edited out of television programs. If a witch had to be portrayed, she had to be pictured as young.

Newsrooms rewrote their guidelines. Reporters were forbidden to describe a woman as "spry for her age" or even to suggest it indirectly by saying that she skied, if there was no other purpose to the reference. Ages were reported only when relevant to the story, and even the word was suspect. College credits were no longer, for instance, allowed to "age"; in print, at least, they were required to "become obsolete."

AGE DISCRIMINATION BACKFIRE. Firefighters, police officers, FBI agents, and other workers whose jobs required physical stamina were allowed to work as long as they could demonstrate their fitness. In order to get rid of an elderly lifeguard, the city of Palm Beach, Florida, decided to require all lifeguards to prove that they could run five miles and swim four.

To the chagrin of the city fathers, all of the younger guards failed the test.

AGE-FREE OLYMPICS.   At the 2012 Olympics, a sixty-five-year-old woman won the 10,000-meter race against a field of men and women of all ages, some of them physically handicapped. Running only five minutes over her Rated Potential, she edged out a twenty-three-year-old man who came within six minutes of reaching his. It was the first open Olympics ever to be judged on the new basis.

Under the Percent of Potential System, competitors are not given handicaps based on previous scores. Instead, a sports physician tests the heart, lungs, muscles, and reflexes of each competitor and applies these data to a formula that establishes the maximum achievement of which the competitor is physically capable. Developed originally to rate the physical performance of male and female cadets on a sex-fair scale of equal effort, the system was adapted to golf, tennis, skiing, swimming, and running.

PPS increased interest in national competitions, because every amateur in the country could compare his or her own performance with the scores of the winners.

AGE INTEGRATION. Retirement communities, nursing homes, foster grandparent programs, senior citizens centers—all of the programs that treat the elderly as a welfare target—have been discontinued or converted to other uses. Like the orphan asylums of the nineteenth century, they disappeared with the problem they were founded to solve.

Housing varies widely with taste, but there is no specifically geriatric architecture. Grab bars in bathrooms, lower shelves, higher wall sockets, and even doors wide enough for wheelchairs will be standard because they are convenient for adults of any age. Monitoring devices will be available so that adults who are indisposed may stay at home alone if they wish. A popular model is an improvement on a sensing device invented in the 1980s. It counts how often the bathroom or refrigerator door is opened, and sounds an alarm if there is no action for more than a specified number of hours.

LOST BORDER. During the 1980s Mexico grew faster than the United States both in GNP and in population. A program of literacy drove many more Mexicans to the cities in search of a higher standard of living. On some unidentified day in the 1980s, Mexico City surpassed New York in population. Their aspirations raised by schooling, young Mexicans were even more eager to get into the United States.

It was soon apparent that we lacked the will, the money, and finally the heart to turn the rising tide of Mexicans back at the border. As their numbers rose many people began to argue that if we couldn't keep the Mexicans out we ought to join them. A binational group that called itself the Committee for Mexicamerica campaigned in both countries for a merger of the nations.

The first step was taken in 1998, when both countries were requiring their eighteen-year-olds to do a year of public service. That year a treaty was negotiated for an even swap of Americans doing their service in Mexico and Mexicans doing theirs in America.

Gender

One of the unexpected consequences of the rise in life expectancy is that it is increasing the power of women.

This is hard to see now, because older women of the 1980s are apt to be cruelly and undeservedly poor. Because so many were housewives younger than their husbands, women now over sixty-five are more apt than men their age to have outlived their spouses and to have no income beyond their Social Security benefits. Because of past discrimination, these benefits are typically so low that their recipients are more apt than men to be living on incomes below the poverty line. In the 1980s poverty in the United States is largely demographic, a matter of age (old), race (black), and sex (female).

In the 1980s another problem of women is that they outnumber men their age by a margin that widens over the course of their lives. The gender ratio of later years is sexually and socially unfavorable to women, but there is a flip side to this handicap: older women outnumber men because their health is better. They are apt to remain active forces to be reckoned with at an age when all but a small minority of men are physically fragile.

In the twenty-first century, women over sixty-five still won't be as well off financially as the men their age, but they will be at less of a disadvantage. Most middle-aged women are earning money now, so their future Social Security benefits will be higher than those of women over sixty-five today. Most important, they will have the job experience they need to continue to earn in their later years, and since their health will be better than that of men their age, and many of them won't have been on the job as many years of their lives, they may be more inclined to postpone retirement. Of course, the women who waited to start careers are a transitional generation. Their younger sisters will have incomes even closer to those of men in their later years, because the pattern of working life is becoming more similar for men and women.

Add it all up. In the twenty-first century there are going to be even more older women relative to older men than there are in the 1980s. They are going to be closer to the men their age in education, income, and occupation. If older women of the future continue to be healthier than men and to grow in self-assertion compared with older men, as psychologists observe them doing in the 1980s, then the stage is set for events that reverse the pattern of female dependence even feminists take for granted.

What changes can we expect in a world more responsive than ours to the wishes of older women? The obvious hope is that they will use their influence to moderate the military mentality that has led to nuclear stalemate and the waste of so much of our national income. But that is only one of the reversals that could occur.

The gender wild cards that follow are offered in the heuristic tradition of Aristophanes's play *Lysistrata*, about the women who tried to seize power by threatening to withhold sex from men, which has influenced thinking about the sexual division of power for the past 2,400 years.

MALE PROTECTIVE LEGISLATION. During the last two decades of the twentieth century there was no improvement in the life expectancy of men, although the longevity of women continued to rise. By the end of the century the discrepancy had been traced to a biological mechanism that protected females from the stresses associated with the occupations dominated by males.

In her public statement, the Surgeon General pointed out that precedent already existed for dealing with industrial hazards that affected one sex only. In the 1970s companies had argued that jobs involving chemicals that might adversely affect pregnant women be reserved for men, even when postreproductive women wanted to do them. She accordingly recommended that women be preferred for jobs that were shown to be specially dangerous to the health of men.

So many congressmen were males past middle age that the Congress took a special interest in the progress of this research. After lengthy and well-attended hearings, both houses passed a Male Protective Act. Drawing on the machinery set up by state labor laws of the early part of the twentieth century that attempted to protect women from work regarded as beyond their strength by limiting their hours and the weights they were allowed to lift, the laws protecting males were designed to discourage employers from hiring males in occupations found hazardous to them by restricting their hours, limiting their responsibilities, and providing facilities and time for them to engage in tension-reducing exercises.

The first batch of occupations certified to be dangerous to men included journalist, congressman, assembly-line worker, and President of the United States.

OLD GIRL NETWORK. Early in the twenty-first century the last man on the board of General Motors died, leaving the company entirely under the direction of women. The first tokens brought into management in response to the women's movement of the 1970s outworked the men with whom they were competing, but nobody at the time had foreseen that they would outlive them, too.

Late in the 1980s, mandatory retirement at seventy had been replaced by age-neutral rules permitting mandatory retirement on the basis of physical ability to perform the specific duties of the job in question. Officials in decision-making jobs were required to score higher on tests of resistance to stress than those whose work subjected them to less pressure. The test disqualified many more men than women.

Forcibly retired males brought a class-action suit contending that the regulation violated the new Equal Rights Amendment to the Constitution. After years of litigation, during which the imbalance of the sexes continued to grow, the Supreme Court upheld the regulation on the ground that ability to withstand pressure was a reasonable requirement for the high-level jobs in question, and so exempted as a bona fide sex qualification under the Civil Rights Act of 1964. In an obiter dictum, the majority opinion added that an exemption from the amendment could be justified for officials whose decisions affected the public interest.

MAN SHARING.   Older women and younger men make ideal sexual partners, but during most of history they have discovered this only by accident. But the practice was legitimized as a solution for the sexual deprivation of older women in the twenty-first century. The movement began in 2010, when some of the young women who had patronized male strippers in the 1980s organized a Senior Women's Swinger Exchange.

Senior Swingers maintained a roster of available women for the many occasions on which established swinger groups find themselves short of female partners. They also facilitated more permanent arrangements under which an older and younger woman shared a younger man. Their literature pointed out that older women offer young husbands sexual variety without endangering their primary relationship, because while most of them wanted an occasional weekend of male companionship, very few of them wanted to go back to the traditional status of wife.

SEX LESSONS.   It took some time for the adult society to free sex from the obligations imposed by reproduction and legitimize it as personal recreation of interest to no one except the consenting party or parties. The shift was accomplished in part by a new kind of sex education. Instead of the analogies with birds and bees and the heavily medical information provided in the pioneer sex education courses of the 1970s, sex educators of the twenty-first century offered practical, how-to-do-it instruction of the kind traditionally available only in books that in the 1980s were banned as pornographic.

Courses in "appreciation of sex" were offered for every stage of life. They ranged from lessons in masturbation for children to classes instructing old women how to obtain sexual gratification from each other. Like piano lessons, the practice of sex was primarily taught through private lessons outside of school, but contraceptive techniques were regarded as a public health concern that could not be safely left to private instructors. The required seventh-grade course in contraception was based on a program designed originally to stem the tide of teenage pregnancies that attracted public concern in the 1980s.

GAY LIBERATION. In 1990 the Civil Rights Act of 1964 was amended to bar discrimination on the basis of sexual preference in employment, education, and housing.

Technology

Biologists believe they are on the verge of discovering why human beings age, and many of them think that they will find a way to slow that process in time to prolong the lives of people already on earth in the 1980s. If so, young people now alive may be called upon to make, in their later years, the unforeseen trade-offs that will confront a society in which most people expect to live to be one hundred years old. That day of reckoning is being speeded by computers that enable scientists to unravel the complicated genetic code that controls the development of all living things.

More immediately, computers are changing everyday life as decisively as the printing press and telephone did, and though the changes are painful at first, they offer us a new kind of freedom. Elaborate communications networks will enable us to work and live wherever we please and relate in many more ways to many more different kinds of people.

At first, at least, we will find the options disorienting. We are going to have to learn to deal with masses of information and relate to large numbers of people we will never see face-to-face. We know this is possible, because almost everyone has had the experience of developing fairly complicated relationships with people known only through telephone conversations.

Technology always scares us at first. Nothing is more disruptive than having to make decisions or deal with information or new relationships for which we have no guidelines. Yet once we adapt to the new dimension, we seldom seriously consider giving it up for the comfort of a limited life. When the telephone was new it was condemned as an intolerable invasion of personal privacy that forced the subscriber to talk with unwanted strangers. We sometimes feel that way today, but not when the telephone is out of order. Once we are used to computer networks, on-line access to data bases, and instant printouts, we will feel as isolated without them as we do when deprived of access to a car or telephone.

In the 1980s we are just beginning to experiment with computer networks that free work, shopping, games, training, education, socializing, access to information, and even services like medical attention from specific locations. We think of them now as cold and impersonal, but they will inevitably enable us to reach out and relate to many more people in many more ways than we now imagine.

Wild cards are one of the ways to explore the human face of machines that bring people together.

COMPUTER GAMES.   When personal computers were new, young people gathered around the first ones in the neighborhood and fell into the habit of playing games with each other. As computers became more common, dedicated fans hooked their computers up by phone and played without leaving home. Later on, when long-distance phone rates dropped, computer games were played by people in different cities.

Long-distance chess became one of the popular pastimes of the 1990s, in part because it was a way two busy people could use odd moments of time to maintain a relationship with each other. When one party wanted to play, he called up the board on his screen and made a move that changed the position of the pieces pictured on the screen. When the other party wanted to play, he called up the board, noticed the changes, and made a countermove. Grandparents played chess this way with their grandchildren.

Computers did as much as the telephone to keep friends and relatives in touch with each other. College roommates, cousins, bridge clubs, and people who had worked together arranged to subscribe to the same computer networks. Then, when one of them had an item of news, he typed it on his screen and transmitted it to the computers of all the others, where it was stored until the recipients had time to check for messages. The method was easier than writing a number of letters, and less intrusive than phoning in person.

Computer networks also created new family relationships by making genealogical searches easier and cheaper. When home computers became as common as telephones, it was easy to locate people of the same name, query them about the names and birth dates of their parents, and process the information to produce a family tree. Many acquaintances discovered, to their surprise, that they were also relatives.

STOCK EXCHANGE MUSEUM. By 2010 the New York Stock Exchange had become a twenty-four-hour computer that repriced a stock the instant a buy or sell order was plugged into it from any one of the thousands of brokers with access to the machine. The right to trade was still called a seat, but it was actually a secret code that accepted messages from any terminal.

The old New York Stock Exchange was maintained as a tourist attraction, where a lone broker eked out a modest living making sample trades for visitors. He also sold samples of old-fashioned ticker tape and plates picturing J. P. Morgan. Serious brokers set up their terminals in places where the weather is attractive.

The most successful bought up secluded little South Pacific islands, from which they beamed their trades to the computer by satellite. They didn't need a staff, because the computer printed out the paper work of their transactions. Research did not require an army of analysts: specific data on listed companies was retrieved from computer data banks. The market was more stable, because relevant information could no longer be hoarded but was instantly available to everyone.

CASHLESS SHOPPING.   By 2020 actual cash became ceremonial, like the five-dollar gold pieces procured from banks in the early twentieth century to put under the Christmas tree for gifts. Payrolls and payments were transactions between computers.

There were no tellers in banks, no cashiers in stores, no billing and payroll clerks, and while there were display centers where you could see actual goods, you seldom went out of the house to do ordinary shopping. Like purchasing agents for big organizations, you set up the specifications for most of the things that you needed to buy and checked them against the products offered. If you wanted to compare the products, you called them up on your video screen and got accurate, updated answers to the questions you put to the vendor's computer program.

But the very computers that saved you trips to the store made it easier to buy on impulse. You loved to visit antique shows, where you could see and handle objects that were common in your childhood in the twentieth century. So many older people remembered them that they had become very expensive. A Cuisinart food processor that caught your eye cost the money you thought it would take to live for a month, but you decided on the spot to buy it anyway. You stepped to the nearest terminal, called up your personal finance program, and asked it what you could best do without if you decided to splurge. When you decided to buy, another program automatically transferred the funds from your account to the account of the merchant, or debited your credit account with the bank.

VIDEO TRIPS.   Video trips were introduced during an energy crisis of the 2010s that temporarily limited foreign travel, and some people liked them so much that they became a permanent alternative to travel.

Video travel centers looked like small hotels. They rented you a berth that looked like an astronaut's couch and hooked you up to a complex of machines that brought you the sights, sounds, and even smells of whatever foreign scene you wanted to visit.

If you were visiting Versailles, you could, by working the controls, choose where you wanted to go in the gardens. You could put yourself on the scene live, in real time, or if you preferred, you could put yourself in the gardens as they were recorded in the spring.

Opinion was divided on video travel. Purists wanted to be there in person. Others said they could see more than if they were on the ground. The argument continued the debate of the 1980s between those who preferred to attend a sports event and those who insisted that they got a better and more comfortable view of it over television.

THE REDEFINITION OF LIFE. Steadily increasing control over the aging process dusted off a long-neglected theological controversy over the right of God to give or take an individual human life.

In the 2010s molecular biologists began discovering the errors in the genetic code that accumulate in later years and result in softened bones, stiff joints, hardening arteries, white hair, inelastic skin, wrinkles, and defects in the immune system that expose older people to infections. Then, in 2015, came the jackpot: the Rockefeller Institute announced that its scientists had identified the master key to the aging process and were workng on a vaccine that would slow all the symptoms down. Normally cautious, the spokesman warned that the vaccine was not yet developed, but he admitted, under questioning, that the vaccine under trial was expected to work well enough to add at least ten years to the average life.

The announcement precipitated a financial crisis. The stockmarket plunged. Analysts pointed out that the prolongation of life would bankrupt the private pension funds, which had become the nation's principal investors. And before the end of the trading day, the chairman of the Social Security Commission demanded an immediate, emergency rise in payroll taxes to cover the longer years of income to which current workers would eventually be entitled, or an immediate reduction in existing benefits so that the money available for each annuitant would last for a longer life.

The very next day, unions and organizations of the retired joined forces to defend existing pension rights. The American Association of Retired Persons and the AFL-CIO demonstrated together outside the Washington office of the Social Security Commission. AARP signs said, FREEZE BENEFITS. Union signs said, FREEZE PAYROLL DEDUCTIONS.

Alerted to the danger over their computer networks, big investors consulted their friends in the fundamentalist churches. An evangelical preacher with a national following decided that the Bible was against a vaccine against aging: "Threescore and ten is God's plan for man," he told his multimillion television audience.

Liberals dusted off RIGHT TO CHOOSE signs left over from their campaign to liberalize abortion laws. Every individual, they asserted, has the right to decide how long he or she wants to live. Those who oppose the vaccine on moral grounds need not take it, but they have no right to force their views on those who do not agree with them.

Fundamentalists launched a nationwide protest against human interference with God's plan for man. They had gone underground when they lost the fight against abortion rights. By the end of the 1980s American law reflected the majority view that the decision to have a baby belonged not to God but to the individual woman involved, yet the religious mystique faded slowly. Even in the twenty-first century, some young couples were not entirely comfortable making the decision to have a baby on the basis of the costs and benefits to them alone.

This time the battle was long and bitter, but the American tradition of respect for individual religious beliefs once again prevailed. The vaccine appeared, and the death rate fell faster than actuaries working on the basis of the first clinical trials had expected. The opponents delayed, but could not finally prevent, the administration of the vaccine in publicly funded medical institutions. Americans are pragmatists, so they eventually tired of the debate about the relative roles of God and man. In order to prevent the bankruptcy of pension funds, retirement was redefined in terms of ability to work, rather than age.

Most people took the vaccine, including a great many of the fundamentalists who had opposed it on theological grounds. It could not, of course, reverse the decrements already being experienced by older people, but it maintained the vigor of those who began it early. Then, when the first of these approached the milestone of one hundred, doctors reported what looked like an epidemic of psychosomatic deaths.

According to the Surgeon General, there was nothing mysterious or even new about psychosomatic death. She pointed out that some individuals had always slipped out of life for no apparent medical reason when they had come to the end of their agenda, as my great-grandmother Sawin had done when the celebration of her hundredth birthday convinced her that living that long was unseemly. The vaccine had simply increased the number of people who were physically able to outlive their agendas.

But some people always seemed to have another agenda. When they finished one project, they simply went on to another and another, growing in wisdom and in daring. As the twenty-first century wore on, they became the innovators, drawing on their lengthening historical perspective to see a wider canvas of the human experience.

In the twenty-first century, hardy centenarians will become the astronauts on whom we rely to explore and expand the human condition.

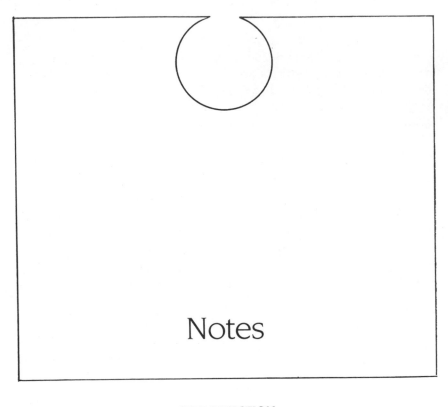

Notes

INTRODUCTION

The decline in hope and happiness between 1957 and 1978 is based on continuing studies by the Institute for Social Research at the University of Michigan, reported in *The Sense of Well-Being in America, Recent Patterns and Trends*, by Angus Campbell (New York: McGraw-Hill, 1981). The percentage who said they were "very happy" dropped from 40 percent to 29 percent for young people age twenty to twenty-nine, but rose from 25 percent to 31 percent for those over sixty, so that in 1978, the old were more apt to be happy than the young.

A 1977 survey conducted for this institute by Robert P. Quinn and Graham L. Staines reported declines from 1969 and 1973, years in which similar surveys were made. The 1977 survey included 1,515 respondents from seventy-four different geographic areas and was representative of all employed adults. The decline in job satisfaction was found to be "pervasive, affecting virtually all the demographic and occupational subclasses examined." It continued the decline reported in *Work in America, Report of a Special Task Force to the Secretary of Health, Education, and Welfare*, prepared under the auspices of the W. E. Upjohn Institute for Employment Research (Cambridge, Massachusetts: MIT Press, 1973).

The poor suffered most, as usual, from attempts to cut budget deficits in the 1980s. More than 700,000 families with dependent children lost their benefits. These and other economies increased the proportion of Americans in poverty from a low of 11.1 percent in 1973 to 14 percent in 1981, when nearly 32 million Americans were subsisting in poverty, then defined by the Census as an income below $9,287 for a family of four. For a comprehensive report on welfare cuts during the first eighteen months of the Reagan Administration, see *The Reagan Experiment, an Examination of Economic and Social Policies under the Reagan Administration*, ed. John L. Palmer and Isabel V. Sawhill (Washington, D.C.: The Urban Institute Press, 1982).

Cuts in federally subsidized jobs for teenagers were so drastic and unemployment so high that many people feared that there would be riots in the summer of 1982, but the inner cities were quiet. Riots and revolutions occur when expectations are rising, not when standards of living are falling.

Productivity is classically measured by dividing the gross domestic product produced in a given period by total employee hours. This figure rose steadily up to 1977, and has wobbled a bit above and a bit below the 1977 rate ever since. The measure is more accurate for manufacturing than for retailing, banking, education, government, and other services that are the growing end of the economy.

Born Female: The High Cost of Keeping Women Down (New York: David McKay Co.) was first published in January 1968, shortly after the foundation of the National Organization for Women.

For comparison between blacks, women, and the elderly, see "Ageism Compared to Racism and Sexism" by Erdman B. Palmore and Kenneth Manton, *Journal of Gerontology* 28, no. 3 (1973): 363–369.

We have some idea of how many people will be over sixty-five in 2030 because all of them are alive today. But we don't know what proportion they will be of the population of 2030 because we don't know how many of them will survive or how many children we will add between now and then. Assumptions on future fertility and mortality keep changing. In 1982 the projection of people over sixty-five in 2030 was usually given at 18 percent, according to Paul M. Siegel, chief, Education and Social Stratification Branch of the Population Division of the Bureau of the Census. He adds that high, low, and medium (the favored) assumptions about fertility yield projected proportions of the population age sixty-five and over in 2030 of 14, 22, and 18 percent, respectively, which correspond to median ages of 31.2, 43.2, and 38.0, for the population as a whole. But he warns, "Don't overlook the possibility of improvements in health and survivorship."

1. THE RISE AND FALL OF YOUTH

Evidence that colonial Americans tried to look older is presented by David Hackett Fischer in *Growing Old in America* (New York: Oxford University Press, 1977).

The highest birthrate in the United States was 55 per 1,000 population in 1800, and it fell with every census thereafter for more than a hundred years, reaching 41.4 at the outbreak of our Civil War, according to Series B 19-30, *Historical Statistics of the United States, Colonial Times to 1957,* U.S. Bureau of the Census (Washington, D.C.: U.S. Government Printing Office, 1960). Now only the fastest-growing African countries attain the U.S. rate of 1800. In 1982, the United Nations Population Division projected 1980–85 crude birthrates over 50 per 1,000 for Kenya, Malawi, Botswana, Mauretania, and Niger.

For American attitudes toward children, see Alexis de Tocqueville's "Influence of Democracy on the Family" in his *Democracy in America* (Boston: John Allyn Publishers, 1882), vol. 2, pp. 233–240, and Richard L. Rapson, *The Cult of Youth in Middle-Class America* (Lexington, Massachusetts: D. C. Heath, 1971).

"The Club of Rome Plan: Killing the American Dream," by Mark Burdman in *Fusion* (July 1980): 12–15, is a useful account of the affiliations of the club's members.

For a thoughtful analysis of the dangers of the backlash against children, see "Perceptions of Childhood and Youth" by Alan Pifer (New York: Annual Report of the Carnegie Corporation of New York, 1978). For discrimination against children in housing, see "Measuring Restrictive Practices Against Children in Rental Housing: A National Perspective" (Washington, D.C.: Department of Housing and Urban Development, July 11, 1980). For an update on the legal rights of children, see "Constitutional Rights of Children," a report prepared for the Subcommittee on the Constitution of the Committee on the Judiciary, U.S. Senate (Washington, D.C.: U.S. Government Printing Office, 1978). For implications of the aging of the population for marketers, see a report of 1980 by a New York marketing and advertising consulting company called Brain Reserve, which predicted calmer politics, greater acceptance of women returning to work, increased use of male cosmetics, and improved television programming.

Virginia Mekos, a labor specialist with Cornell University's School of Industrial and Labor Relations in New York City, points out that neither age nor an unemployed status provides a sufficient reason for violent criminal behavior by youths. She contends that a mix of cultural prescriptives, an economically impoverished background in an affluent environment, irrelevant and depersonalized schooling and limited career options, and lack of adolescent role responsibilities fuel the phenomenon of higher violent-crime rates for male youths.

On the declining birthrate, the authoritative U.S. source is the National Center for Health Statistics, 3700 East-West Highway, Hyattsville, Maryland 20782. The estimate that half the fall in marital fertility in developed nations is due to better birth control and half due to a decline in the number of wanted children was made by G. T. Acsadi and G. Johnson-Acsadi in *Social, Economic and Health Aspects of Low Fertility,* Center for Population Research, NIH and World Health Organization (Washington, D.C.: U.S. Government Printing Office, March 1977).

Although outdated, *Population and the American Future, The Report of the Commission on Population Growth and the American Future* (New York: New American Library, 1972) is an authoritative attempt to analyze all the different impacts of the aging of the population. Dr. Charles Westoff, the mainstream U.S. demographer, warns that slight upturns in the birthrate do not mean a return to the rapid population growth following World War II. "The theory that the historical demographic transition will terminate in a magical balance of births and deaths at low levels may be more aesthetic than realistic," he wrote in the *Population Bulletin of the United Nations,* no. 11 (1978).

Childless women are at least twice as apt to be in the labor force as parents of small, planned families, and their earnings are a higher proportion of the family income, according to a study of childlessness made by William D. Mosher and Christine A. Bachrach of the National Center for Health Statistics published in the *Journal of Family Issues* (December 1982). Analyzing data from the 1973 and 1976 National Surveys of Family Growth, they found 17.8 percent of ever-married women childless, of whom 13.3 percent were planning to have children in the future. Their study confirmed previous ones suggesting that voluntarily childless persons tend to be disproportionately well educated, employed, well paid, and nonreligious, and they found that the temporarily childless were similar to the voluntarily childless in these respects.

The estimate of $134,414 for the out-of-pocket cost of raising a child to the age of eighteen is for a child born in 1979 and reared at a moderate cost level in the urban North Central region of the United States, in a family with no more than five children, on the assumption of an annual inflation rate of 8 percent. It was made for the U.S. Department of Agriculture; see Carolyn S. Edwards, *USDA Estimates of the Cost of Raising a Child: A Guide to Their Use and Interpretation,* Miscellaneous Publication 1411 (Washington,

D.C.: U.S. Government Printing Office). Budget items include food at home and away from home (that is, school lunches), clothing, the child's share of family housing costs, medical care, education, transportation, and the child's share of miscellaneous family expenditures for reading, recreation, and personal care. This is, of course, a very modest estimate. For a longer analysis of the cost for working couples, see Caroline Bird, *The Two Paycheck Marriage* (New York: Rawson, Wade Publishers, Inc., 1979).

Richard A. Easterlin's theory is presented in his book *Birth and Fortune*: *The Impact of Numbers on Personal Welfare* (New York: Basic Books, 1980). Dr. Charles F. Westoff is frequently called upon to dispute it. See his "Marriage and Fertility in the Developed Countries," *Scientific American* 239, no. 6 (1978): 51–57.

On the subject of declining populations, the Federal Republic of Germany, Great Britain, and Austria are among the countries that have registered more deaths than births in recent years; see *Demographic Yearbook 1979* (New York: United Nations Department of International, Economic, and Social Affairs) and Jean Bourgeois-Pichat, "The Economic and Social Implications of Demographic Trends in Europe up to and beyond 2000," *Population Bulletin of the United Nations*, no. 8 (1976): 34–89.

On happiness, the older one gets, the higher one rates one's present life, according to a nationwide survey made by *Psychology Today*, and reported in the September 1981 issue in an article by William Watts entitled "The Future Can Fend for Itself." This confirms Gail Sheehy's survey; see the "Life-Happiness Graph," with the scores for both men and women rising with age, in *Esquire* (October 1979), and the finding by Leo Srole and Anita Kassen Fischer that the survivors of the Midtown Manhattan Study made in the 1950s whom they were able to locate twenty years later had fewer symptoms of mental illness than when they were younger.

Sterilization rates come from the National Survey of Family Growth conducted periodically by the National Center for Health Statistics.

On life stages, Erik H. Erikson's are in *Childhood and Society* (New York: W. W. Norton & Co., 1950); Gail Sheehy's are in *Passages, Predictable Crises of Adult Life* (New York: E. P. Dutton, 1976); Christine L. Fry's are in "The Ages of Adulthood: A Question of Numbers," *Journal of Gerontology* 31, no. 2 (1976): 170–177.

Christine Fry is an anthropologist at Loyola University in Chicago and one of the founders of the Association for Anthropology and Gerontology. Her original study is being expanded into a major cross-cultural study on aging. She believes that people create the number of age categories needed to explain those around them. "Perception of the way life is divided, however, is not a direct product of age and accumulated experience," she writes in a personal communication. "Position in the reproductive cycle and the resulting age differences within a family shape the way life careers are seen."

Age categories of adulthood should be less salient in the age-irrelevant society predicted by Bernice L. Neugarten in "Time, Age, and the Life Cycle," *The American Journal of Psychiatry* 136, no. 7 (July 1979).

The suggestion for reversing the traditional sequence of life stages was made by Willard Wirtz in his *The Boundless Resource* (Washington D.C.: The New Republic Book Company, 1975).

For the premature aging of sports figures, see Roger Kahn, "Past Their Prime," *Playboy* (May 1979).

Marie L. Blank's indictment of the ageism of social work advocacy is in "Ageism in Gerontologyland," a paper she presented at the Gerontological Society Conference on November 17, 1978, in Dallas, Texas. Andrew Achenbaum, a historian at Carnegie-Mellon University, faults the "excessive rhetoric used by well-intentioned reformers to gain government help for the aged."

The myths of age have been well documented by gerontologists Robert N. Butler and Alex Comfort. Dr. Robert N. Butler is a psychiatrist and a gerontologist who was the first director of the National Institute on Aging. His book *Why Survive? Being Old in America* (New York: Harper & Row, 1975) was a best-seller. On September 1, 1982, he joined the Mount Sinai Medical Center in New York City to establish the first department of geriatrics in a U.S. medical school.

Although now outdated, the classic reference on social science data on the influence of chronological age is the encyclopedic three-volume work *Aging and Society*, vol. 1, *An Inventory of Research Findings*, Matilda White Riley and Anne Foner (New York: Russell Sage Foundation, 1968); vol. 2, *Aging and the Professions*, ed. Matilda White Riley, John W. Riley, Jr., and Marilyn E. Johnson (New York: Russell Sage Foundation, 1969); vol. 3, *A Sociology of Age Stratification*, Matilda White Riley et al. (New York: Russell Sage Foundation, 1972).

Careful examination of the data revises many commonly held notions about the influence of age. In a paper delivered at the American Sociological Association meetings of 1979, Matilda Riley pointed out that "disengagement," the supposed mode of the old, was associated with joblessness rather than chronological age. Young men out of work in the Great Depression became disengaged, too, and so are black teenagers who can't find jobs.

Regression to immature defenses is related to disability rather than chronological age. A young woman of my acquaintance who was confined to her room with hepatitis grew fearful of going out, busied herself with handiwork and cleaning her bureau drawers, tired of company, took to sleeping and dozing, and behaved in other ways regarded as senile. Dr. Philip G. Zimbardo, an experimental psychologist at Stanford University, found that college students rendered temporarily deaf through posthypnotic suggestion became "irritated, agitated, hostile, and unfriendly," characteristics that, when they occur in older people, are usually ascribed to their age.

Poverty is not a direct consequence of age and retirement. Many older workers have lower incomes because they never acquired the skills that enable their juniors to earn high incomes over the course of their working lives. Then, too, a great deal of attention is paid to the decline of income in later years because the retired who experience a dramatic drop in income and lifestyle are articulate, highly paid professional workers. Social Security, private pensions, and, since inflation, their investments have not been able to replace as high a percentage of their preretirement earnings as Social Security for the millions of lower-paid workers. A common rule of thumb says that two-thirds of work-life income is required for comfortable retirement. Social Security replaces two-thirds of the income of the lowest-paid workers, but executives who have been living elaborately may have to cut their expenses by more than half even if they have a private pension and income from investments. In addition, of course, the retired enjoy tax breaks and help from Medicare in paying for the expense of illness.

Finally, the decline of the generation gap shows that the old are not impervious to the changes in values that have occurred over the course of their lifetimes. According to James O'Toole, a professor at the Center for Futures Research at the University of Southern California, "There is some evidence—although it is far from conclusive—that instead of young people growing out of their values, older Americans are growing into the boom babies' values."

2. THE ADULT SOCIETY

Although they are frequently compared, the unemployment of 1982 was not as damaging as the unemployment in the Great Depression of the 1930s, but we cannot take comfort from the relative rarity of individuals suffering from pangs of hunger or sleeping in subway stations. Although more common, people in obvious want were surprisingly invisible in the 1930s.

Eli Ginzberg, the human resources economist, wrote a good, short overview of the Social Security system in the January 1982 issue of *Scientific American*. For explanations of the Social Security laws, I am indebted to Morris Ordover, Director External Affairs Staff, Region II of the Social Security Administration, but needless to say he is not responsible for my errors or opinions.

The idea of reducing Social Security benefits to conceal the federal deficit was a bright idea of David Stockman, President Reagan's feisty young Director of the Office of Management and Budget. He deliberately used the aging of the population as an excuse, although this demographic squeeze was far in the future. "The Social Security problem is not simply a matter of satisfying actuaries," he told William Greider, the journalist who wrote "The Education of David Stockman" for *The Atlantic* (December 1981). "It's one of satisfying the here-and-now of budget requirements."

For data and insights on the economy I am indebted to *Our Overloaded Economy: Inflation, Unemployment, and the Crisis in American Capitalism*, Wallace C. Peterson (Armonk, New York: M. E. Sharpe, Inc., 1982).

A conscientious presentation of the major income and employment issues affecting older Americans was prepared by the Urban Institute of Washington for the U.S. Special Committee on Aging: "Emerging Options for Work and Retirement Policy" (Washington, D. C.: U.S. Government Printing Office, 1980).

For work values, I am indebted to the landmark study *Men and Women of the Corporation*, Rosabeth Moss Kanter (New York: Basic Books, 1977). A widely used measure of values is described in *The Nature of Human Values*, Milton Rokeach (New York: The Free Press, 1973). Individuals are invited to rank the order in which they hold such values as "a world at peace," "a comfortable life," and "equality," which makes it possible to compare differences of values on the basis of age, race, sex, income, education, occupation, etc.

The futurists who have predicted the rise of nonmaterial values with improvements in the standard of living have been listed in "U.S. Long-Term Economic Growth Prospects: Entering a New Era," a staff study prepared for the Joint Economic Committee of the Congress, January 25, 1978. The authorities quoted include Herman Kahn, who talks about "risk aversion, localism, leisure, health, environmental protection, and anti-technological, anti-industrial attitudes" and predicts that economic growth will drop when the U.S. median income reaches $20,000 per capita. Others quoted include John McHale, Gardiner Ackley, Herman Daly, and Willis Harman. Some of these forecasters think that the real limit to growth will be cultural and social attitudes, rather than a shortage of energy or materials.

The shorter schooling of the elderly of the 1980s accounts for many rigidities we associate with age. According to *Aging and Society*, vol. 1: *An Inventory of Research Findings*, Matilda White Riley and Anne Foner (New York: Russell Sage Foundation, 1968), p. 4, the less-educated majority of older people "are more likely to retire and less likely to belong to voluntary associations or to read or to want to learn more. They have lower incomes. They are distinctly less happy and less optimistic about the future; but at the same time, they are less introspective and less ready to doubt their own adequacy as spouses or parents."

3. THE HUMAN YEARS

Margaret Mead's speech at Houston is reported in *The Spirit of Houston, The First National Women's Conference, An Official Report to the President, the Congress, and the People of the United States* (Washington, D.C.: National Commission on the Observance of International Women's Year, March 1978), for which Caroline Bird was the chief writer.

The definition of the disengagement theory was made by James E. Birren in his 1964 text *The Psychology of Aging* (Englewood Cliffs, New Jersey: Prentice-Hall, Inc.), pp. 237–238, but the theories of the text do not necessarily reflect his views in 1982.

The classic books on life stages are *Childhood and Society*, Erik H. Erikson (New York: W. W. Norton & Co., 1950); *Seasons of a Man's Life*, Daniel J. Levinson et al. (New York, Alfred Knopf, 1978); *Transformations, Growth, and Change in Adult Life*, Roger L. Gould (New York: Simon and Schuster, 1978); and *Passages, Predictable Crises of Adult Life*, Gail Sheehy (New York: E. P. Dutton, 1976). Most of the theories of behavioral scientists are at least mentioned in the monumental *Adult Development and Learning*, Alan B. Knox (San Francisco: Jossey-Bass, Inc., 1977) and in *The Life-Span Perspective in Social Science Research*, a long review of current research to 1980, by David L. Featherman of the University of Wisconsin at Madison, commissioned by the Social Science Research Council for the National Science Foundation's Second Five-Year Outlook on Science and Technology.

Most of the metaphors for the life course come from a question I used to stimulate the ageless individuals I interviewed: "If you had to choose a metaphor, would you liken the course of your life to: a river flowing through different kinds of country, as the River Nile; an obstacle race; a journey along a well-mapped road; a novel with turning pages; a voyage of discovery through stormy seas." Some of the metaphors came from interviews reported by Jane Seskin in her book *More Than Mere Survival, Conversations with Women Over 65* (New York: Newsweek Books, 1980).

Pauli Murray, the civil rights advocate, prefers to be called a Negro rather than a black. She studied at Yale under Thomas I. Emerson, the noted professor of constitutional law and civil rights advocate whom she calls the Clarence Darrow for the Equal Rights Amendment.

On length of life, the heartbeat measure of longevity comes from *The Panda's Thumb*, Stephen Jay Gould (New York: W. W. Norton, 1980).

The film *Eleanor, First Lady of the World*, on Eleanor Roosevelt's life, with Jean Stapleton in the title role, is a memorable document of her United Nations career. See also *Mother and Daughter: The Letters of Eleanor and Anna Roosevelt*, ed. Bernard Asbell (New York: Coward, McCann & Geoghegan, 1982) and *Eleanor Roosevelt, An American Conscience*, Tamara K. Hareven (Chicago: Quadrangle Books, 1968).

Rosser Reeves points out that he has made history as well as money in advertising. He invented the spot commercial and liberated programs from direct control of sponsors. And although increasing his fortune is no longer his primary objective, he does remain active in a number of business ventures all over the world.

Robert N. Butler, the first director of NIA, is a psychiatrist who believes that many older people naturally engage in an active, purposeful form of reminiscence he calls life review. See his "The Life Review: An Interpretation of Reminiscence in the Aged," *Psychiatry: Journal for Study of Interpersonal Processes* 26, no. 1 (February 1963).

Dr. Karl H. Pribram's speculation on the electrical basis for the loss of memory in later life is in a personal communication. He is affiliated with the Neuropsychology Laboratories and the departments of psychology, psychiatry, and behavioral sciences at Stanford University. Walker Percy's novel *The Second Coming* was published in New York by Farrar, Straus and Giroux in 1980.

Margaret Mead is the best authority on her own life. See her *Blackberry Winter: My Earlier Years* (New York: William Morrow and Co., Inc., 1972) and *Letters from the Field, 1925–1975* (New York: Harper & Row, 1977).

4. A HUMAN DEFINITION OF HEALTH

"The Deacon's Masterpiece Or, The Wonderful One-Hoss Shay,' A Logical Story" comes from *The Complete Poetical Work of Oliver Wendell Holmes, Poems from the Autocrat of the Breakfast Table, 1857–1858* (Boston: Houghton Mifflin Co., Cambridge ed., 1908).

> Have you heard of the wonderful one-hoss shay,
> That was built in such a logical way
> It ran a hundred years to a day,
> Now in building of chaises, I tell you what,

> There is always *somewhere* a weakest spot,—
> You see, of course, if you're not a dunce,
> How it went to pieces all at once,—
> All at once, and nothing first,—
> Just as bubbles do when they burst.

Aunt Bee Bee's real name was Louise Shaw. When my friend Dorothy Roberts was learning to talk she called her Bee Bee because she was always busy as a bee.

Dr. James F. Fries of the Stanford University Medical Center points out that the curve describing the numbers of persons surviving at each successive age has become a rectangle. This has happened because the average length of life has increased from forty-seven to seventy-three years in this century, while the maximum life span hasn't increased at all. He proposes that medical policies aim at postponing not death but illness, so that senescence is concentrated in fewer years at the end. He believes that chronic illness can be postponed by changes in lifestyle. The effects this would have on medicine, medical costs, and society are analyzed in *Vitality and Aging: Implications of the Rectangular Curve*, James F. Fries and Lawrence M. Crapo (San Francisco: W. H. Freeman & Co., 1981).

For the wonders of medicine to come I am indebted to progress reports on research compiled by futurists, especially *Future Facts: A Forecast of the World As We Will Know It before the End of the Century*, Stephen Rosen (New York: Simon and Schuster Touchstone Book, 1976); *The Book of Predictions*, David Wallechinsky, Amy Wallace, and Irving Wallace (New York: William Morrow and Co., Inc., 1980); and *Breakthroughs, Astonishing Advances in Your Lifetime in Medicine, Science, and Technology*, Charles Panati (Boston: Houghton Mifflin Co., 1980). The most carefully researched popular report on prolonging the life span itself is *Prolongevity* (New York: Avon Discus Book, 1976), by Albert Rosenfeld, then science editor of *The Saturday Review*.

On healthier lifestyles, Dr. James A. Schoenberger and his colleagues were able to lower cholesterol levels and blood pressure and reduce smoking in a large sample of men by special programs to help them change their way of living, but the control group of similar men getting no special care cut down on their own, biasing the experiment. See *Medical World News* (May 11, 1981): 10, 11, 15.

For the impact of medicine on longevity, see *Who Shall Live? Health, Economics, and Social Choice*, Victor R. Fuchs (New York: Basic Books, Inc., 1974). Fuchs is an economist specializing in health who anticipated the health care crisis of the 1980s. When he wrote this book, he was vice-president of the National Bureau of Economic Research and professor of economics at Stanford University and of community medicine at the Stanford Medical School.

René Dubos summarizes the decline of the tuberculosis death rate prior to the development of a drug attacking the germ, in his well-documented *Man Adapting* (New Haven: Yale University Press, 1965), pp. 235–236: "The tuberculosis mortality in New York City was 700 per 100,000 in 1812; it had fallen to 370 in 1882 (the year Koch discovered the tubercle bacillus); to 180 in 1910 (when bed rest was just beginning to be accepted as a method of treatment); and to fewer than 50 in 1945 (before the beginning of chemotherapy)." Fuchs points out that the decline fell more sharply after the adoption of penicillin, streptomycin, and PAS (para-aminosalicylic acid) in the late 1940s and of isoniazid in the early 1950s.

Inner-city housing today is luxurious compared with the conditions endured by immigrants who crowded into tenements without plumbing at the turn of the century. See *Encyclopaedia Britannica*, 1955 ed., s.v. "Slum."

On the medical neglect of the concept of health, Dr. Paul T. Costa, Jr., of the Gerontology Research Center, National Institute on Aging at Baltimore, agrees that only 2 percent of the money spent on health research goes to studying what constitutes health. It is easier to get money for work that could prevent or cure a specific illness.

The summary of the biological changes of aging came from *Aging in Culture and Society: Comparative Viewpoints and Strategies*, ed. Christine L. Fry (Brooklyn, New York: J. F. Bergin Publishers, Inc., 1980). Fry is one of the anthropologists who helped to organize the Association for Anthropology and Gerontology, which promotes a cross-cultural approach to gerontology. For a good account of measures of biological aging, see *Second Conference on the Epidemiology of Aging, March 28–29, 1977* (Bethesda, Maryland: National Institutes of Health Publication No. 80–969, July 1980).

Suspicion of drugs is not new. Oliver Wendell Holmes, Jr., the Supreme Court Justice, was the son of Oliver Wendell Holmes, the physician. Dr. Holmes was professor of anatomy and physiology at Harvard University and very suspicious of drugs; see his *Currents and Counter-Currents in Medical Science with Other Addresses and Essays* (Boston: Ticknor and Fields, 1861).

There is dispute about the odds of living to be a hundred, largely because official figures have been distorted by the number of elderly citizens who habitually inflate their ages, by the growth in the population, and by the large number of immigrants among today's elderly. The best analysis was made by Osborn Segerberg, Jr., for his book *Living to Be 100: 1,200 Who Did and How They Did It* (New York: Charles Scribner's Sons, 1982). He figures it this way: In 1879, about 1,524,000 people were born in the United States. In 1979, a century later, there were 4,548 people 100 years old. But not all the centenarians were born in this country. By subtracting the 18.5 percent estimated to have been born outside the United States, the odds for an American living 100 years become 410 to 1.

The National Center for Health Statistics, 3700 East-West Highway, Hyattsville, Maryland 20782, is the authority on vital statistics collected by the United States government. Careful information on the qualities that go with survival is being developed by longitudinal studies, especially those under way at the Baltimore laboratory of the National Institute on Aging and at Duke University. Segerberg gives a convenient summary of these studies.

Life expectations for groups with special characteristics, such as occupation or health habits, are usually based on small series undertaken by private researchers, and their accuracy varies widely. Of these, the most responsible are those calculated by the Metropolitan Life Insurance Company and published in that company's *Statistical Bulletin*, available free from the company at 1 Madison Avenue, New York, New York 10010.

Dr. Reubin Andres, Clinical Director of the National Institute on Aging, says that he likes to poke fun at articles that contain questionnaires inviting individuals to predict how long they will live. He warns that such guidelines are not to be taken for gospel. "Some of the questions are legitimate: Do you smoke cigarettes? then deduct x years. Others are stupid and some are cruel. You can't do anything about selecting the age of your mother when you were born—and it's a trivial effect anyway."

He warns, however, that longevity isn't totally a matter of good luck. "Cigarette smoking, heavy boozing, gross obesity, freaky diets, fast driving are not the result of bad luck, but they will certainly increase your chances of dying."

Once income rises to a level that ensures adequate nutrition, housing, water, and waste disposal, further increases in income have much less significance for life expectancy, and according to Fuchs, most Americans are now above that level. He cites a study published in 1972 and based on 1964–66 data that showed appreciable declines in infant death rates as family income rose from under $3,000 to the $5,000 to $7,000 range. Above that income level, however, there was no further decline with rising income.

Older people living with their age peers perceive themselves to be healthier than those who are in daily contact with people younger than themselves, according to Eunice Boyer's "Health Perception in the Elderly: Its Cultural and Social Aspects," in *Aging in Culture and Society*, ed. Christine L. Fry, pp. 198–216.

Dr. Butler believes that the old can profit by psychiatric help. He points out that despite the myth that they are resistant to change, they are, in fact, experienced in adaptation.

For a heroic fight against medical odds, see Norman Cousins, *Anatomy of an Illness as Perceived by the Patient* (New York: W. W. Norton, 1979).

While diet and exercise programs can make people of every age feel better, your own family doctor is likely to warn that they cannot cure serious illnesses and are dangerous if they are undertaken as a substitute for medical attention.

Large-scale clinical trials of the effect of vitamin C on the common cold conducted since Pauling's pronouncement on its efficacy in 1970 have produced conflicting results, according to "Ascorbic Acid and the Common Cold: Reviewing the Evidence," an analysis of the literature by J. L. Coulehan in *Postgraduate Medicine* 66, no. 3 (September 1979): 153. "Benefits shown have been modest, and positive findings have not been reproducible," Coulehan concludes. "Reported benefits probably are due to statistical artifact, minor vitamin-produced physiological changes, the placebo effect, or a combination of these."

According to Dr. Fries, a runner in middle life who completes a marathon in 3½ hours is in the ninety-ninth percentile for this endeavor; yet not until age seventy-three would that time set an age-group record. These marathon data are important in that they show the maximum rather than the average performance. The age-related decrement in maximal performance is only 1 percent a year between ages thirty and seventy. See *The New England Journal of Medicine* (July 17, 1980): 134.

There have been several perceptive reports on how it feels to grow old. For a sympathetic account that reflects the British admiration for feisty old people, see Ronald Blythe, *The View in Winter: Reflections on Old Age* (New York: Harcourt Brace Jovanovich, Inc., 1979).

Donald O. Hebb, the authority on the psychology of perception, charmed the 1978 convention of the American Psychological Association in Toronto with an address entitled "On Watching Myself Get Old," reprinted by *Psychology Today* (November 1978). Not to be outdone, B. F. Skinner made the headlines of the 1982 APA convention in Washington with a first-person account of how he copes with failing memory and diminished intellectual powers. He suggested sticking to an outline, tackling broader intellectual issues, writing down ideas as soon as you have them, and hanging the umbrella on the doorknob to avoid forgetting that the forecast you read at breakfast was for rain.

Eleanor Clark's book *Eyes, Etc., A Memoir* (New York: Pantheon Books, 1977), is an excellent example of the use the ageless intuitively make of calamities that are supposed to daunt the old.

For a useful review of recent social research on aging, see "The Life-Span Perspective in Social Science Research," January 1981, by David L. Featherman of the University of Wisconsin at Madison, commissioned by the Social Science Research Council. The research he reviewed suggests that "constructive environments, practice, and encouragement can offset or reverse losses of mental functions associated with biological senescence." He concludes that "it is not at all unlikely, given the overall improvements in levels of education, health, and economic security, that the pattern of future research such as Schaie's will show smaller declines in mental ability at every age in successively more recent birth cohorts."

Feelings of health are highly subjective. According to the sociological theory of relative deprivation, elderly people in retirement communities should feel healthier than they would in a college dormitory of young people. If so, they will feel better in the adult society of the future.

The proportion of Americans in poverty declined with the Great Society programs that put an income floor under the poorest and has risen again as a result of attempts to balance the federal budget.

On programs for reducing the self-induced stress of the heart attack–prone "Type A," see *Type A Behavior and Your Heart* (New York: Alfred A. Knopf, 1974), by Dr. Ray Rosenman and Dr. Meyer Friedman, two San Francisco cardiologists.

For the American seaman in the Arabian jail, I am indebted to Jeff Beaubier's "Biological Factors in Aging," in the Fry anthology, *Aging in Culture and Society.*

Comparison of life expectancy among nations is presented in the *Demographic Yearbook, 1975,* published by the World Health Organization of the United Nations. The values in the text came from a table printed in *Health—United States, 1981* (Hyattsville, Maryland: U.S. Department of Health and Human Services, DHHS Publication No. [PHS] 82-1232, December 1981).

Contrary to myth, American families are not dumping their older members into nursing homes. Most people over sixty-five who require care are getting it from their own relatives. Little more than 5 percent are in nursing homes, and most of these are childless. According to a government study, 21.4 percent of women born between 1906 and 1911 were childless, and the proportion of women sixty-five and older who head a household containing no kin increased from 18 percent in 1950 to 39 percent in 1975. For an analysis of demographic trends affecting the care of elders, see *The 1981 White House Conference on Aging: Report of the Technical Committee on Creating an Age-Integrated Society: Implications for the Family.*

Women live longer than men, and this sex gap is in fact rising, so it is tempting to conclude that sex equality is improving the life expectancy of women relative to men in the same way that race equality appears to be improving the life expectancy of blacks relative to whites. But the case of women is complicated by real biological differences. In *Second Conference on the Epidemiology of Aging, March 1977,* cited earlier, Erdman Palmore of Duke University's Center for the Study of Aging and Human Development ascribed half of the greater longevity of women to genetic differences and half to differences in lifestyle, such as less hazardous occupations, more careful driving, less smoking.

However flattering, the natural superiority of women cannot explain all of the sex gap. It doesn't exist in India today and did not appear in America until the twentieth century. Since then, the sex gap has grown, along with our GNP, from two years in 1900 to nearly eight in 1970. The big jump came with the widespread prosperity following World War II.

A good summary of the existing evidence was presented by Dr. Ingrid Waldron of the department of biology of the University of Pennsylvania at the Second Conference on the Epidemiology of Aging. She warned that the life-expectancy advantage of women might decline with sex equality, but the decline has not yet appeared. In spite of the stress of employment and the added burden of homemaking, working women live longer than homemakers.

A psychiatrist by training and a feminist by conviction, Dr. Butler predicts that women who go back to work after their children are grown will live longer than those who stay at home because of the psychological boost that comes with participation in the mainstream of the society.

5. HUMAN WORK

The decline in work satisfaction was documented by *Work in America, Report of a Special Task Force to the Secretary of Health, Education, and Welfare,* prepared under the auspices of the W. E. Upjohn Institute for Employment Research (Cambridge, Massachusetts: MIT Press, January 1973). A pervasive decline for all demographic groups between 1973 and 1977 was reported in a survey conducted for the U.S. Department of Labor by

Robert P. Quinn and Graham L. Staines of the University of Michigan's Institute for Social Research in Ann Arbor in 1977.

Flexible work rules and more autonomy for workers have been proposed as remedies by Fred Best of the Quality of Life Research Associates and James O'Toole of the Center for Futures Research at the University of Southern California. In 1979 the Public Agenda Foundation and the Aspen Institute for Humanistic Studies launched an elaborate study of the mismatch between jobs and workers entitled "Jobs in the 1980s: Bridging the Gap between People and Work." News of research in these areas is collected and presented by Work in America Institute, Inc., 700 White Plains Road, Scarsdale, New York 10583.

According to a study by Louis Harris and Associates reported to the House Select Committee on Aging in 1979, 51 percent of a broad sample of American workers and retirees preferred to continue working after retirement age, though not necessarily full time.

Peter F. Drucker, the prolific writer on the economy, warns that retirement age will have to rise in the future, and he urges employers to adopt flexible work plans that will make work more attractive. See his *Managing in Turbulent Times* (New York: Harper & Row, 1980). *Working Free*, John Applegath (New York: Amacom Books, 1982), is a useful compendium of the alternative work styles that are attracting followers in the 1980s.

In *The Third Wave* (New York: William Morrow and Co., Inc., 1980), Alvin Toffler predicts that work will decentralize into small units and that many homes will become electronic cottages.

The underground economy is by definition unmeasurable. It refers to goods and services that are off the books and so uncounted in official government statistics. These include services on which no income or Social Security taxes are paid, sales made in cash to avoid records, and most barter transactions. Broadly speaking, it also includes the substantial volume of services done without pay at home or incidentally for friends. Some economists think that consumption that never gets on the books is adding as much as 20 percent to the GNP.

In Washington retired defense officials who monitor military spending give their information to Dina Rasor's Project on Military Procurement, which is supported by the Fund for Constitutional Government. One of its contributors is Stewart Mott, a liberal philanthropist who has been a generous supporter of the women's movement.

6. THE LOVE PIONEERS

Carl Lerner died on August 26, 1973. Gerda Lerner's book *A Death of One's Own* (New York: Harper & Row, Colophon Books) was published in 1978.

A generation earlier, Lael Tucker Wertenbaker wrote a similar book about the death of her husband, the *Time* writer Charles Wertenbaker, on January 8, 1955: *Death of a Man* (New York: Random House, 1957).

The *Starr-Weiner Report on Sex and Sexuality in the Mature Years*, Bernard D. Starr and Marcella Bakur Weiner (New York: Stein and Day), was published in 1981.

Kinsey's groundbreaking study, *Sexual Behavior in the Human Male*, Alfred C. Kinsey, Wardell B. Pomeroy, and Clyde E. Martin (Philadelphia: W. B. Saunders Co., 1948), was published in 1948, but the interviews on which it was based began in 1938 and extended over a period of years in the 1940s.

In combing the sociological literature, Dr. Barbara H. Vinick of Boston University found several studies that reported more restrictive attitudes toward old-age sex and remarriage among older people than among younger ones. Her paper "Some Considerations Concerning the Future of Remarriage among the Elderly," was presented at the annual meeting of the Eastern Sociological Society at Philadelphia in 1978. Her doctoral dissertation on remarriages of older people in the Boston area was summarized in "Remarriage in Old Age," *The Family Coordinator* (October 1978). Elderly brides and grooms gave stereotypical reasons for remarrying, such as, "She was a good housekeeper." Vinick did not ask about sex, but some of her subjects brought it up.

Reliable evidence on the decline of sexual activity in later years was collected by the Duke Longitudinal Study of Aging that followed 268 local volunteers over age sixty from 1955 to 1979.

Two-thirds of the Starr-Weiner subjects said that lovemaking was the same or better than it had been when they were young. All those participating were over sixty.

The word *limerence* was coined by Dorothy Tennov, professor of psychology at the University of Bridgeport. She elaborates the concept in *Love and Limerence, The Experience of Being in Love* (New York: Stein & Day, 1979).

Dr. Gerald Hodan is a clinical psychologist with a special interest in the problems of older people who practices in a professional corporation, Behavior Management, Inc., in Milwaukee.

7. LIFESTYLE

College life wasn't free until students rebelled against parietal rules in the 1960s. One advantage, if you can call it that, was that students didn't regret graduating into what they now call the real world.

Many older people, perhaps a majority, really prefer to live with contemporaries. Like a women's college, a community for the elderly gives individuals opportunities that might be denied them in a mixed community. For a thoughtful defense of retirement communities, see Christine L. Fry, "The Community as a Commodity: The Age Graded Case," *Human Organization* 36, no. 2 (Summer 1977).

The experience of attending college and living "on one's own" was rated higher than academic instruction by employers as well as by the graduates themselves. See Caroline Bird, *The Case Against College* (New York: David McKay Co., Inc., 1975).

Western Washington University at Bellingham no longer maintains a separate staff for older students, but an intergenerational living unit called "The Bridge" has been integrated into the Fairhaven College complex of that campus. Washington state residents over age sixty can enroll for courses on a fee-waiver basis. Inquiries should be addressed to the Office of Student Life, Western Washington University, Bellingham, Washington 98225.

The Academy for Educational Development has published two guidebooks on college education for older people: *Never Too Old to Learn*, a report submitted to the Edna McConnell Clark Foundation, 250 Park Avenue, New York, New York, June 1974; and *Never Too Old to Teach*, Judith Murphy and Carol Florio, 1978. At the April 1977 Life Cycle Planning Conference sponsored by Holt, Rinehart and Winston/CBS, Inc., in Washington, former Secretary of Labor Willard Wirtz suggested that people over sixty who missed out on high school in their youth be staked to a year of college.

Some economists believe that unpaid work in the home may be adding as much as a third to the GNP, and all of it, of course, tax free.

For a frank statement of the value of the traditional family in motivating men to accept the conditions of paid employment, see self-confessed male chauvinist and supply-sider George Gilder's *Wealth and Poverty* (New York: Basic Books, 1981), which attracted wide attention during the first, honeymoon year of the Reagan Administration.

Calvin L. Beale of the Economic Research Service of the U.S. Department of Agriculture has written and spoken widely about the population shifts between country and city.

For data on the housing situation of older people, see *Report of the Technical Committee on the Physical and Social Environment and Quality of Life*, prepared for the 1981 White House Conference on Aging.

8. 2010

A full discussion of the origins of the wild cards would do grave injustice to some of the sources and require another book.

Scenarios of the future are always extrapolated from the present, most often in ways that cannot be blamed on or credited to the precipitating suggestion, fact, trend, or fantasy. A few examples illustrate how the wild cards originated.

Some are based on straightforward predictions of specialists. The rationale for *Freebies*, for instance, draws on "Free! Free! Free! The Priceless World of Tomorrow," an article written by economist Burnham P. Beckwith in *The Futurist* (October 1978), which predicts that free goods and services will account for more than half of the GNP in 2100.

In the winter of 1982, many quite sober economists were warning of the possibility of a financial collapse as dramatic as the Crash of 1929. For a parallel, see "A Scenario for a Depression," by Benjamin J. Stein in the *New York Times Magazine* (February 28, 1982).

Many of the wild cards develop suggestions or proposals seriously discussed by public figures. In 1980, for instance, Jack Kemp, the author of what came to be known as supply-side economics, actually suggested a return to basing the currency on gold.

Others depart from a provocative fact, such as the U.S. Treasury's estimate that OPEC countries held $40 billion worth of U.S. government securities, reported in the *New York Times* (July 9, 1981). Reducing the national debt by making them take stock for these bonds occurred to me as one way of getting some of our own back again.

The wild cards of demography simply apply a little imagination to current population trends reported by sober authorities such as the Bureau of the Census or "Entering the Twenty-first Century," *The Global 2000 Report to the President*, A Report Prepared by the Council on Environmental Quality and the Department of State, Washington, D. C., 1980.

The wild cards of technology draw on articles in *Business Week*, *Time*, and specialized publications, as well as the informal suggestions of computer hardware enthusiasts and sales promoters. For *Video Trips*, see a report by Michael Schrage, "Good-bye, 'Dallas,' Hello, Videodiscs," *New York* (November 17, 1980), on the laboratory of Dr. Nicholas Negroponte at the Massachusetts Institute of Technology.

One of the most provocative recent views of the future is *Megatrends: Ten New Directions Transforming Our Lives*, by John Naisbitt (New York: Warner Books, Inc., 1982).

Index